WEB CACHING AND ITS APPLICATIONS

THE KLUWER INTERNATIONAL SERIES IN
ENGINEERING AND COMPUTER SCIENCE

WEB CACHING
AND ITS
APPLICATIONS

by

S. V. Nagaraj
Chennai, India

SPRINGER SCIENCE+BUSINESS MEDIA, LLC

Library of Congress Cataloging-in-Publication
WEB CACHING AND ITS APPLICATIONS
by S. V. Nagaraj
ISBN 978-1-4757-7915-8   ISBN 978-1-4020-8050-0 (eBook)
DOI 10.1007/978-1-4020-8050-0

Contents

List of Figures

List of Tables

Preface

The last decade has seen a tremendous growth in the usage of the World Wide Web. The Web has grown so fast that it seems to be becoming an unusable and slow behemoth. Web caching is one way to tame and make this behemoth a friendly and useful giant. The key idea in Web caching is to cache frequently accessed content so that it may be used profitably later.

This book focuses entirely on Web caching techniques. Much of the material in this book is very relevant for those interested in understanding the wide gamut of Web caching research. It will be helpful for those interested in making use of the power of the Web in a more profitable way.

Audience and purpose of this book

This book presents key concepts in Web caching and is meant to be suited for a wide variety of readers including advanced undergraduate and graduate students, programmers, network administrators, researchers, teachers, technologists and Internet Service Providers (ISPs).

The purpose of this book is to bring to light key ideas that have been published in the area of Web caching in the past few years. Web caching research is growing by leaps and bounds as may be seen by the scores of research articles that have appeared in less than five years. There have been important developments in many aspects of Web caching. It is not easy to keep up to date with such developments as they are scattered in various professional journals.

The objective of this book is to aid the reader in understanding the latest developments in Web caching research. It is intended to help the reader in applying the knowledge for solving practical problems related to Web caching and Internet performance. Practitioners will benefit from the experience of others who experimented with various aspects of Web caching and gain some helpful tips.

What is covered in this book?

This book covers the following topics related to Web caching:

- Architectural aspects

  - Proxy cache deployment options
  - Caching architectures
  - Techniques for caching dynamic data

- Aspects requiring co-ordination among caches

  - Inter-cache communication
  - Routing requests to caches
  - Cache replacement algorithms
  - Cache coherency

- Aspects related to network traffic

  - Web traffic characteristics
  - Forecasting patterns of access

- Techniques that complement caching

  - Prefetching
  - Load balancing
  - Replication

- Practical aspects

  - Fault tolerance
  - Caching for libraries, ISPs and others
  - Building cache friendly Web sites
  - Caching at the global level

- Aspects related to performance

  - Measuring performance
  - Zipf's law and its role in Web caching

Several chapters in this book include exercises to test the reader's understanding of the subject matter. The book includes an exhaustive list of references so that the interested reader may easily obtain access to the relevant literature to pursue further study on the subject.

What is not covered in this book?

The basics of computer networking, in depth coverage of fundamental protocols such as TCP/IP and HTTP, aspects related to languages such as HTML and CSS, security related aspects and coverage of products (except for freely available open source products). Particulars about topics not covered in this book may be obtained from numerous text books or from widely available documents on the Web.

Course Information

Although, a deep background in the field of computer networking or Internet technologies is not expected from the readers, nonetheless, a sound understanding of the basic principles will be of immense help. The reader must be familiar with the basics of computer networking and be thorough with concepts such as HTML, DNS, HTTP, TCP/IP etc. and also possess some knowledge about their functioning. Adequate exercises have been included in this book to help the learner in grasping the subject. Some of these exercises may aid the student in selecting a thesis topic or a semester project. The book may be used for teaching courses in the areas of Internet technologies, Web applications, system performance, information storage and retrieval and computer networking (especially network architecture and design, and networking protocols).

This book is dedicated to
users of the World Wide Web.

Acknowledgments

Much of the information presented in this book is a bird's eye-view of the research insights of several hundred researchers in diverse fields related to the World Wide Web and computer networking. Their contribution to various disciplines has to be gratefully acknowledged.

My special thanks to the folks at Kluwer especially S. Lagerstrom-Fife and S. Palleschi for being very helpful during all phases in the production of this book.

Acknowledgments

Introduction

The World Wide Web (or Web for short) is very popular and is being used by people all over the world. However, its utility is being threatened by its ever growing popularity. Web users are getting frustrated because Web pages take too long to show up. Web sites are losing patronage because users find them too slow for their needs. As a result, it is no surprise that Web users want to overcome this situation.

Traffic on the Web is increasing continuously because the user population is growing steadily. Many people access the Web for various reasons: to get the latest news, to send and receive emails, for e-commerce applications, for playing on-line games and so on. The number of such applications is also growing very rapidly. Hackers and spammers generate large amounts of redundant traffic that further slows down access to the Web. All this has resulted in the World Wide Web being referred to jokingly as the World Wide Wait.

Web application developers have often wondered if something could be done to make the Web surfing experience a more enjoyable one. The speed at which the Web may be surfed by a user depends greatly on the capacity of the links connecting the user with the Web. A vast majority of Web users continue to depend on slow dial-up connections that get disconnected frequently. However, a small fraction of Web users have switched to faster technologies such as cable modem, Digital Subscriber Line (DSL) and T1 links (1.5 Mbps links). High speed broadband connections seem to induce more demand in the form of newer applications such as Webcasts, networked games and so on. Although newer technologies provide more bandwidth than older technologies, nevertheless, they do not cut down the transmission of redundant data being sent across the Web.

A surprising fact is that many people tend to access the same piece of information repeatedly. This could be weather related data, news, stock quotes, baseball scores, course notes, technical papers, exchange rate information and so on. If too many people attempt to access a Web site at the same time then they may experience problems in getting connected to the Web site. The Web site is unable to cope with the load and the responses received from it are either slow or perhaps absent.

Web caching is a technology aimed at reducing the transmission of redundant network traffic. Its main objective is to improve access to the Web. It can be beneficial to a wide spectrum of users including those dependent on slow dial-up links as well as those relying on faster broadband connections. The word caching refers to the process of saving data for future use. Web caching is the process of saving copies of content (obtained from the Web) closer to the end user, in order to enable quicker access to the content. Web caching is a fairly new technology whose history is linked to that of the Web. See Krishnamurthy and Rexford [314] for more details about the history of the Web and its evolution.

The reader may have the following questions in mind: what exactly does Web caching achieve? why is it needed? and where could it be used? This book is primarily concerned with such questions and presents a picture of the key ongoing Web caching related research accomplishments.

Some of the main reasons for which a user would opt for Web caching include the following:

- to increase the bandwidth availability by curbing the transmission of redundant data,

- for reducing network congestion,

- for improving response times and

- for achieving savings in terms of cost (for e.g. cost of bandwidth).

Web caching deals with problems such as redundant data transmission, limited bandwidth availability, slow response times and high costs and aims to provide better performance in these areas. Its success is measured by the satisfaction experienced by its users in terms of response times, costs etc. The performance of a Web caching solution needs some standard benchmarks (see the chapter on measuring performance) in order to judge whether a Web caching solution is indeed suited for the problem at hand.

Caching can happen at various levels for e.g. the Web browser of an user, the user's hard disk, servers located in the institution in which the user is employed, the institution's Internet Service Provider (ISP), the regional Internet hub, the national Internet hub or at the global level. Caching can be accomplished by Web browsers; by specialized caches known as *proxy caches* and by Web servers. Many popular Web browsers cache the Web pages browsed by the user. Very often such browsers enable the users to view the content downloaded earlier, by pressing a back button. In this case, the Web page is fetched from the browser's cache instead of fetching it again from the original source on the Web, thereby avoiding unnecessary downloads.

A proxy cache can store the Web pages retrieved by users located within an organization. The pages may have been retrieved from the Web directly or they may have been retrieved from servers operating within the organization. A common cache for a large number of users (say hundreds or thousands) with diverse interests implies that the contents of the cache may have to be replaced frequently.

The Web relies on a fundamental protocol known as the *Hypertext Transfer Protocol* (HTTP). When a user accesses a Web page, HTTP acts on behalf of the user and sends requests (HTTP requests) and receives responses (HTTP responses) so that the user may view the contents of the Web page on a Web browser. In Web caching, HTTP responses are cached so that they may be used later. However, not all responses may actually be cacheable. There are some features in HTTP that assist the process of caching. Needless to say, an in depth understanding of the caching process can be obtained only by studying the HTTP protocol in more detail. The current version of the HTTP protocol is known as HTTP 1.1. Earlier versions of HTTP include HTTP 1.0 and HTTP 0.9. The latest version of HTTP operates in ways somewhat different from that of earlier versions and includes more features. HTTP offers mechanisms known as *methods* to facilitate communication between a Web client and a Web server. A good starting point for understanding the functioning of HTTP is the authoritative document on HTTP 1.1 by the Internet Engineering Task Force (IETF) [200]. The reader may also refer the book by Krishnamurthy and Rexford [314] for details about HTTP that are beyond the scope of this book.

Figure I.1. Communication between a Web client and a Web server

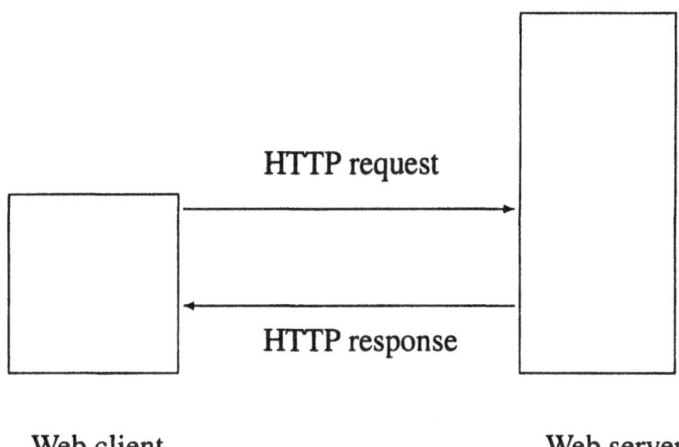

Web client   Web server

Table I.1.   Versions of the Hyper Text Transfer Protocol (HTTP)

Version	Defining document	Web link
HTTP 1.0	RFC 1945	http://www.ietf.org/rfc/rfc1945.txt
HTTP 1.1	RFC 2616	http://www.ietf.org/rfc/rfc2616.txt

Table I.2.   HTTP method headers in HTTP 1.1

Method	Details
GET	Get the specified data
PUT	Enables the client to put a new item in a specified location on the server
DELETE	Enables the client to delete the specified item
POST	Enables the client to post information to the server
HEAD	Similar to GET, the server returns no page content except for HTTP headers
TRACE	The client gets to trace the request it made to the server
OPTIONS	Helps the client to ascertain the options for communication at the server

The fundamental question in Web caching is how do we know if something can be cached or perhaps cannot be cached. Krishnamurthy and Rexford [314] mention protocol and content specific considerations that determine whether a response is cacheable or uncacheable. The HTTP protocol forces some constraints that must be satisfied by a Web cache. Hence, it dictates which responses are cacheable and which are uncacheable.

It is not hard to guess that certain types of content may not be worth caching. For example, cookies (see Glossary for a definition), personalized content and dynamically generated content. However, it would be desirable to cache some of these (if it was possible to do so) for the sake of efficiency, by adopting some means or the other. It may of course be worthwhile to cache content that is requested often. On the other hand, it may not be beneficial to cache content that is not likely to be requested frequently. Hence, we see that there are many factors that determine the cacheability of content. It is worthwhile to explore how we could increase the cacheability of content.

One important point to be noted is that the content obtained from a Web cache may not be up to date with the original content on the Web server containing the master copy. The Web server hosting the original content is known as the origin server. Hence, we see that maintaining cache consistency becomes an important requirement so that stale or outdated content is not served to the end user.

Managing the content within a cache becomes important because caches have a finite storage space at their disposal. Hence placing content in the cache if space is available and removing content from a cache if there is no space becomes important due to space constraints. The process of removing some content from a cache and replacing it with some other content is known as cache replacement. Many algorithmic techniques are used to facilitate this process. Such algorithms are known as cache replacement algorithms.

A number of commercial and free software and hardware products for facilitating Web caching are currently available in the market (see appendix for a list of Web sites that contain details of such products). Squid is a popular open source Web caching software that has been well studied. There have been numerous extensions and modifications to various versions of Squid in order to obtain better performance. Users and system administrators who are interested in setting up a Web cache (or a system of Web caches) will benefit by reading the documents available on the Squid Web site http://www.squid-cache.org. A hands on experience with Squid may go a long way to supplement the understanding obtained by studying textbooks or research articles on the subject of Web caching. The reader may also experiment with tools that could assist in understanding various aspects of Web caching (some of these are listed in the Index).

Effective use of cached information is more important than merely caching content. An organization may benefit by employing multiple caches depending on the requirements. When multiple caches are used, techniques to organize or coordinate them become important. Inter-cache communication (viz. communication between the caches) is essential if caches have to communicate among themselves and cooperate, so that maximum advantage can be obtained from them. Several protocols are used for inter-cache communication and also for other purposes. We look at some of the important protocols in this book.

The main goal of Web caching is to improve response times by bringing content closer to the end user. A technique that has a similar goal but operates in a different way is known as *replication*. In replication, content hosted by Web servers is mirrored (duplicated) at various locations so that a user may access a Web server that is nearest. Such Web serves containing duplicated content are known as *mirrors*. Web caching and replication are therefore complementary techniques although they operate in dissimilar ways but have the common objective of bringing content closer to the end user. Replication may be thought of as an alternative to Web caching.

The benefits of Web caching

Web caching systems when properly deployed can provide substantial of bandwidth wastage. This leads to cost savings, reduction in network traffic, improved access and better content availability. Content may be fetched from nearby caches instead of far away origin servers. This also helps when connections to the origin servers are not readily available.

The drawbacks of Web caching

If Web caches fail to regularly update the Web content stored by them then they may be returning stale content to the users. If sought after content is not found in a cache then a *cache miss* occurs and this results in an increase in the response time. Caching systems may themselves become a bottleneck if they are down or if they don't ensure a high quality of service (QoS). A poorly configured caching system may actually degrade performance instead of bringing benefits. Cost considerations may also dissuade the deployment of caching systems. In certain cases, the effort involved in setting up a caching system or using it may also be a negative factor. Security and privacy issues that arise when caches are maintained can never be overlooked.

Although it may appear that there are many drawbacks in using a Web caching system, we will see in this book that a properly configured caching system will bring positive benefits.

I

ARCHITECTURAL ASPECTS

Chapter 1

VARIOUS FLAVORS OF WEB CACHING

The common kinds of caching include proxy caching, reverse proxy caching, transparent caching, Adaptive Web caching, push caching and Active Cache.

1. Cache deployment options

Caches are often deployed as forward proxy caches, reverse proxy caches or as transparent proxies.

Table 1.1. Popular cache deployment options

Forward proxy caching
Reverse proxy caching
Transparent caching

1.1 Proxy caching

In plain proxy caching(also known as *forward proxy caching*) a proxy cache server gets hold of HTTP requests from clients, and on tracing the object asked for in its cache, gives the object to the user. If the object asked for was not found in the cache then a request is sent on behalf of the user to the *origin server* (see Glossary for definitions). The object is then fetched from the origin server and a copy of it may be stored in the cache before forwarding it to the user.

Proxy caches are generally positioned at the edge of a network. This is done so that a large number of internal consumers may be serviced. A judicious placement of proxy caches can lead to bandwidth savings, quicker response times, and enhanced accessibility to static Web objects. However, a standalone proxy cache set up could become a problematic single point of failure in the network. In the event of the failure of the cache, the network (or the Web as the case may be) appears to be out of bounds to the users. With this approach, all the Web browsers of the users have to be set up by hand to make use of the relevant proxy cache. In addition, in the event of failure, all users may have to make changes to their Web browsers so that they may use a different cache. However, these problems have got lessened to an appreciable extent due to the advent of automatic browser configuration.

Figure 1.1.   Forward proxy caching

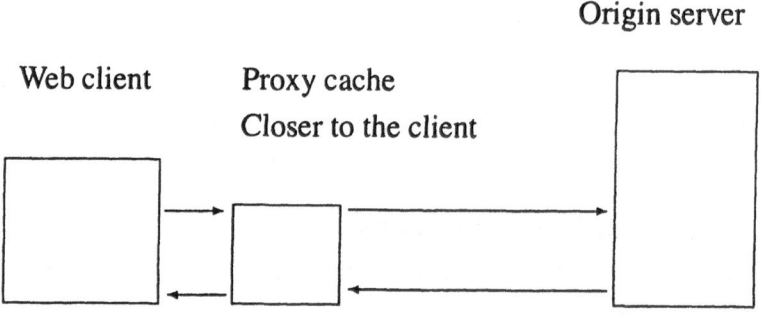

Figure 1.2.   Failure in a standalone proxy caching system

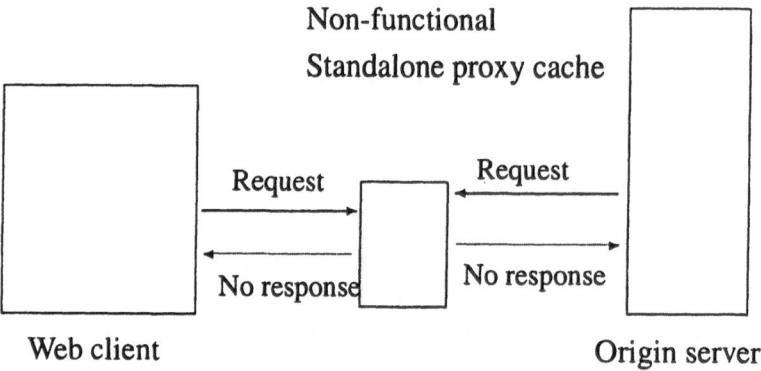

1.1.1   Browser auto-configuration

Due to the above mentioned problems associated with the manual config-uration of Web browsers of users, a technique for automatic configuration of

Web browsers has become a necessity. The Web Proxy Auto-Discovery Protocol (WPAD) (see the Squid Web site http://www.squid-cache.org and documents therein for more particulars) is a mechanism for identifying neighborhood proxy caches. WPAD makes use of resource finding aids such as domain name system (DNS) records and the Dynamic Host Control Protocol (DHCP) (see [183]) to find an automatic proxy configuration file.

Table 1.2. Browser configuration options

Manual browser configuration
Automatic configuration files
Web Proxy Auto Discovery

The difficulties normally encountered with large proxy cache systems have to some extent got mitigated due to the use of proxy configuration URLs. WPAD conduces to this by making it hands free at the client side. In addition to DHCP and DNS records, it also uses several protocols in addition to a protocol known as the Service Location Protocol (SLP) to find a configuration URL. Once this URL has been located, the client can fetch the configuration file that possesses the desired proxy configuration information. To find a URL, a WPAD-capable Web browser initially makes use of DHCP after which it makes use of SLP. In case the desired URL was not found, the browser seeks the URL inside DNS records. In order to accomplish this it enquires starting with the most pertinent host name with the prefix *WPAD*. It then goes up the DNS hierarchy until a record is located. This way the Web browser recovers the most appropriate proxy configuration worthy of consideration despite some superfluous attempts. As we may guess, the use of WPAD-capable browsers in networks with a substantial number of users could bring positive benefits. For instance, by diminishing the need for assistance to clients with erroneous browser configurations. WPAD is in the experimental phase and is used only within an administrative domain.

1.2 Reverse proxy caching

This is a variation of regular proxy caching (which is otherwise known as forward proxy caching). In reverse proxy caching, caches are placed near the source of the content (viz. the origin server) rather than the destination of the content (viz. the client). This type of deployment of caches is helpful for servers that anticipate a substantial number of requests and desire to maintain a superior quality of service. Reverse proxy caching is particularly beneficial for Web hosting farms as it can ameliorate their performance and also protect them

Figure 1.3.   Browser auto-configuration gets around non-functional proxy cache

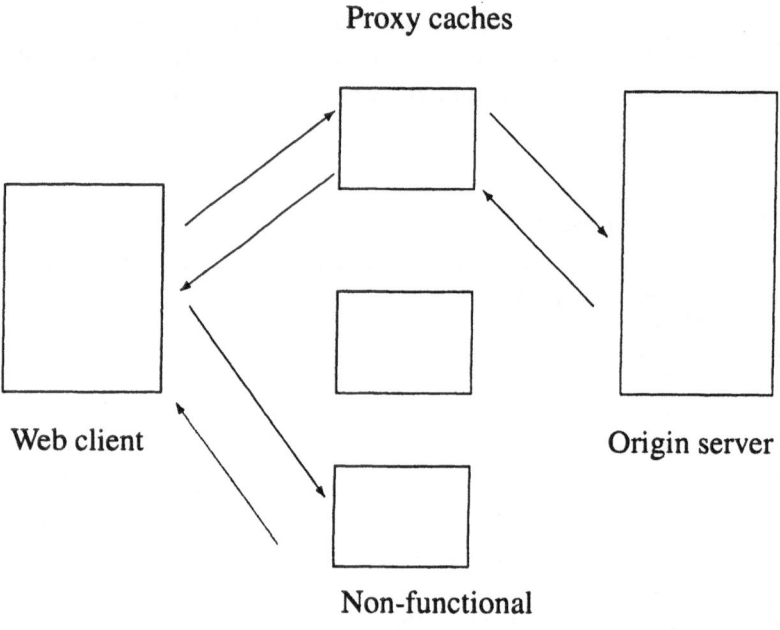

from attacks by hackers. A notable characteristic of reverse proxy caching is that it is totally autonomous from client-side proxy caching. Hence it may be feasible to make both of them work together in a harmonious fashion. Doing so may improve the functioning significantly by exploiting the advantages offered by both the techniques.

Figure 1.4.   Reverse proxy caching

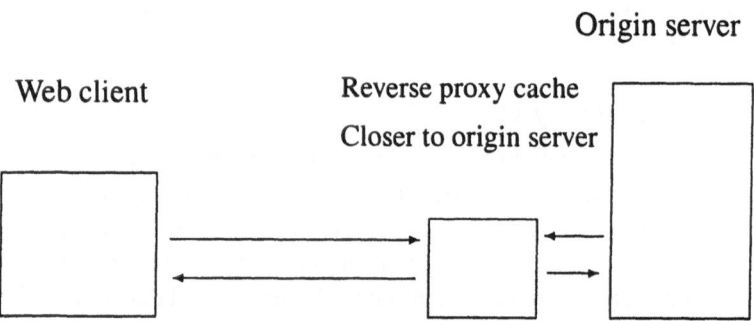

Figure 1.5. Combining forward proxy caching with reverse proxy caching

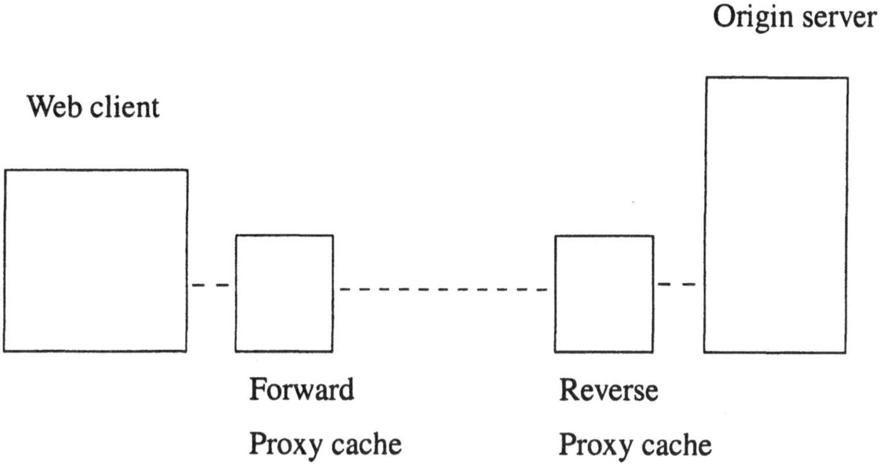

1.3 Transparent caching

As we have seen earlier, one significant shortcoming of the proxy caching technique is the need for configuration of Web browsers of users. Although automatic browser configuration and WPAD help to deal with this shortcoming, other options are definitely worth considering. Transparent proxy caching offers the opportunity to surmount the problem of configuration of Web browsers encountered in proxy caching. In transparent caching, the caches intercept HTTP requests and channel them to Web cache servers or bunches of Web caches. This approach offers flexibility in decision making for various purposes, for instance in load balancing (viz. balancing requests amongst Web servers).

There are at least two different ways to set up transparent proxy caching. One is at the router level while the other is at the switch level. The router based approach employs policy-directed routing in order to forward requests to the pertinent caches. The switch-based approach utilizes the switch for the purpose of load balancing. When the two approaches are compared, the switch based approach seems to offer some definite advantages. For instance, the overhead is less than what is seen with policy-directed routing. In addition, switches are often cheaper than routers. From the above discussion, we see that various network elements (such as routers and switches) play a pivotal role in the efficacy of a Web caching strategy. Barish and Obraczka [52] mention the applications of network components for the purpose of load balancing.

There are several possibilities for arranging caches in a transparent caching system. The caches may be arranged as an Ethernet bridge or they may be orga-

Figure 1.6. Transparent caching

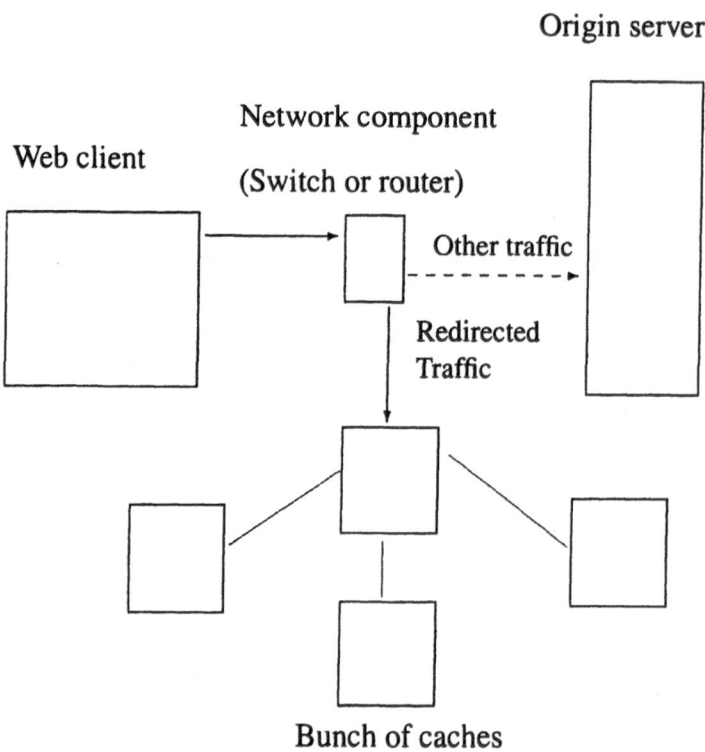

Origin server

Network component

Web client

(Switch or router)

Other traffic

Redirected
Traffic

Bunch of caches

Table 1.3. Transparent caching options

Router-based
Switch-based

nized as a network's default gateway. Another possibility is by the application of protocols such as Web Cache Communication Protocol (WCCP) [514] to get hold of traffic at either a switch or a router. The most suitable arrangement is often dictated by the configuration of the network. It should be noted here that the introduction of a cache as a bridge or as the default gateway may bring in a new single node of failure that could even result in the breakdown of all network traffic. As a result, network supervisors often opt for a proxy based option. The use of a WCCP-capable network component such as a router or a switch could lead to more burden on crucial components of the network (for e.g. routers and switches) although it circumvents the possibility of a single node of failure.

WCCP makes use of an arrangement of Web caches that is akin to a cluster. The inbound request on being seized by a network component is channelled to a particular Web cache. As a result, a few caches may service a major portion of the content if the traffic is restricted to a particular Web site or only a few Web sites.

Despite the fact that transparent caching confers the benefit of avoiding the requirement of having to set up Web clients to make use of particular Web caches, nevertheless, there is still a major pitfall. The client may be unable to bypass a cache that is non-functional or may even be unable to sense that a breakdown has occurred (due to the transparent nature of the caching mechanism). As a consequence, such failure could affect traffic throughout the network. Therefore we see that it is desirable to search for fault-tolerant solutions. In this direction, a few commercial products make use of techniques such as clustering and also employ solid sate devices for the purpose of fail-over.

Abba et al. [1] describe the results of their experiments concerning transparent caching and outline its advantages and disadvantages. They mention that they were able to obtain improvements in the quality of service in addition to a small savings in the bandwidth. In addition, redundant traffic was not sent to the Web because of the application of transparent caching. The reader may refer [551] for a discussion on transparent Web caching and the application of commercial products to facilitate it.

1.4   Translucent caching

Obraczka et al. [418] discuss strategies for scalable Web caching. They introduce the concept of *translucent caching*. This is intended to provide another option in the place of transparent caching. Translucent caching relies on the idea that requests are sent along the most suitable path from a client to the origin server. On this path routers may send the request in the direction of a cache picked from a cluster of translucent caches in the proximity. Translucent caches differ from transparent caches because they avoid the need for TCP connection go-betweens. This is due to the fact that they depend on routers only for getting the next-hop cache related data.

Rodriguez et al. [474] investigate translucent proxying of TCP. They state that although transparent proxies support numerous functions such as Web proxy caching, service differentiation and load balancing, nonetheless, they have a major shortcoming. They must be deployed at key points in a network in order to make sure that all the IP packets of an intercepted TCP connection are viewed by an intercepting transparent proxy. Translucent proxying of TCP surmounts this drawback by employing TCP-OPTIONs (a feature of TCP) and IP tunnelling in order to guarantee that every IP packet in the possession of a

TCP connection will get across the proxy that happened to intercept the first packet. This guarantee permits the unplanned deployment of such proxies at any location in the network. As a consequence, we see that translucent proxies offer some extra benefits when compared to transparent proxies.

2.   Adaptive Web Caching

An important problem encountered in Web caching is the *hot spot phenomenon* viz. some Web sites become very popular overnight, although, they may not attract any interest after the passage of a short span of time. Adaptive Web caching (see [589, 395, 394]) can be used for dealing with the problems posed by the hot spot phenomenon. Adaptive Web caching makes uses of several distributed Web caches (see the chapter on caching architectures for more details about distributed caching) that dynamically become part of groups of caches (known as cache meshes) or quit such groups. The adaptivity and the self organizing nature of the cache meshes assist in coping with instances when the requirement of Web objects either grows slowly or peaks. They also help when the demand happens to be erratic.

Adaptive Web caching relies on two protocols: the Cache Group Management Protocol (CGMP) and the Content Routing Protocol (CRP) (see [589, 395, 394]).

The first protocol viz. CGMP outlines how cache meshes are created, and also how a particular cache may become part of such meshes or quit such meshes. The caches are arranged as overlapping multicast groups. The admissibility or rejection criteria of a particular cache into such groups is often determined by using mechanisms such as feedback and voting.

The second protocol viz. CRP is used to detect cached content inside the current set of meshes. When compared to hierarchical caching (see the chapter on caching architectures for more on hierarchical caching), CRP may be thought of as a more settled version. As something that makes use of the overlapping structure of the meshes for distributing requests for Web objects amongst groups and also for spreading popular Web objects all over a mesh. This in turn depends on multicast messaging among constituents of a cache group. In addition, URL tables (see [394]) may also be employed to cleverly guess to which overlapping meshes a request ought to be transmitted.

An important premise in Adaptive Web caching is that bunches of Web caches may be positioned so that they may transverse frontiers being managed by different organizations, without encountering any difficulty. However, this may not always be possible and could cause some administration related problems. Consequently, it becomes a necessity to weaken control so that cache groups may evolve without any hindrance at appropriate places within a network that happens to span different organizations.

3. Push caching

One of the important goals of Web caching is to bring content close to the requesting client. Push caching is a caching technique that follows this precept.

Gwertzman [226] introduces the concept of *geographical push-caching*. Unlike other caching schemes which are often client initiated, geographical push-caching is server initiated. The server is allowed to make good use of its familiarity with the network topography, the geography, and the patterns of access in order to diminish network traffic and load on the servers. Gwertzman mentions that while plain client caching could diminish server load and network bandwidth consumption by about 30%, incorporating server-initiated caching diminished the server load by an extra 20% and also curtailed the bandwidth utilization by an extra 10%. Gwertzman reports that geographical push-caching also offers cache space savings.

In a couple of articles [227, 228] related to the above discussion Gwertzman and Seltzer analyzed geographical push-caching. In their technique, data is systematically distributed to co-operating Web servers once the origin server gets to know from where the requests are coming. Therefore the origin server's knowledge of the contrived network topology is put to good use. Both push caching and Adaptive Web caching (see the section on Adaptive Web caching) depend on the requirement of managing caches under the purview of different organizations.

López-Ortiz and Germán [364] discuss a multi-collaborative push-caching HTTP protocol. Their protocol is meant for mirroring highly accessed Web pages automatically in a distributed and temporal fashion. The caching protocol is dissimilar to other caching protocols because it caches by reckoning the load characteristics in the server side as an alternative to access patterns in the client side. The protocol of López-Ortiz and Germán is independent of other extensions that have been proposed for the HTTP protocol.

Malan et al. [371] describe a push-based wide-area network (WAN) data dissemination substrate known as Salamander, for use by groupware and Webcasting Internet applications. Salamander is designed to supply many kinds of delivery semantics.

Tewari et al. [520] studied various distributed caching techniques (see the chapter on caching architectures) for bettering the response time. They performed their experiments under a broad spectrum of workloads. Based on their studies they listed four fundamental design principles for implementing distributed caches in an adept manner. One of these important design principles suggests the need to share data amongst caches while another highlights the importance of bringing cached content near the clients. Tewari et al. mention that correctly implemented push caching strategies could improve the performance nearly 1.27 to 1.43 times that obtained by conventional cache hierarchies (see the chapter on caching architectures for discussion related to hierarchical caching).

One shortcoming of push caching is that although space and effort is expended to transmit copies of Web objects, the performance becomes better only if such objects are actually asked for. This is a common pitfall in many Web caching strategies.

4.   Active Cache

Cao et al. [103] considered the problem of caching dynamic documents on the Web (also refer the chapter on caching dynamic data). Caching dynamic data is becoming a major topic of research because it is a fact that caching such data is not trivial and poses problems when only conventional caching strategies are used. Web pages are often personalized for users by placing *cookies* in their computers. Cookies are HTTP header elements for signalling that the content needs to be personalized. Personalization of Web content is currently becoming commonplace. These days many Web users tend to prefer personalized services. Caceres et al. [97] mention that the study of a large ISP trace disclosed that more than 30% of client requests carried cookies.

Active Cache enables a server to move a part of its work to a proxy when requests come from an user. It permits servers to furnish Java applets that may be appended to documents. This enables customization of Web objects that may otherwise not be cached. Active Cache necessitates that proxies make use of *cache applets* when there is a *hit* (see Glossary for definitions), so that there is no need to interact with the server. Hence, when a request for personalization comes for the first time, the server supplies the required Web objects and related cache applets. In case of future requests for the same Web content the cache applets do the required processing at the *cache itself.* That is to say, without interacting with the server. Consequently, the additional expense of contacting the origin server after the first request for personalization is dispensed with. Cao et al. [103] demonstrate that Active Cache is a practical scheme that can provide bandwidth reduction at the cost of marginal processor overheads.

5.   Further reading

The advantages of caching were understood even prior to the HTTP era. Danzig et al. [160] mention that it is worthwhile to cache file objects in interconnected networks. Their study was conducted in the context of caching for file transfer accomplished by the use of the File Transfer Protocol (FTP). They mention that careful placement of file caches could diminish the amount of FTP traffic by about 42% and NFSNET backbone traffic by about 21%. They also mention that the savings would be about 27% if the clients and the servers employed data compression. They state that although their experiments were conducted for FTP traffic, the observations as a result of their experiments should also be capable of being utilized for caching objects in interconnected networks. Spasojevic et al. [507] study the application of wide-area file systems for hoarding and fetching documents within the World Wide Web.

Bestavros [65, 66] studied demand-based data dissemination schemes in which data (including multimedia data) is pushed from the source to servers that are closer to the client. This also helped to diminish network traffic and perform some load balancing among the servers.

Bestavros et al. [71] studied the functioning of application-level document caching in the Internet by means of trace-driven simulations (simulations employing a collection of information concerning requests and responses) and highlighted the need for distinguishing between documents that were produced locally and documents that were produced remotely. They state that this could be exploited by caching policies.

Markatos [379] conducted a study of main memory caching of Web documents. A strategy is proposed for diminishing the burden due to continuous requests for Web resources. An insignificant proportion of the main memory is stated to be sufficient for caching nearly 60% of the Web documents that were sought. Markatos mentions that conventional file-based cache maintenance techniques are not suitable for main memory Web caches.

Oguchi and Ono [420, 419] study proxy cache mechanisms for wide area distributed networks and also give some proposals concerning them. They mention that some files such as multimedia files may not get cached because they may exceed size limits set for caching files. In order to overcome this, they suggest that the quality level of the files may be reduced so that such files may be cached. Another issue raised by them is the absence of relationship between neighboring proxy caches which results in the absence of sharing among them. For this, they propose the formation of a cluster by utilizing such proxy caches and by means of hyperlink information.

Caughey et al. [109] mention that prevailing caching processes do not offer much aid for Web caching techniques that have to be tailor-made or happen to have a complicated structure. They also state that such processes are for the most part transparent to their users and work with objects which are mostly read-only. Caughey et al. propose an approach to tackle such problems.

Inoue et al. [258] study an adaptive Web caching technique for a satellite network serving many countries. Many factors require that such a caching system be adaptive to the environment.

Kangasharju et al. [292] describe the design and implementation of a soft caching (viz. caching after recoding images to lower resolutions) proxy. They discuss a set of alterations to existing proxy caching algorithms so as to implement a soft caching proxy. They describe the functioning of a soft caching test bed founded on the Squid proxy cache.

Kim et al. [307] analyze buffer management policies for a Web proxy. They describe caching strategies for objects with variable size and mention that it does not seem possible to optimize for both hit ratio and byte hit ratio simultaneously.

It may actually be possible to utilize techniques that assist Web caching schemes in ways that are not readily apparent. Santos and Wetherall [487] describe a technique for augmenting the operational link bandwidth by curbing replicated data. They use cheap hardware to develop a link layer caching and compression technique that diminishes bandwidth usage. Their strategy works alongside application-level systems such as Web caches that attempt to curtail bandwidth utilization, and offers an option when such systems are not worthwhile. Santos and Wetherall observe that there is substantial replication of data at the packet level that is attributable to Web traffic. They develop a link compression protocol that is practically realizable in a cost effective manner.

Hada et al. [231] studied the behavior of Web proxy caching servers in low bandwidth environments. They mention that the efficient functioning of a proxy cache server is crucial for providing better service. They gauge the performance of a proxy cache server by studying the time taken by clients to fetch Web objects using the proxy caches. They demonstrate that the external bandwidth connectivity to the Internet is a paramount factor affecting the performance of a proxy cache server.

Krishnan et al. [323] discuss transparent en-route caching (TERC) in wide area networks (WANs). Although TERC is easy to implement in LANs, however, there are a number of issues to be tackled when they need to be utilized for WANs. Krishnan et al. look at these difficulties and outline approaches to tackle them and state that the use of TERCs for WANs appears promising. In a related article, Krishnan et al. [324] discuss a problem related to the location of TERCs.

Markatos et al. [381] study secondary storage management techniques for Web proxies. They look at the encumbrances often attributed to disk I/O in Web proxy cache systems. They suggest the implementation of secondary storage management techniques as a viable choice for the purpose of bettering the functioning of Web proxy cache systems. They come up with various file management techniques to diminish the burden attributable to disk I/O by a magnitude of nearly 25. This in turn helps to improve the single-disk service rate.

Tomlinson et al. [524] describe a high-capacity proxy cache service that functions on a tailor-made operating system. The specially built operating system is meant for effectively sustaining large scale Internet middleware. Tomlinson et al. mention that such an operating system would offer advantages when compared to operating systems that are not designed specifically for addressing such issues. They demonstrate the performance and scalability of the proxy cache service.

Cooper and Dilley [143] list out some problematic aspects of Web proxy caches and cache servers. They discuss various approaches used to overcome the known problems. Typical problems include breaking of cache directives by some proxies and problems due to the Internet Cache Protocol (ICP) (see the chapter on inter-cache communication) which could make ICP traffic more prevalent than HTTP traffic.

Michel et al. [394] discuss URL forwarding and compression in Adaptive Web caching. The Adaptive Web Caching system (AWC) makes use of a forwarding table to identify the closest cache containing a copy of the sought after URL's objects. In AWC, a URL table compression algorithm permits the partaking of content related data between caches that are in the vicinity.

Mogul [399] mentions that conventional Web caches stash away HTTP responses expecting a future citation to the URL of a cached response. However, this approach may not go far because numerous responses are of value only on one occasion. Mogul reports on trace-based studies of a plan based on automatic recognition of duplicated content.

Wills and Shang [560] look at the role played by Domain Name System (DNS) lookup costs for retrieval of Web objects. They conducted experiments as a result of which they reason that the DNS lookup technique was faster for popular Web servers when contrasted with random Web servers. They state that the functioning of the DNS lookup technique was more favorable for popular Web servers in terms of factors such as cache hit ratios, and authoritative and non-local, non-authoritative response times.

Chandranmenon and Varghese [114] look at the reduction in Web latency achieved by the application of a technique which they refer to as *reference point caching*. If a document is cited in another document then they get data cached at the latter. Chandranmenon and Varghese study two specific aspects of their technique:

- caching IP addresses in order to refrain from doing DNS lookups at clients and

- the potential benefits of caching data concerning documents, in order to overcome the requirement for establishing new connections.

Chandranmenon and Varghese report that time savings is obtained by adopting the above two approaches. They state that it is possible to make use of the ideas to design new services such as search engines that throw up IP addresses to help quicken the search process, and also for caching at servers at the regional level.

Shaikh et al. [500] studied the effectiveness of Domain Name System (DNS) based server selection. DNS-based server selection is one way to enable clients approach the nearest server that provides the desired content. Shaikh et al. study the following aspects of DNS-based server selection:

- the drawbacks of diminishing the cache lifetimes of DNS data

- the effect of dispensing with cache lifetimes of DNS data

- the usually taken for granted assumption that client nameservers reflect the true location of the clients and their performance.

Shaikh et al. measure the effect of decreasing the DNS TTL (see Glossary for a definition of TTL) values on Web access latency and establish that doing so will worsen the domain name resolution related latency by nearly two orders of magnitude. They also recommend alterations to protocols in order to ameliorate the effectiveness of re-routing strategies that are based on the Domain Name System.

Yocum and Chase [581] describe a technique known as *payload caching*. It is meant for improving the performance of host-based network intermediaries such as firewalls, content routers, protocol converters, caching proxies, multicast servers and static Web servers for forwarding data from storage to the clients. Yocum and Chase expand the capability of network adapters to cache parts of an inbound packet stream, thereby allowing a system to forward data directly from the cache. They state that payload caching was able to better the forwarding performance by nearly 60% for TCP/IP traffic.

6.   Exercises

1 List various flavors of caching. Compare and contrast them.

2 What is browser auto-configuration? What are the advantages of using it?

3 What is WPAD? Explain how it works.

4 What is reverse proxy caching? How is it different from normal proxy caching?

5 Explain the role of WCCP in transparent caching.

6 How do network components such as routers and switches help in load balancing?

7 What are CGMP and CRP? Explain how they are used in Adaptive Web caching.

8 Describe the functioning of push caching and Active Cache.

Chapter 2

COMPARING CACHE DEPLOYMENT OPTIONS

As we have seen in the earlier chapter, there are various cache deployment options. Caches may be positioned near the destination of the content or near the source of the content. It is also possible to deploy caches at key points in a network on the basis of factors such as user access patterns and network topology or on the basis of other requirements. Caching may be accomplished at the clients, the proxy caches and the servers.

1. The benefits and drawbacks of these options

Forward proxy caching is perhaps the most popular cache deployment option. In forward proxy caching (as described in the previous chapter), the cache is positioned near the consumer of the content (the Web client). Hence, the proxy cache behaves like a Web server for the Web client and like a Web client for the Web server. The end users can therefore deploy the forward proxy cache themselves. They often tend to convert a proxy server into a proxy cache as it performs two useful functions: proxying and caching. As the cache is close to the user, performance gains are readily visible in terms of factors such as response times, bandwidth saved etc. It is also possible to use the proxy to filter undesirable content before it reaches the end user. As a consequence this is beneficial for various organizations which allow Web access to their users.

Security administration gets simplified by the application of forward proxy caching because of the dual use of the proxy cache for caching as well as for filtering content. However, care must be taken because a standalone forward proxy cache can become a single point of failure that could block all access to external Web sites. Scalability aspects must not be ignored as an increase in the number of users diminishes performance. If users tend to access the same kind of content then the forward proxy cache deployment option is a good choice. It can improve response time by servicing requests locally and is therefore beneficial to end users. However, issues such as browser configuration or proxy discovery have to be handled by the use of techniques that were discussed in the previous chapter.

Transparent caching avoids the need for configuring browser's of users. Despite the fact that it offers the same advantages as forward proxy caching (because it is deployed near the end user), the cost factor comes into play. Network elements such as routers and switches involve a non-zero cost. As discussed in the previous chapter, adequate safeguards must also be provided for fault tolerance in order to avoid a single point of failure.

Positioning caches near the source of the content is beneficial to the content provider. This approach is followed by reverse proxy caching and push caching. Delay-sensitive content (such as video or audio) may require a deployment mechanism of this kind. This helps to improve performance and throughput. Caches which are positioned near the source of the content may be pre-filled with content. Provision for security in reverse proxy caches helps to safeguard the origin servers. Content providers benefit by the improved response times to their Web sites.

Needless to say, there are compromises in both source-oriented caching and destination-oriented caching. Security constraints might prevent organizations subscribing to a common ISP from using a cache positioned at the ISP's end. However, the compounded use of both source-oriented caching (e.g. reverse proxy caching) and destination-oriented caching (e.g. forward proxy caching) techniques could be an effective approach since it combines the advantages of both while simultaneously diminishing the disadvantages of each one.

It is likewise possible to deploy caches in a dynamic and need-based fashion. This can be accomplished at bottleneck points in the network as they surface. However, difficulties related to administration may prevent the use of such techniques as network boundaries of organizations may have to be crossed in order to create cache meshes.

2.   Further reading

Huston [251] describes proxy caches and discusses their deployment in Internet Service Provider (ISP) networks.

Li et al. [346] study the optimal placement of Web proxies in the Internet. They argue that much of the prevailing research has been concentrated on Web caching strategies without paying much attention to strategies for proper positioning of proxies. Keeping this in mind, they try to discover the optimal placement policy for Web proxies. They study how to place M proxies amongst N probable sites in an optimal manner. They demonstrated that this could be done by formulating the problem as a dynamic programming problem. They come up with an algorithm for arriving at the optimal solution in $O(N^3 M^2)$ time.

Jamin et al. [267] study constrained mirror placement in the Internet. Mirror sites are used primarily for decreasing the response time and also for diminishing the load on Web servers. Jamin et al. look at the gains obtained by employing additional mirror sites when different placement algorithms are utilized. They make the plausible assumption that mirrors can be placed only in some specific locations.

The subject of suitable positioning of Web server replicas is crucial for Content Distribution Networks (CDNs) (see Glossary for a definition of a CDN). Qiu et al. [453] study appropriate positioning strategies for Web server replicas in order to better the functioning of Content Distribution Networks (CDNs). Qiu et al. list several placement algorithms and study the effect of factors such as network topography on them.

Chapter 3

CACHING ARCHITECTURES

The following architectures are popular: hierarchical, distributed and hybrid.

Table 3.1. Popular caching architectures

Hierarchical
Distributed
Hybrid

1. Hierarchical caching

It is possible to set up caches hierarchically in a tree-like construction so that when a request for a Web object comes, the caches can obtain strategic advantage by working together. This can happen when the cache which received the request did not possess the object asked for. In hierarchical caching, caches are classified into parent caches and child caches. As a rule, in a hierarchical caching structure, parent caches never query their children although they may be queried by them. This causes a trickle down effect wherein data progressively goes down the hierarchy until it reaches the leaves.

Adaptive Web caching (see the chapter on flavors of caching) is an example of a caching strategy that makes use of hierarchies. In Adaptive Web caching the cache groups can be considered to constitute a cache hierarchy. Adaptive caching helps to propagate information from the hot spots (which occur dynamically) to clusters of caches that are relatively far off. In Adaptive Web caching the parent/child kinship is set up for every object. Therefore the hierarchies in this case are contemporary oriented. As an illustration, a group of caches might

Figure 3.1.   A cache hierarchy

A: Root cache
B: Parent cache
D, E: Child caches
D, E, F, G: siblings

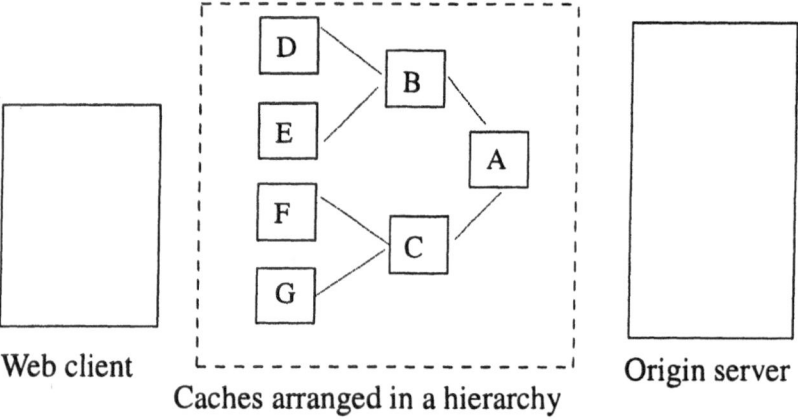

Web client   Caches arranged in a hierarchy   Origin server

function as a parent for a particular object but may also function as a child for another object. This therefore leads to some flexibility in dealing with content.

One major shortcoming with the hierarchical caching approach is that parent caches could get overburdened because of too many queries from their children. One way to deal with this problem is to employ clustering. Many commercial products make use of clustering to overcome the inundation effect on parent caches.

It is possible to identify several tiers in a caching hierarchy. For instance, caching may be feasible at the browser of the user, at the institution or organization of the user, at the regional, or at national and global levels. A Web page found in a browser's cache may be sent to the user. If not, a request may be placed with caches at the institutional tier. If it is found at this tier then it may be forwarded to the user after putting a copy in the browser's cache. If not, a request may be placed with the caches at the higher tiers and ultimately with the origin server.

Chankunthod et al. [116] debate the design and performance of a hierarchical proxy cache system aimed at better scalability of Internet information systems. They mention that it is often believed that hierarchical caching is not a suitable architecture due to the possibility of high access latency due to the hierarchical structure. They present the results of their experiments and challenge the conventional thinking that hierarchical caching is not worth considering by showing that superior results are possible by employing it. Their system performs better in the case of load that happens to be concurrent.

Rodriguez et al. [475] compare the performance of two competing architectures: hierarchical and distributed (see the next section for more on distributed caching). As mentioned earlier, in hierarchical caching, caches may be placed at several tiers in the network. On the other hand, in distributed caching, caches are placed only at the lower tiers of the network. In addition, there is no concept of intermediate caches. The metric used by Rodriguez et al. to compare the performance of the architectures is the access latency to fetch a Web object. They discover that hierarchical caching has smaller connection times when compared to distributed caching. In addition to this, keeping copies at intermediate tiers in hierarchical caching diminishes the access latency for documents of modest size. However, distributed caching was found to have lesser transmission time in spite of the fact that its bandwidth requirement is more than hierarchical caching. They report that the network traffic produced by a distributed caching approach is better spread out and also makes use of bandwidth at lower tiers to a greater extent. This helps because lower tiers are not so clogged.

Rodriguez et al. [475] also study a hybrid approach. In this strategy a fixed number of caches work together at every tier of a caching hierarchy by employing distributed caching. They report that a properly set up hybrid scheme can club together the benefits of both hierarchical and distributed caching. For instance, diminishing the connection time and also the transmission time. They mention that contingent on factors such as the hybrid caching architecture chosen; the load on the incumbent parent caches; the document size etc., a lower bound may be derived. This bound specifies the minimum number of caches that must work together at every tier of the network in order to keep the total retrieval latency to a minimum. Rodriguez et al. also propose changes to cache sharing protocols for choosing the extent of collaboration at all tiers of a hybrid caching strategy. Also refer [476].

Hierarchical caching is also employed by Adaptive Web Caching (see Michel et al. [395]) and the access driven cache (see Yang et al. [571]). The Adaptive Web caching strategy is explained in the chapter on flavors of Web caching. In addition, refer to Tewari et al. [520]. A hierarchical caching strategy is beneficial when some collaborating cache servers do not have high speed links. This is due to the fact that it does not consume much bandwidth. Hence, in such situations it becomes feasible to effectively propagate hot Web pages in the direction of the demand. On the negative side, there do exist problems with hierarchical caching, some of which we discussed earlier. A few of the major difficulties with hierarchical caching are recapitulated here. The set up of a caching hierarchy often involves placing cache servers at important locations in the network. As a consequence, this may necessitate substantial collaboration amongst cache servers involved in the scheme. Slowdown may occur at various tiers in the hierarchy. Caches at the higher tiers could get inundated with requests from the caches at lower tiers thereby causing long queuing times. A huge number of copies of a particular document could get duplicated at different tiers in the hierarchy. This could make it difficult for maintaining cache consistency (see the chapter on cache coherence for more on cache consistency).

Listed below are the salient features of hierarchical caching. Compare with those of distributed caching (see next section).

Table 3.2.   Salient features of hierarchical caching

Parent caches in a hierarchy may get overburdened
Possibility for high access latency due to the hierarchical structure
Short connection times
Bandwidth required is low when compared to distributed caching
Beneficial when some cooperating cache servers do not have high speed links
Hierarchies with more than four tiers are not worth considering due to high access latencies
Transmission times could be high when compared to distributed caching
Network traffic is unevenly distributed amongst caches
Scalable architecture: possibility for institutional, regional, and national tiers
Disk space usage is significant when compared to distributed caching
Fault tolerance is low when compared to distributed caching
Load distribution is not uniform
Placement of caches at strategic locations is vital
Too many copies of objects may get duplicated at various tiers
Ensuring freshness of objects is not easy
Responses times are worse for clients that are close to the lower tiers of a hierarchy
Useful in WANs but not in LANs
Significant communication delays
Slowdowns at various tiers add up
Possibility for collaboration amongst siblings at various tiers

---

2.   Distributed caching

Distributed caching is an alternative to hierarchical caching. In distributed caching there do not exist any intermediate tiers except for the institutional tier. All caches at the institutional tier are made to possess meta-data concerning the content of participating caches. This makes it possible to fetch documents in the event of a cache miss (refer Glossary for a definition). In order to obtain a scalable approach for dispersing meta-data particulars we may make use of a hierarchical scheme. The hierarchy is used only for sharing information about the directories in which content is available. See Povey and Harrison [450] for more particulars about a distributed caching scheme.

Distributed caching offers some advantages over hierarchical caching some of which we discussed earlier. To recap, caches at the lower tiers are not congested and there is no need to deal with intermediate tiers because they do not exist in distributed caching. As a result, disk space usage in distributed caching is less than in hierarchical caching. Other benefits of distributed caching include a higher degree of fault tolerance and more uniform load distribution. The reader may consult the following references for more on the benefits of distributed caching: Tewari et al. [520], Rodriguez et al. [475, 476] and Povey and Harrison [450].

Listed below are the salient features of distributed caching. Compare with those of hierarchical caching (see previous section).

Table 3.3. Salient features of distributed caching

No concept of hierarchy, nevertheless, a meta-data hierarchy may be used
Caches at lower tiers are not congested
Access latency is lower when compared to hierarchical caching
Connection times could be long when compared to hierarchical caching
Bandwidth required is high when compared to hierarchical caching
Transmission times are low when compared to hierarchical caching
Network traffic is more evenly spread out
Scalability concerns exist due to communication overheads
Disk space usage is low when compared to hierarchical caching
Fault tolerance is high when compared to hierarchical caching
Load distribution is more uniform when compared to hierarchical caching
No requirement for placement of caches at strategic locations
Duplication of objects is low when compared to hierarchical caching
Ensures freshness to a higher degree when compared to hierarchical caching
Response times are better when compared to hierarchical caching
Useful for both LANs and WANs
Possibility for higher hit ratios when compared to hierarchical caching

Povey and Harrison [450] discussed a distributed caching scheme wherein directory servers keep pieces of information otherwise known as location hints about the location of documents that are maintained in all the caches. These servers were intended to overcome the need for maintaining caches at the higher tiers of a caching hierarchy. A meta-data hierarchy was employed to obtain an effective dispersal of such location hints.

Tewari et al. [520] studied a distributed caching strategy akin to that of Povey and Harrison [450]. In their system location hints are duplicated at caches in the institutional tier. Gadde et al. [209] discussed the use of CRISP, a distributed caching system. A CRISP cache comprises of a set of collaborating servers that make use of a common directory of cached Web objects.

Some caching protocols that are often used particularly for distributed include the Internet Cache Protocol (ICP) and the Cache Array Routing Protocol (CARP) (see the chapter on inter-cache communication and refer to [550, 532]).

ICP

Wessels and Claffy [550] mention the practical aspects of ICP, its construction and application in Squid. Squid is a popular open source software used for implementing Web caching. ICP may be thought of as a light messaging mechanism for communication between Web caches. Caches use such messages for determining the most suitable cache to fetch an object. Hence, ICP provides the capability for locating and fetching documents from neighborhood caches and also parent caches.

CARP

The Cache Array Routing Protocol (CARP) was described by Valloppillil and Ross [532]. CARP splits the URL-space between a group of caches. The linkage between the caches is deliberately made slack. CARP permits a cache to hold only those documents for which the URLs are hashed to it.

In some distributed caching systems such as the CacheMesh system (see Wang [543]) cache servers may set up a routing table to be shared among themselves. In CacheMesh every cache server is made to become the preferred server for a select number of Web sites. Any incoming requests are then directed to the appropriate cache server on the basis of the entries in the routing table.

Many caching systems such as Summary Cache (see below and refer to Fan et al. [194]), Cache Digests (see below and refer to Rousskov and Wessels [480]) and the Relais project (see Makpangou and Bérenguier [369])allow for the possibility of exchange of information among caches. This exchange could help in locating content and in maintaining local directories.

Summary Cache

Summary Cache is a wide-area Web cache sharing protocol developed by Fan et al. [194]. In this protocol, every proxy maintains a *summary* of the cache directories of other proxies. These summaries are examined by the proxy for possible hits prior to sending requests to other proxies. Two major advantages of this protocol include the following: summaries are made up to date occasionally and the representations are very space efficient. Fan et al. [194] use trace-driven simulations and deduce that their implementation brings down the quantum of inter-cache protocol messages substantially; curtails bandwidth usage by at least 50 %, and also gets rid of the protocol related processor burden to a significant extent. It is stated that Summary Cache does all this with a cache hit ratio comparable to that of ICP. In addition, Summary Cache is reported to be quite scalable.

Cache Digests

Cache Digests (see Rousskov and Wessels [480]) is a protocol for distributed caching. In this protocol, information concerning the contents of data in a cache are made available to its peers. This information is provided in a compact manner by the use of *digests*. Digests are used by a cache to find whether its neighbors possess a given Web object. Cache Digests may be considered as an alternative to conventional designs obtained by the use of ICP. Wessels and Rousskov explain the reasons for using Cache Digests and also mention their application in the Squid caching software. They compare the performance of Cache Digests with ICP in real-world situations and demonstrate that it performs better in many cases.

Tay et al. [518] describe a distributed Web caching system. In their system, every client computer in the network takes up the supplementary role of a cache server. This enables the client to serve objects that it had earlier asked for and obtained, to different client computers that seek the same objects. Tay et al. develop a protocol to deal with functions such as access, storage and serving. Their protocol ensures consistency between the object in the master server and that in the cache. Tay et al. state that their system has the maximal storage capability and also the highest level of reliability imaginable for a network of the stipulated structure.

3. Hybrid caching

In hybrid caching, caches may collaborate with other caches at the same tier of the cache hierarchy or at a higher tier by means of distributed caching. The ICP protocol (see Wessels and Claffy [550]) is a representative example of hybrid caching. Rodriguez et al. [475] listed the benefits of a hybrid caching approach (see the discussion under hierarchical caching). Rabinovich et al. [458] suggested that the amount of collaboration between adjacent caches could be curtailed. This is done to shun fetching documents from caches that are either distant or slow and that could otherwise have been fetched directly from the origin server at a lesser expense.

4.   Further reading

There may be definite advantages in preferring a particular architecture when compared to others. Worrell [566] states that a hierarchical caching scheme throws up the possibility for implementing offbeat cache consistency approaches (see the chapter on cache consistency).

Dahlin et al. [155] study four cooperative caching algorithms. Their study indicates that cooperative caching can cut the number of disk accesses by nearly 50% and better the file system read response time by almost 73%. They state that simple cooperative caching algorithms are adequate to obtain the performance improvement.

Kwan et al. [332] describe the architecture of a Web server located in the National Center for Supercomputing Applications (NCSA). This server was a frequently accessed Web server. Kwan et al. looked at the logs of this server in order to grasp how users accessed the NCSA Web server. See also [333].

Jeffery et al. [268] look at proxy cache servers that share their contents with neighbors within the proximity. They argue that good performance and scalable solutions demand the use of non-hierarchical structures.

Sarkar and Hartman [489] describe a decentralized algorithm for cooperative caching. They mention that their algorithm has insignificant overheads and performs on par with several centralized algorithms. They propose a hint-based approach that enables Web clients to exercise control on the functioning of the Web caches in a decentralized manner. They mention that their algorithm achieves performance comparable to the centralized algorithms in existence but at the same time has the following advantages:

- diminishes the manager load by a factor of at least 15

- cuts down the block lookup traffic by about 66%, and

- curtails the replacement traffic by a factor of at least 5.

Baggio and Pierre [36] discuss the working of Oléron. Oléron is a system of collaborating proxy caches. It permits sharing of small sets of documents among groups of users. It also allows for efficient Web browsing in mobile environments.

Gadde et al. [206] study several choices for maintaining directories in distributed Web caches. They employ trace-driven simulations to evaluate multicast-based queries of local maps (as in a system known as Harvest) with unicast queries of a global map (as in CRISP). They develop a CRISP structure that merges the beneficial features of various distributed cache structures without compromising the hit ratio (see Glossary for a definition).

Gadde et al. [207] modify the Squid cache to obtain a variant known as Crispy Squid. This variant epitomizes numerous CRISP cache structures. Gadde et al. assess these structures using a tool known as Proxycizer. This tool is employed for playing back traces of the witnessed request traffic into the Web cache epitomes. CRISP caches are organized as an agglomeration of independent Web proxy servers that use their cache directories jointly by means of a shared mapping service. This mapping service may be interrogated by incurring at the maximum only one message interchange. In the CRISP system, every independent server may be permitted to duplicate content in order to reduce overheads and the access costs.

Danzig [157] gives a description of the architecture of a commercial proxy cache known as NetCache. The article deals with topics such as choosing the most advantageous size of proxy caches, the benefits and drawbacks of transparent caching and approaches for ensuring high availability in caches. Danzig also describes the experience gained as a consequence of employing the proxy cache at Internet Service Providers (ISPs) and commercial organizations.

Inoue et al. [259] altered Internet Cache Protocol (ICP) (see the chapter on inter-cache communication) message contents in order to accommodate what they call as hints. Their system known as WebHint automatically makes up-to-date the data concerning peer caches. The modified ICP messages are employed for a variety of useful functions.

Krishnan and Sugla [325] discuss the utility of cooperating proxy caches. They look at a commercial intranet setup supporting several Web proxies. As a result of their experiments, they deduce that hit ratios improved because of co-operation among the proxies by about 0.7% to 28.9 % on a daily basis. They come up with metrics that proxies may utilize in order to assess the efficiency of caching.

Kurcewicz et al. [329] describe the design of a distributed Web cache. Their cache did not possess a single point of failure. It made use of filtering algorithms (see [330]) for placing objects in memory caches. Load sharing between the components of the cache is accomplished by the use of routing arrays.

Nishikawa et al. [415] describe a memory-based architecture for a distributed Web proxy cache. They come up with such an architecture for Web proxy caches in order to deal with the disk I/O constrictions in such caching systems. They report that their technique has the following characteristics:

- only routinely accessed Web pages are fetched

- a mechanism is employed for the effective utilization of cache space between collaborating proxy caches, in an unattended fashion.

They mention that when compared to conventional proxy caches, their method requires only about a tenth of the cache space without suffering any deterioration in the cache hit ratio. Another important advantage is that fast DRAMs may be employed in the proxy caches due to the diminished cache space requirement. Thus their approach overcomes the disk I/O bottleneck problem.

Pierre and Makpangou [440] describe Saperlipopette!, a distributed Web caching system evaluation tool. This tool is intended to aid decision making while building Web caching systems. As an illustration, some of the common questions while designing a large scale caching system could include the following:

- how many caches are to be used,

- what must be their sizes, and

- how they must collaborate in a beneficial fashion.

Saperlipopette! is designed to answer such questions and ease the task of building a Web caching system. It offers the possibility of assessing beforehand the quality that would be provided by every possible configuration of the distributed cache infrastructure. In order to achieve this, Pierre and Makpangou observe the Web activity of an organization over a period of time so as to obtain data regarding the patterns of Web access. They then replay the access patterns during their simulations. By running their tool for every potential configuration, it then becomes possible to determine the best one. They report that as a result of their experiments they found that after reaching a particular cache size the performance tends to be constant although cache consistency happens to deteriorate.

Rodriguez et al. [469, 471] discuss two approaches for the dispersion of documents in the World Wide Web. In the first approach, the sender sends a Web document in a recurring fashion to a multicast IP address. The receivers become members of the pertinent multicast tree without any synchronism in order to obtain a copy of the document. In the second approach, the document is sent to the receivers by means of a Web cache hierarchy. Rodriguez et al. contrast the two approaches with respect to parameters such as latency and bandwidth consumption. They observe the following:

- In case of documents that change very often, the multicast approach:
  - lowers latency,
  - does not consume much network bandwidth and hence conserves it, and also
  - diminishes the burden on the origin server.

- In case of documents that remain more or less unmodified most of the time, the approach that makes use of the Web cache hierarchy produces reduced latency and consumes less bandwidth than the multicast approach.

They mention that combining both the approaches cited above would be requisite in order to obtain the best performance from the Web.

Asaka et al. [30] describe a hash-based query caching technique for distributed Web caching in wide area networks (WANs). They state that although distributed Web caching permits multiple clients to rapidly access Web pages, there do exist problems with traditional distributed Web caching schemes. For example, ICP and hash-based routing both necessitate that numerous queries be sent amongst cache servers. They may also burden cache servers that happen to be far away. In order to deal with these issues, Asaka et al. suggest a hash-based query caching scheme that makes uses of a hash function and also a query caching technique. They state that their scheme is able to locate cached objects in various cache servers by making use of only one query message and diminishes cache server burdening and retrieval latencies.

Baker and Moon [42] discuss a system known as DCWS (Distributed Cooperative Web Servers). They mention that by convention, techniques for a distributed Web server design have resorted to utilizing centrally located resources such as routers or Domain Name System (DNS) servers in order to disperse requests intended for a single IP address to multiple Web servers. The DCWS system controls hyperlinks contained within documents for reducing the constrictions or loads on centralized resources. DCWS is stated to be completely capable of working together harmoniously with prevailing HTTP protocols and also Web client software.

Dykes et al. [189] propose a taxonomy for distributed network caching on the basis of techniques used for discovery, delivery and dissemination. They also describe a cooperative caching protocol by which servers locate copies by searching in local metadata directories. Dykes et al. mention that their technique does well when compared to standard proxy caching techniques.

Wolman et al. [561] analyze Web object sharing and caching from an organizational point of view. They mention that although many caching techniques exploit the fact that some documents are asked for by several clients in a repetitive manner, studies have not been directed at understanding how clients within an organization share documents. They state that it is essential to understand sharing of documents from an organizational point of view because caches are often configured for an organization as a whole. They study document sharing between:

- clients located within an organization

- clients located in various organizations.

For their study they consider a big university as an example of a set of different organizations.

Wolman et al. [561, 562] study the functioning of cooperative Web proxy caching in a large sized Web set up. They make use of analytic and also trace-based approaches for determining the benefits and shortcomings of cooperation between proxy caches. They study the possibility for collaboration between 200 small Web proxies in a university set up. They also study the collaboration between two large proxies within the university. One of which is capable of dealing with 23,000 clients, while the other is capable of working with 60,000 clients. Wolman et al. try to go beyond these numbers and predict the collaboration behavior of cooperative proxy caches when there are millions of clients. In order to do achieve this, they make use of their analytic approach. By their study, they infer that cooperative proxy caching is beneficial only when the number of Web clients is not very big.

Bhattacharjee et al. [74] study self-organizing wide-area network (WAN) caches. In their article, they perform a detailed critical inspection of the gains of linking caches with switching nodes throughout a network rather than barely at a few locations. They study the use of several self-organizing cache management schemes for the purpose of organizing cache content. They conclude that efficient use of cache space and self-organizing caching schemes can provide more beneficial average round-trip latencies than normally used techniques.

Hufftaker et al. [247] describe a tool for visualizing the growth and topology of the NLANR cache hierarchy. They mention the visualization capabilities of an enhanced version of a tool known as Planet Cache that was used earlier. The new version provides for both topological and geographical portrayals of the hierarchy and is Java based.

Melve [386] describes the design of a Web caching system. Useful guidelines are presented for setting up a cache server. In related articles, Melve et al. [389, 390] discuss the architectural aspects when designing a Web caching system.

Melve [387, 388] mentions that there are no good methods in existence for evaluating the benefits of relationships between proxy cache servers with respect to factors such as cost advantages, latency reduction, and network bandwidth savings. The objective of their work is to find a limiting value for relationships between servers based on the above mentioned factors. The limiting value is intended to be useful for automatic configuration of large scale proxy cache systems having several servers. Melve also presents a formula for estimating the efficacy of relationships between caches. This formula could be used for deciding when to break a relationship.

Menaud et al. [392] develop a protocol for efficient cooperation among caches that form part of a transverse Web caching system. The protocol reduces demands on both bandwidth and traffic and is stated to distribute work between caches in a balanced fashion. In a related article Menaud et al. [393] state that either it is possible to increase the storage capacity of a single cache or improve the cooperation among a group of caches. The second option would often be economical when compared to the first for several reasons. Menaud et al. describe two cache replacement algorithms (see the chapter on cache replacement algorithms) known as LRU-HOT and LRU-QoS that perform better than earlier algorithms in terms of parameters such as the hit rate, byte hit rate (refer Glossary) and the response time to service requests from Web clients. They also make use of their cache cooperation protocol for keeping the load on the network, processing overheads and storage uptake by caches to a minimum.

Yu and MacNair [585] study the performance of a collaborative method for hierarchical caching in proxy servers. They are mainly concerned with the task of minimizing or diminishing the duplicate caching between a proxy and caches at the higher tiers in the hierarchy. This is intended to help decision making at the time of caching. Yu and MacNair employ a collaboration protocol for aiding decision making. The protocol sends information beneficial for caching along with the Web object to caches at the lower tiers of the hierarchy. Yu and MacNair report that their collaboration protocol has positive benefits.

Bouthors and Dedieu [84] give an account of Pharos, a collaborative infrastructure for sharing the knowledge acquired from the Web. Pharos has been implemented by using the Java programming language. Scalability issues are tackled in Pharos by dispersing servers widely and by duplicating the contents of their databases. The infrastructure used by Pharos permits users to index and judge the worth of documents on specific topics.

Kawai et al. [298] look at the scalability concerns in distributed Web caching systems in which proxy caches make use of the Internet Cache Protocol (ICP) for intercommunication. ICP is often used for bettering the hit ratio. Kawai et al. assess the volume of traffic produced by the ICP and HTTP protocols in systems with siblings and also in systems without siblings. They arrive at the conclusion that a distributed caching system based on ICP cannot be of great help in diminishing Web traffic. They base their conclusion on the fact that a proxy having only one sibling has a very low hit ratio.

Chiang et al. [125] develop a scheme for re-routing requests in dynamic Web caching hierarchies. In an earlier work, they had suggested a Web caching technique that was supported by the Caching Neighborhood Protocol (CNP) (see [126]) and made use of dynamic Web caching hierarchies. CNP is intended to be an alternative to ICP (used by Harvest and Squid). Chiang et al. [127] make use of a mathematical model to estimate the response times of schemes that made use of Cache Digests, CNP, ICP and a simple hierarchy and demonstrated that CNP does well for a particular target size.

When compared to static Web caching hierarchies, the dynamic Web caching hierarchies are somewhat different in the way they operate. In the dynamic variety, proxy servers construct hierarchies in a need-based manner on the basis of every incoming request. In the static variety, proxy servers are built up into hierarchies beforehand. Chiang et al. argue that dynamic Web caching hierarchies can turn out to be as beneficial as static Web caching hierarchies.

Belloum et al. [59] propose a caching architecture in which confederations of Web servers are distributed globally and also cache data partially. They argue that doing so reduces the burden on global caches and also enables a scalable configuration. They discuss algorithms for confederation of Web servers and techniques for identifying probable cache collaborators. Bellow et al. [60] extend their ideas for developing a scalable Web server architecture that makes use of distributed databases instead of file systems.

Busari and Williamson [94] employ trace-driven simulations to study the performance of Web proxy caching hierarchies with multiple tiers. They look at heterogeneous cache replacement policies in a two-tier cache hierarchy and also study the effect of size-based partitioning across the tiers of the hierarchy. They mention that both heterogeneous cache replacement policies and size-based partitioning offer some improvement in the performance of caching.

Che et al. [119] study the basic design precepts for hierarchical Web caching. They develop an analytical modeling technique for characterizing a two-tier hierarchical caching system that does not employ cooperation between caches. The hierarchical caching system makes use of the Least Recently Used (LRU) cache replacement algorithm (see the chapter on cache replacement algorithms) locally at every cache. Che et al. make use of the modeling technique to learn how the caching processes work. As a consequence, they discover some basic design precepts. They put forward for consideration a cooperative hierarchical Web caching architecture on the basis of these precepts. They demonstrate that their cooperative architecture does better than a hierarchical caching architecture that does not employ cooperation. It performs better by making use of cached resources in a more beneficial way. Also refer [118].

Cohen and Kaplan [135] note that the *age of content* in caches situated at the higher tiers of a hierarchy becomes an important performance determining factor. They study the magnitude of the *age penalty* (see the chapter on cache consistency) for content served by large caches.

Dykes and Robbins [190] conduct a viability analysis of cooperative proxy caching. They model the response time speedup for various cooperative arrangements and appraise the viability of proxy cooperation on the basis of experimentally ascertained hit rates and calculated Web response times. They discover that proxy cooperation is not very profitable if average response time happens to be the only criterion. Nevertheless, they state that proxy cooperation can diminish the unevenness in response times and the quantum of inordinate delays. In addition, proxy cooperation provides an alternative to prevent the occurrence of network congestion because of which the gross output gets better.

Gadde et al. [208] make use of an analytical model due to Wolman (see [562]) for studying the behavior of interior cache servers in multi-tier caching systems. They accomplish the following:

- use the model for large caching systems in which the inner nodes are owned by third-party content distribution agents

- study the efficiency of content distribution agents as traditional Web proxy caching becomes more widespread

- compare the model's forecasts of the behavior of inner caches with real world data obtained from the root caches of the NLANR (National Lab for Applied Network Research) cache hierarchy.

Li and Moon [349] describe the design and implementation of the Distributed Co-operative Apache (DC-Apache) Web server. They feel that dispersing documents amongst a group of collaborating Web servers would improve the performance of a caching system as a whole. Their DC-Apache system has the following capabilities:

- the ability to spread and duplicate documents within a group of collaborating Web servers

- the ability to distribute requests between servers in order to achieve load balancing by the application of dynamic hyperlink creation

- the ability to ensure consistency between documents that have been duplicated across the collaborating group of Web servers.

Li and Moon mention that their system is highly scalable and also performs well. It is also stated to be suitable for tackling the hot spot phenomenon.

Paul and Fei [432] study in depth the benefits and drawbacks of a distributed caching architecture in which caches are organized by means of a central controller. They contrast the performance of a set of autonomous caches against the performance of a set of coordinated distributed caches. They observe that a distributed architecture facilitating a set of coordinated caches has the following advantages:

- attains better hit ratios

- ameliorates the response time

- ensures freshness to a higher degree

- accomplishes load balancing

- betters the capability of the network to deal with more traffic.

All these benefits are obtained at the cost of some extra control traffic. Paul and Fei state that by their approach they observed improvements to the extent of:

- 40% in the hit ratio

- 70% in the response time

- 60% in ensuring freshness

- 25% in the traffic wielding capability of the network.

Selvakumar and Prabhakar [496] discuss the implementation of two distributed caching schemes and also contrast them. They study how a group of shared Web caches can work together in a coordinated fashion by looking at two approaches. The first approach makes use of the Internet Cache Protocol (ICP). The second approach makes use of hash-routing. In hash-routing, the Web client viz. the browser gets to know the hash value of the URL for the Web page asked for. It then directs the request to the pertinent cache server. In contrast to hash routing, in the ICP approach Web caches query peers and seek the requested Web pages from the caches in the vicinity that possess them. Selvakumar and Prabhakar implement the two approaches mentioned above. They study these two approaches by looking at:

- the latency in fetching Web pages

- the flexibility of cache servers in the event of failure of a compeer cache server.

They observe that hash routing offers substantial performance benefits when compared to the ICP approach as regards average latency under ordinary circumstances. However, ICP offers good flexibility when the failure rate of cache servers becomes considerable. Selvakumar and Prabhakar also note that the hash function used in the hash routing scheme must be able to:

- compute the hash values rapidly, and also

- offer uniform dispersion of Web pages amongst the cache servers.

Buchholz and Schill [92] mention the application of hierarchical caching in a pervasive computing environment. They state that the hierarchical proxies are able to adapt content for the needs of the mobile devices and also offer the benefits of caching.

In hierarchical caching systems users located close to the leaf level of a caching hierarchy are likely to encounter a higher miss rate and delayed response time than users who are at higher levels. Therefore techniques must try to surmount this drawback. Hou et al. [243] develop a prefetching technique (see the chapter on prefetching) for alleviating the bias against users near the leaf level of a cache hierarchy.

Rodriguez et al. [470] discuss mechanisms for automatic delivery of updates to documents by means of a caching infrastructure. They study both push and pull techniques and also discuss the benefits of multicast and caching hierarchies to enable the automatic delivery of updates to documents.

Laoutaris et al. [336] state that although hierarchical caching is widely used, it has one drawback. Regardless of the replacement algorithms used in the individual caches belonging to the hierarchy, a feature of current hierarchical caches is that a hit for a document at a cache in tier k results in the caching of the document at all intermediate caches (i.e tiers $k - 1, \ldots, 1$) on the path leading to the leaf cache that got the original request. Laoutaris et al. describe several algorithms that try to be more preferential in selecting caches that get to store a local copy of the requested document. These algorithms are known as *meta algorithms* because they function at liberty irrespective of the replacement algorithms used in the individual caches.

Laoutaris et al. develop three meta algorithms and contrast them with the de facto algorithm and another due to Che et al. They state that meta algorithms are advantageous for dealing with multimedia objects such as stored music files or short video clips. They also develop a simple load balancing algorithm based on the ideas used for designing the meta algorithms. They state that their algorithm is capable of balancing load efficiently and may also be an answer to the filtering effect in hierarchical Web caches noted by Williamson (see [554]). This effect is caused by the existence of multiple tiers in a cache hierarchy. The characteristics of workload bestowed to a tier get affected by the previous tier since a tier is accessed only if there are misses in the previous tiers.

Ahn et al. [13] study content-aware cooperative caching for cluster-based Web servers. They argue that traditional cooperative caching methods were designed for network file systems and are not suitable for file systems in Web servers. They develop a new cooperative caching scheme that is more suited for file systems in Web servers. The scheme makes use of a cache replacement policy that does not cache unwanted data that would be generated in the course of serving requests. Ahn et al. mention that their cooperating caching scheme reduces the disk access ratio by nearly 29% and also diminishes block access latency by almost 26% when contrasted with traditional cooperative caching schemes.

5. Exercises

1 Mention different caching architectures. Compare and contrast them.

2 Investigate the benefits and drawbacks of using a cache hierarchy.

3 Try to come up with alternatives for avoiding the use of cache hierarchies.

4 Explore ways of preventing overburdening of caches at the higher tiers in hierarchical caching.

5 What factors determine the most beneficial depth in a caching hierarchy?

6 Explain how hierarchical caching is employed by Adaptive Web Caching.

7 Mention different protocols commonly used in distributed caching. Make a comparative study of these protocols and list their advantages and disadvantages.

8 Explore how ICP works in Squid.

9 Investigate different caching architectures with respect to scalability.

10 What are the advantages of employing a hybrid caching architecture?

Chapter 4

CACHING DYNAMIC DATA

There may not be much benefit in caching data such as personalized data, data that is generated by servers dynamically, authenticated data etc. Therefore the advantages from Web caching get lowered by the presence of such data. Experiments by Caceres et al. [97] and Feldman et al. [199] have demonstrated that almost 30% of the requests possess cookies (see Glossary for a definition). Feldman et al. mention that cookies can drastically reduce the hit ratio and also render several documents uncacheable. Therefore it becomes necessary to find ways of making such data more cacheable. In order to improve the performance we must also diminish the latency of accessing data that does not appear to be cacheable. Feldman et al. also mention that aborted connections may result in wastage of bandwidth, much more than what could be saved by the application of caching.

There are at least two alternatives for caching dynamic data. They are Active Cache and server accelerators.

Table 4.1. Alternatives for caching dynamic data

Active Cache
Web server accelerators

1. Techniques for caching dynamic data

1.1 Active Cache

Active Cache described earlier in the chapter on flavors of caching was developed by Cao et al [103]. It provides for caching of dynamic documents at

Web proxies by permitting servers to furnish *cache applets*, which are meant to be appended to documents. It expects the proxies to call on cache applets in case of a cache hit so that it can act without the need for interacting with the server.

Although, the Active Cache technique does result in substantial network bandwidth savings, it puts extra burden on the CPU. Hence, in some situations it might be better to avoid caching dynamic objects.

1.2   Web server accelerator

Levy-Abegnoli et al. [345] discuss the design and performance of a Web server accelerator which runs on an embedded operating system. They mention that it can enable the Web server to serve a huge number of Web pages per second. They also state that it is an order of magnitude better than what could be got without using it. A Web server accelerator can be positioned as the forepart of a Web server for the purpose of accelerating Web access. It supplies an API (Application Program Interface) that permits the addition, deletion or updating of cached data by application programs. The API makes it possible to cache both static and dynamic data. Levy-Abegnoli et al. study the SPEC Web96 benchmark and demonstrate that their technique can attain high hit ratios and performance on par with the benchmark.

2.   DUP algorithm

Challenger et al [110] describe a scalable system for consistently caching dynamic data. Their system uses an algorithm known as the Data Update Propagation (DUP) algorithm. This keeps data dependence information in a graph. On detecting changes to the inherent data, the system employs graph traversal algorithms to find out which cached objects are influenced by the changes. Cached objects detected to be obsolete are updated or may be invalidated. The DUP algorithm was used by its authors for designing an Olympic games Web site. They mention that they were able to achieve hit ratios close to 100% as compared to an earlier version which achieved only 80% without employing DUP. They mention that this allowed for high quality service when the requests were at their peak.

Iyengar [262] discusses the design and performance of a general-purpose software cache. It is meant for bettering the functioning of Web servers and databases. It is designed to handle cache hits amounting to many hundred thousands per second. The general-purpose software cache makes use of the Data Update Propagation (DUP) algorithm described earlier, in order to invalidate objects. The inclusion of the general-purpose software cache does not contribute to any worsening of the performance of the system. A more effective algorithm is stated to be valuable for dealing with obsolete objects.

3. Further reading

Dan and Sitaraman [156] study multimedia caching strategies for heterogeneous application and server environments. For a multimedia system, bandwidth and storage are undoubtedly crucial. Multimedia documents may be cached in local storage in order to mitigate bandwidth requirements. Multimedia documents are often heterogenous in size. So a caching policy for multimedia data has to adjust with dynamic changes in the workload and size variations. Dan and Sitaraman develop a caching policy that is able to deal with such issues and also helps to route requests to heterogenous servers and balances load among them.

Douglis et al. [181] report on an extension of HTML known as HPP (HTML pre-processing). HPP allows for pre-processing of HTML macros in order to enable dynamic document caching. In their approach, Douglis et al. split a resource (viz. a Web object) into two halves corresponding to its static and dynamic components. This makes it possible to cache the static component. The dynamic component may then be procured on every access in a need-based manner. They report that their approach has the potential for diminishing significantly the network traffic, the access latencies, and the burden placed on servers.

Iyengar et al. [261] study the performance of Web servers under high CPU loads. Efficient functioning of Web servers is a crucial requirement for Web sites, especially for those that handle a huge number of requests. Iyengar et al. observe that performance of Web servers diminishes considerably due to requests for dynamic Web pages. Hence, where possible it is beneficial to restrict the fraction of dynamic pages to a bare minimum. It is also worthwhile to utilize techniques for dealing with dynamic Web pages in an efficient manner. Iyengar et al. state that when a Web server functions at virtually the highest capacity, the performance is better if a higher proportion of requests are abandoned.

Holmedahl et al. [241] studied cooperative caching of dynamic content on a distributed Web server. They put forward for consideration a technique for bettering the average response time of Web servers. They accomplish this by caching the results of requests for dynamic content by adopting a cooperative approach. They devised a distributed Web server known as Swala. In this Web server, the nodes cooperatively cache the results of CGI requests and also the cache meta-data that happens to be preserved in a replicated global cache directory. They mention that the application of caching results in better performance. They also state that the cache hit ratio is better when cooperative caching is employed.

Smith et al. [505] mention that requests for dynamic Web content could also include significant locality for identical requests. They categorize locality in dynamic Web content into three categories:

- identical requests,

- equivalent requests, and

- partially equivalent requests.

By the phrase *equivalent requests* they refer to requests that are not identical to earlier requests but which lead to the creation of identical dynamic Web content. For *partially equivalent requests* the content created is not identical but may be used to serve as a temporary place holder as the actual document is being created. Smith et al. describe a new protocol known as the (). They explore the working of the protocol by making use of real world data.

Wills and Mikhailov [558] report that by their experiments they are able to deduce that there are possibilities for reprocessing a greater proportion of cached resources than was being done before. They attribute this to the earlier use of cache directives (refer [200]) that were either imprecise or even absent. They also emphasize that the kinship between the objects used to make up a Web page must be taken into account. For example, they suggest that images contained in Web pages may often be used again even if the Web pages get modified. Such Web objects could be thrown away if they are not likely to be used again. Wills and Mikhailov mention that static resources can be cached whereas dynamic resources may be fetched when needed. Therefore it helps to identify the static and dynamic portions of Web pages. Needless invalidation of cached resources can be avoided this way.

Wills and Mikhailov [557] continue their studies aimed at obtaining a deeper understanding of the nature of resource changes at Web servers. They examine the cacheability of Web resources that have been asked for by users. They report that nearly one out of three HTML resources did not get altered in their experiments. However, the resources did not possess any information concerning the time when the last modification was made or did not supply any cache directive in the response. Due to the absence of these valuable pieces of information such resources were not cached and hence could not be validated by consulting the origin server. Wills and Mikhailov also report that the addition of a cookie as a constituent of a request does not necessarily render a response uncacheable. They mention that they were able to obtain matching responses from two requests for a particular URL, both of which happened to possess distinguishable cookies. They state that such responses can be cached and employed for validation provided cache directives permit this.

Brewington and Cybenko [90] study the dynamic nature of the Web. They present data on the frequency and on the nature of Web page alterations and also conduct a statistical analysis. They calculate the rate at which Web search engines must re-index the Web in order to continue to be up-to-date. They do this by employing models derived from experiment and observation rather than theory and also develop a new metric of recency.

Challenger et al. [111] give an account of a publishing system for producing dynamic Web data in an efficient manner. In their system, complex Web pages are fabricated from simpler shards which may themselves engraft other shards. Challenger et al. use object dependence graphs for depicting the affinity between the Web pages and the shards. They present algorithms for effectively discovering and updating Web pages after alterations have been made to the shards. They also present algorithms for publishing sets of Web pages in an orderly manner. Their publishing system has many other features and is said to have been implemented in many Web sites regarded with great favor.

Gruber et al. [220] state that multimedia streams which have been originated by the Web often encounter high start-up delay due to several reasons for e.g. significant protocol overheads. They state that Internet service providers (ISPs) can ensure better performance by caching the first segment (or the prefix) of multimedia streams that are in high demand, at proxies that are closer to the clients initiating requests for such streams. The proxy can then start the transmission of this segment to the client while at the same time seeking the balance portion of the stream from the server. Gruber et al. discuss how caching partial contents of multimedia streams poses new problems in cache coherency. They also describe a real world implementation of their technique.

Martinez et al. [383] study how large images may be browsed by using a protocol known as the Internet imaging protocol. They mention that caching at the client and server ends helped to obtain better performance.

Almeida et al. [18] analyze client workloads for educational media servers at two universities. The objectives were to understand caching techniques for streaming media content, and to measure the amount of server bandwidth that could be conserved by employing new multicast streaming techniques for stored content.

Deolasee et al. [169] discussed a mechanism for disseminating dynamic Web data. Their mechanism is known as *adaptive push-pull*. A significant proportion of Web data is highly time-dependent for e.g. scores of sports events and exchange rates of currencies. For such data, it is important to maintain time-dependent coherency i.e. temporal coherency. Servers may possess the capability for pushing or pulling data. They may pull data as per the needs of a user. They may also push only those modifications that a user expects or wants. Deolasee et al. demonstrate how the pull and push techniques may be merged so that the best of both the techniques can be realized. Their method adapts the dissemination of data from the servers to the clients on the basis of the following:

- the load on the servers and the proxies and their potential

- the coherency needs of the client's.

Their experiments demonstrate that this kind of adaptive dissemination is required for matching the varied time-dependent coherency needs and also for reasons such as effectiveness, scalability and fault tolerance.

Rejaie and Kangasharju [463] describe the design and implementation of Mocha, a quality adaptive multimedia proxy cache for layered encoded streams. Mocha has the capability to adapt the quality of cached streams on the basis of factors such as their popularity and the usable bandwidth between the proxy and the clients. Mocha applies fine-grained replacement and prefetching. Rejaie and Kangasharju describe an implementation of Mocha for the Squid proxy cache and discuss issues such as the management of streams that have been cached only partially.

It may indeed be possible to design specialized caching algorithms for handling specific types of data such as multimedia data. Wu et al. [568] discuss segment based proxy caching for streams of multimedia data.

In the real world, many popular and highly loaded short-lived Web sites such as sites reporting events pertaining to sports often deal with huge amounts of dynamic data. It may become necessary to review the functioning of cache consistency protocols employed in such cases. This may have to be accomplished in order to ensure reliability and good performance. Yin et al. [579] study the use of server-driven cache consistency protocols for massive dynamic Web workloads. They implement a server-driven cache consistency protocol for a sports Web site that was quite popular when the events were taking place. Yin et al. studied the cacheability and scalability issues concerning dynamic Web content. They study the consequences of caching dynamic data by means of server-driven cache consistency protocols and incorporate their cache consistency protocols for Squid.

Zhu and Yang [590] describe a class-based cache management approach for dealing with dynamic Web content. They state that caching dynamic pages at a server site is helpful for diminishing server resource demands and also facilitates caching of dynamic Web pages at proxies. Earlier work made use of fine-grain dependence graphs amongst separate dynamic pages to enable consistency. Zhu and Yang describe an approach for applications that necessitate coarse-grain cache management. They split dynamic pages into classes on the basis of URL patterns. Zhu and Yang also develop a system known as Cachuma that integrates their techniques and works alongside standard Web servers. It enables Web sites to incorporate the ability to cache dynamic Web pages with small changes. Zhu and Yang on the basis of empirical results conclude that their methods help in enabling coarse-grain cache management.

Almeida et al. [17] develop cost models for purveying content distribution networks that make use of a particular protocol for streaming. The protocol has utilitarian attributes such as simplicity, scalability, and low bandwidth consumption. Almeida et al. study the following aspects:

- how cost-efficient proxy servers are in multicast streaming systems

- the most useful streaming protocol

- the best proxy content in terms of the workload and the system parameters.

From their analysis, they infer that proxy servers are cost efficient only under some conditions such as the following: the origin server does not possess multicast ability or the file request rate is low and hence multicast is not very effective and so on.

Lee et al. [341] mention that caching of streaming media must be accomplished in a manner different from that of conventional non-streaming objects. They develop a caching system that makes use of a video abstraction and summarization technique. Their amalgamated video delivery and caching system makes use of content-aware segmentation, prefix caching, prefetching, and also cooperative caching.

Psounis [451] discusses the application of class-based delta-encoding for caching dynamic Web content. Class-based delta-encoding is a variation of traditional delta-encoding, the difference being that in the former documents are split into classes and one document for every class is stashed away in the server-side. Psounis presents an architecture that does not affect either the clients, the proxy caches or the servers. It is reported that class-based delta-encoding when merged with compression brings enormous benefits. For example, it constricts the bandwidth utilization to about 1 in 30 of its original value and also curbs the user perceived latency to nearly one-tenth of its original value without putting exorbitant storage demand on the server side.

Chen et al. [121] study an adaptive and lazy segmentation based proxy caching mechanism for streaming media objects. They delay the segmentation so that it occurs as late as possible and also determine the segment length based on the client access behaviors at real time. They state that their method reduces network traffic by about 30%.

Laoutaris et al. [336] mention that their meta algorithms (see the discussion in the chapter on caching architectures) are beneficial for dealing with multimedia objects such as stored music files and also short video clips.

4. Exercises

1 In the context of Web caching explain what is dynamic data.

2 Explain why it is not easy to cache dynamic data.

3 What is a cookie? Why is it difficult to cache responses containing cookies?

4 Explain two widely used techniques for caching dynamic data.

5 What is a cache applet?

6 Study in depth how the Web server accelerator technique works. Try to develop a Web server accelerator for your favorite open source Web server.

7 Describe in detail the functioning of the Data Update Propagation algorithm.

8 Compare and contrast the Active Cache and Web server accelerator techniques. Analyze their plus and minus points and determine which scheme would be better and why?

II

ASPECTS REQUIRING CO-ORDINATION

Chapter 5

INTER-CACHE COMMUNICATION

Web caching systems often consist of multiple distributed caches for the purpose of improved availability and scalability. Therefore caches must query each other to provide better service. Thus, inter-cache communication comes into the picture. There are several popular inter-cache communication protocols. Of these protocols Internet Cache Protocol (ICP) [550], Cache digests [550], Content Routing Protocol (CRP), Cache Array Routing Protocol (CARP) [532], and Web Cache Communication Protocol (WCCP) [514] are widely used.

Table 5.1. Protocols for inter-cache communication

Internet Cache Protocol (ICP)
Cache digests
Content Routing Protocol (CRP)
Web Cache Communication Protocol (WCCP)
Cache Array Routing Protocol (CARP)

1. Inter-cache communication protocols

1.1 Internet Cache Protocol

Internet Cache Protocol (ICP) is probably the oldest and most widely studied inter-cache communication protocol. It has its origins in the Harvest project. It was studied in great depth when it was used by the Squid caching software (see Wessels and Claffy [550]). We discussed ICP in short in the chapter on caching architectures. In ICP, caches pass queries to other caches to find out the most appropriate cache for fetching the Web object requested by the user. ICP makes use of a request-reply model. One drawback with multiple distributed caches is that although they may improve scalability, they may also be a hindrance to it. This was revealed during studies concerning ICP.

Baentsch et al. [33] suggest the most beneficial depth of a caching hierarchy. They mention that trees with more than four tiers can cause significant time-lags and are therefore unworthy of being considered. If the number of peers in a caching system goes up then so does the number of ICP messages exchanged. Hence, there will be concerns about the scalability of protocols such as ICP. Wessels and Claffy [550] mention the application of *multicast* (see Glossary) along with ICP for querying caches. Multicast is an important technique for adaptive caching.

1.2   Content Routing Protocol

The Content Routing Protocol (CRP) discussed briefly in the chapter on flavors of caching uses multicast for querying cache meshes. Adaptive Web caching employs CRP (see the chapter on flavors of caching) for finding out the possible paths of origin of the content so that the path of the meshes that have to be queried may be optimized. However, the scalability of the multicasting approach has not been well studied.

1.3   Cache Digests

Cache Digests offer another approach for facilitating inter-cache communication. Cache Digests were implemented by Wessels and Claffy [550] for the Squid caching software and also by Summary Cache (see the chapter on caching architectures and refer to [194]). Digests diminish the need for frequent inter-cache communication by listing a summary of Web objects present in caches. Therefore requests are sent in a more effective manner. In Adaptive Web caching, URL routing tables are used for effective dispatch of requests.

1.4   Web Cache Communication Protocol

Web Cache Communication Protocol (WCCP) [514] is used by some commercial products. It allows HTTP traffic to be rerouted from the network routers in a transparent manner.

1.5   Cache Array Routing Protocol

Cache Array Routing Protocol (CARP) [532] uses a hashing strategy to locate proxies possessing the desired content. Upon receipt of a request from a client, a proxy computes the hash of the requested URL with the names of the proxies it is aware of. The proxy with the maximum hash value is considered to be the possessor of that content. The CARP hash-routing protocol was developed in order to overcome the scalability problems associated with inter-cache communication as well as the overheads. Hence, we see that though inter-cache communication is a definite requirement, nonetheless, it must be kept to a minimum in order to obtain positive benefits.

2.   Hash-based Routing

Ross [477] studied the application of hash-routing for collections of shared Web caches. One primary application of hash based routing is for load balancing in clusters of caches. Hash-routing makes use of a *hash function* to identify a URL or a domain name with a cache located within a cluster. Ross compared the effectiveness of ICP and hash-routing with respect to cache server overload and the latency of fetching objects for collections of shared Web caches. Ross determined that hash routing is better in both cases. He outlined how to develop a robust hash-routing scheme for balancing requests among caches according to any preferred distribution, robust in case of cache failure and suitable for heterogeneous caches (viz. caches having different sizes).

As we may expect, well chosen hash-functions are necessary for spreading load uniformly between caches or cache clusters. As an illustration of the application of hash routing in real-world applications, we may consider the example of NetCache [157]. NetCache makes use a hash function called MD5 (see Glossary for a definition of MD5). In NetCache URLs for which MD5 has been applied are used to seek clusters of caches that have no imbricated URLs.

Hashing can be employed for cache selection at the time of fetching Web objects. Hashing can diminish or nullify the necessity for caches to pass requests between themselves. When CARP is used (see the discussion earlier on CARP), caches never search peer caches directly. On the other hand, requests are routed by the use of hashes of URL keys. Hash routing may also be used to guide the requests towards the location where the content can be found. This approach is employed by Adaptive Web Caching.

The employment of schemes based on hashing for routing requests demands that caution must be exercised since requests may be hashed to proxies that are either far away in a geographical sense or perhaps overburdened already. Wu and Yu [567] assess a hashing scheme sensitive to latency for use in collaborative Web caching. The reasons they give for considering such a scheme are as follows:

- proxies designed for a collaborative Web caching system often belong to different geographies thereby causing latency delays

- a hash based scheme for such a system could hash URL requests to proxies that are either far off or perhaps overburdened.

In their scheme, the following two steps are adopted:

- every URL request is hashed to a hash bucket each of which translates to a proxy cache

- hash buckets in the neighborhood are accessed to determine the proxy that provides the lowest latency delay to the Web browser.

Wu and Yu assess the performance of their latency-sensitive hashing scheme for collaborative Web caching. They report that their scheme:

- distributed load uniformly by hashing URL requests to proxies that are far-flung geographically despite the existence of hot spot like effects or uneven requests

- efficiently diminishes latency delays by forwarding requests to proxies that are nearer to one another in a geographic sense, when the load on the system is not heavy.

Thus their scheme is able to take into consideration latency delays attributable to either the prevailing network load or the geographical location of proxies.

3.   Further reading

Donnelley [178] discusses Web media distribution by way of an approach known as *hop-wise reliable multicast* (). A model is suggested for the distribution of Web pages that are not only big but also static, by means of mass multicast. Such Web pages are handed out to points within a local area network (LAN), so that access may be confined or restricted to a particular location. Donnelley suggests the application of the HRM technique for reducing the complexity of dependable multicast of mass data that is transferred between LANs in an off-line mode. The HRM mechanism makes use of TCP for dependability.

Hamilton [232] studies the application of multicast approaches for Web caching. Multicast IP (see [233]), an extension of the Internet Protocol (IP) is described along with the scope for applying multicast for Web caching.

Liao [354] studies issues concerning the distribution of Web documents to several points. Liao develops a multicast Web application known as WebCanal that permits the sharing of Web documents amongst a set of users by employing MBONE (multicast backbone) technology. A general purpose light-weight reliable multicast transport protocol (LRMP) is also described.

Kheong and Feng [305] describe a strategy known as *tree-caching* for efficient setup of multicast connections in connection-oriented networks. They propose a tree-caching algorithm to reduce the complexity of tree computations when a new connection is to be established. They state that their tree-caching strategy functions nicely and can considerably diminish the computation complexity for setting up multicast connections.

Touch [525] describes a multicast distributed virtual Web cache known as the LSAM proxy cache. It is intended for supporting unattended multicast push of Web pages. The LSAM proxy cache has been developed with the objective of diminishing the load on the servers and also the network. It is also designed for providing enhanced performance for a group of Web pages that are mutually dependent. These groups keep a record of the varying popularity of Web sites. Groups that are regarded with great favor are automatically cached at suitable locations in the network.

Inoue et al. [259] describe a system known as WebHint for optimizing Web cache utilization. The WebHint system along with a hint server is used for automatically making current the information affiliated with peer cache servers. This is done in order to diminish the quantum of packets interchanged between the servers. This also helps to curtail the access latency. Inoue et al. modified the Internet Cache Protocol (ICP) message contents in order to accommodate hints. The modified ICP messages are then used to perform a number of useful functions. They mention that a hint server does not consume many resources and is quite convenient to implement even in low end computers.

Li and Cheriton [347] discuss a protocol for enabling scalable caching of frequently updated objects by means of reliable multicast. They mention that Web objects that get updated very often, contribute to the inefficiency of the commonly used repeated unicast method of distribution. They study multicast invalidation and distribution of routinely updated Web objects to the proxies. Their protocol known as MMO bunches objects into *volumes*, every one of which translates into a single IP multicast group. They show that with a proper selection of volumes of suitable size and object correlation, reliable multicast offers an advantageous position. MMO is stated to use network bandwidth effectively and also offers scalability. It is also stated to be beneficial for realizing *strong cache consistency* (see the chapter on cache coherence) for dynamic Web objects (see the chapter on caching dynamic data).

Gulwani et al. [223] describe a domain specific language known as WebCal for Web caching. This language is based on an event-action model by means of which new local Web cache policies and inter-cache protocols can be effortlessly defined. Gulwani et al. state that WebCal should make it easy to compose a new policy or protocol rapidly, assess its performance, and also to examine it.

Liang et al. [353] study transparent Web caching using Layer 5 (L5) switches. The L5 switches deal with HTTP requests and redirect them on the basis of their contents. Requests that are not cacheable may therefore get around the cache servers and avoid burdening them. Liang et al. develop a layer 5 switch based distributed Web caching technique known as (LB-L5) that also incorporates load balancing capabilities. It makes use of the basic L5 transparent Web caching technique. Liang et al. mention that LB-L5 does well when compared to ICP, Cache Digests, and the basic L5 transparent Web caching technique on the basis of factors such as load balancing amongst servers and also the response time. It is stated to be more adjustable to high HTTP request rates than the other three techniques.

Lindemann and Waldhorst [357] evaluate the performance of four protocols for cache cooperation: ICP, Cache Digests, CARP and WCCP by means of trace-driven simulations in order to understand how they perform under given traffic conditions. The performance was evaluated on the basis of factors such as bandwidth utilization, user perceived latency and cache utilization. On the basis of their study, Lindemann and Waldhorst give some suggestions for ISPs and Web clients and application service providers (ASPs). They mention that ICP is the best choice for backbone networks having a bandwidth of 155 Mbps due to its efficiency. On the other hand, WCCP is stated to be the better choice for future backbone networks having a bandwidth of 2.4 Gbps because of its potential to save bandwidth despite its low efficiency.

Selvakumar and Prabhakar [496] study a distributed caching scheme that employs hash-routing. In hash-routing, a Web browser client becomes aware of the hash value of the URL for the Web page that was sought. It then forwards the request to the appropriate cache server. Selvakumar and Prabhakar state that hash-routing provides performance advantage when compared to an ICP based approach with respect to the average latency under normal conditions. However, they mention that ICP provides better flexibility when the failure rate of cache servers becomes appreciable.

Escorcia et al. [193] describe a cache distribution heuristic for a mesh of caches and analyze its performance. They study how to reduce the time taken to download documents by allotting fractions of the total storage amongst caches in a mesh. Their objective is to enhance storage in caching nodes that handle more traffic. This is done to obtain diminished average document retrieval latency. Escorcia et al. design a heuristic to calculate the traffic at every cache in the network. This calculation is then used to enable every cache in the network to get a proportionate percentage of the total storage capacity of the network. Escorcia et al. state that their cache distribution technique can diminish document retrieval latency by almost 80% when compared to earlier Harvest-type and demand driven data diffusion algorithms.

Hassanein et al. [236] contrast the performance of a number cooperative caching techniques (such as ICP and Cache Digests) and also transparent caching techniques. They carry out simulations by taking into account several HTTP request saturations, varying delays at the link level and different groups of cache servers that happen to collaborate. They identify the strength of different approaches.

Gu and Helal [222] describe an extension of the Internet Cache Protocol known as the Extended Internet Caching Protocol (x-ICP). It is intended to help wandering users in a mobile computing environment to get the documents desired from the proxy servers in the home network that are nearby instead of origin sites.

4.   Exercises

1 What is meant by inter-cache communication? Why is it required?

2 Mention popular inter-cache communication protocols. Compare and contrast them.

3 What are the overheads in using inter-cache communication techniques?

4 What is hash based routing ?

5 What are WCCP and CARP ? Investigate their application in commercial products. How do they differ from each other?

6 How does hash based routing help in load balancing?

7 What features would a good hash function possess in order to be used for high performance hash based routing?

Chapter 6

ROUTING REQUESTS TO CACHES

One of the fundamental problems in systems employing a large number of caches is the need to instantly identify a cache that has the document being sought. Obsolete information concerning caches will only result in a high incidence of cache misses (see Glossary for definitions). A perfect cache routing algorithm would probably direct requests to a cache most likely to hold the Web objects that are wanted. However, it is not easy to come up with such an algorithm.

Documents which are very popular are likely to be found quickly because such documents will be available in several caches. However, the fact is that majority of the documents are not very popular. This is due to a result of Abrams [5] which states that hit ratios are typically less than 50%. One way to overcome this problem of finding less popular documents could be to use an approach similar to that of Malpani et al. [372]. They make a group of caches function as one unit. The incoming request is forwarded to a cache in a discretionary fashion. If the desired document is found in the cache it is sent to the user. If it is not found then requests are sent to rest of the caches by means of IP multicast. If the requested document was not found in any of the caches then a request is placed with the origin server in order to fetch it.

The Harvest caching system (see Chankhunthod et al. [116]) arranges caches in a hierarchy and makes use of a cache resolution protocol such as the Internet Cache Protocol (ICP) (see Wessels and Claffy [550]). Any requests for Web documents are sent up the hierarchy in pursuit of cached versions of the documents. Caches first query their peers before sending the requests to the higher tiers of the hierarchy. This helps to prevent burdening of caches at the higher tiers. See the discussion in the chapter on flavors of caching.

The Adaptive Web caching strategy of Michel et al. [395] employs a mesh of caches. The caches in the mesh are arranged into multicast groups that intersect. Requests pass through these in pursuit of a cached version of the Web document that is being sought. The Adaptive caching approach is able to reduce the clogging of servers at higher tiers. It is also beneficial when dealing with documents that are only moderately popular provided a restriction is put on the number of caches a request can access.

Povey and Harrison [450] describe a hierarchy that must be spanned by all requests. Their strategy diminishes the load on caches in the higher tiers by maintaining *location pointers*.

Wang [543] mentions a strategy for the CacheMesh system, intended for employing routing tables in caches for specifying for every document/server, the place to access in the immediate future in case the local cache did not possess the required document. However, it is essential to keep the table size within manageable limits. This may be achieved by specifying a default route.

Legedza and Guttag [343] describe a scheme for distributed Web caching that utilizes network-level support for facilitating routing of requests to caches. Due to the fact that requests for documents that are not very popular tend to exhibit long latencies primarily because of ineffective routing, Legedza and Guttag integrate cache routing into the network layer. This quickens the search for cached copies of documents.

1.   Using hashing for routing requests to caches

Hash functions are routinely employed for cache routing. The Cache Array Routing Protocol (CARP) due to Valloppillil and Ross [532] provides for distributed caching by means of a hash function. The hash function is for directing to the cache in which the requested document may be found or likely to be found on being fetched from the Web.

In Summary Cache (see Fan et al. [194]) every proxy maintains a summary of the URLs of cached documents available at collaborating proxies. These summaries are first checked for possible hits before forwarding any requests to other proxies. In order to minimize the burden, the summaries are made current only occasionally and are maintained as *Bloom filters* (see Bloom [79]). Summary Cache has been shown to be economical in terms of bandwidth utilization, processor overheads and also the quantum of inter-cache messages. All this was achieved with essentially the same cache hit ratio as ICP. Therefore Summary Cache might be a much better choice when compared to ICP.

Karger et al. [295] propose a Web caching approach based on *consistent hashing*. The consistent hashing technique could be chosen instead of traditional multicast and directory based alternatives. It is supposed to be the better choice for load balancing and fault tolerance. The approach of Karger et al. constructs distribution trees with superior load balancing characteristics using consistent hashing. A consistent hash function requires only marginal changes when the range of the function changes. Consistent hashing technique is stated to be suitable for tackling the hot spot phenomenon. Also refer [296].

2. Further reading

Grimm et al. [219] study how requests are routed in cache meshes. Their work was motivated by their involvement in the German DFN caching project. They describe the problem of including routing data in neighbor cache selection algorithms. They solve this problem by allowing the caching software to collect routing data by means of Whois requests. This data is then analyzed by the cache selection algorithm. They mention the inadequacies of the prevailing neighbor selection algorithms. They give an elaborate account of an extended neighbor cache selection algorithm that was developed by them in order to overcome the shortcomings with earlier approaches. They also mention how they incorporated their techniques for the Squid caching software.

3. Exercises

1 What is meant by routing requests to caches? Why it is essential to understand how it works?

2 Explore how requests are routed in Adaptive caching.

3 What is a cache routing table?

4 Investigate how the cache routing table size is kept within manageable limits.

5 Mention how network level support would facilitate routing.

6 Study the role played by hash functions in routing requests.

7 Investigate how requests are routed when protocols such as ICP and Summary Cache are used.

8 What is consistent hashing? Explain the advantages of using consistent hashing.

Chapter 7

CACHE REPLACEMENT ALGORITHMS

The efficiency of proxy caches is influenced to a significant extent by document placement/replacement algorithms. *Cache placement algorithms* try to place documents within a cache whereas *cache replacement algorithms* replace documents from a cache. Such algorithms are beneficial only if they can ameliorate the hit ratio (see Glossary for a definition of hit ratio). In contrast to cache replacement, the subject of cache placement has not been well researched.

Cache replacement algorithms often aim to minimize various parameters such as the hit ratio, the byte hit ratio, the cost of access and the latency (refer Glossary for definitions).

The most widely used cache replacement algorithms include Least Recently Used (LRU), Least Frequently Used (LFU), LRU-Min [5], LRU-Threshold [5], Pitkow/Recker [447], SIZE [552], Lowest Latency First [564], Hyper-G [552], Greedy-Dual-Size (GDS) [102], Hybrid [564], Lowest Relative Value (LRV) [467], LNC-R-W3 [492], Bolot/Hoscka [80], Size-adjusted LRU (SLRU) [11], Least Unified-Value (LUV) [38], and Hierarchical Greedy Dual (HGD) [312]. Several of these attempt to maximize the hit ratio.

There are several ways to categorize cache replacement algorithms (see [448] for a representative categorization and for a survey of Web cache replacement strategies). We may follow the approach suggested by Aggarwal et al. (see [11]):

- Traditional algorithms

- Key based algorithms

- Cost based algorithms

Table 7.1.   A list of some popular cache replacement algorithms

---

Least Recently Used (LRU)
Least Frequently Used (LFU)
LRU-Min
LRU-Threshold
Pitkow/Recker
SIZE
Lowest Latency First
Hyper-G
Greedy Dual Size (GDS)
Hybrid
Lowest Relative Value (LRV)
LNC-R-W3
Bolot/Hoscka
Size-adjusted LRU (SLRU)
Least Unified-Value (LUV)
Hierarchical Greedy Dual (HGD)

---

1.   Traditional algorithms

Traditional cache replacement algorithms include LRU, LFU, Pitkow/Recker and some of their variants.

Least Recently Used (LRU) expels the object from the cache that was asked for the least number of times, of late. Least Frequently Used (LFU) expels the object that was retrieved least frequently from the cache. Pitkow/Recker [447] expels objects in LRU order unless all objects are referenced in a single day, in which case the biggest object is replaced.

It is quite possible that some cache replacement algorithms may not perform well when certain parameters such as hit ratios, size etc. are used for evaluating them. Williams et al. [552] mention that proxy servers can possibly diminish the following three quantities: the number of requests sent to favorite servers, the volume of network traffic produced as a result of requests for documents, and the access latency. They look at the first two by employing two metrics: cache hit ratio and byte hit ratio (see Glossary for definitions of these terms). Williams et al. present a taxonomy of cache retrieval policies. By means of trace-driven simulations they measure the maximum feasible hit ratio and byte hit ratio. They conclude that the norms employed by LRU and Pitkow/Recker have the worst performance in their simulation. They suggest that it would be much better to replace documents based on the size as this maximizes the hit ratio in each of their workloads.

2. Key based algorithms

Key based replacement algorithms expel objects from caches on the basis of a primary key. Ties may be broken by the use of secondary or tertiary keys or in other ways. The algorithm SIZE [552] expels the object having the largest size from the cache. LRU-Min [5] favors smaller objects. If there happen to be any objects in a cache with size at least S then LRU-MIN expels (from the cache) the least recently used object satisfying that condition. However, in case there are no objects with size at least S then LRU-Min begins expelling objects of size at least S/2 in LRU order. See Abrams et al. [5] for more details regarding LRU-Min. Abrams et al. also describe LRU-Threshold which is essentially the same as LRU except that objects that are larger than a certain size are never cached.

The Hyper-G cache replacement algorithm described by Williams et al. [552] is an enhancement of LRU. In Hyper-G, ties are broken by checking the recentness of earlier access and also by measuring the size of objects.

Wooster [565] considers optimizing response time instead of hit ratios when studying Web proxy caches. Wooster mentions that several previous studies concerning proxy caches have focused primarily on bettering the cache hit ratio. However, doing so would brush aside the actual time taken to fetch files. Wooster studies cache replacement algorithms that take into account the time taken to fetch a file as one of the factors. Wooster mentions that a cache replacement algorithm that attempts to minimize only the time taken to download a file does not show good performance. An algorithm that overcomes this shortcoming is then developed. It makes use of the following three factors:

- the number of hits of a file

- the size of the file being fetched

- the rate at which a file is fetched.

Wooster compares the performance of the two algorithms mentioned above alongside other popular cache replacement algorithms such as the Least Recently Used (LRU) cache replacement algorithm, the Least Frequently Used (LFU) cache replacement algorithm and a cache replacement algorithm based on the size of a document known as SIZE [552]. Wooster reports that the three factor algorithm mentioned above performs well while diminishing the average latency observed by users.

Wooster and Abrams [564] try to find out whether users do not have to wait for long if proxy caches make use of information about the prevailing network conditions in cache replacement algorithms. They study the two algorithms described in Wooster's thesis [565] (mentioned in the previous paragraph).

They discuss Lowest Latency First. This algorithm keeps the average latency to a minimum by expelling first the document with the lowest download latency. Wooster and Abrams design two cache replacement algorithms that:

- store documents that take the maximum amount of time to fetch

- make use of a combination of multiple requirements such as maintaining in the cache documents from servers that take significant time to connect to, those that need to be fetched from the slowest links, those that have been accessed very frequently, and those that are small.

The first algorithm is known as Lowest Latency First whereas the second one is known as Hybrid. The two algorithms execute by calculating the delay in downloading Web pages or the proxy to server bandwidth by making use of pages recently fetched. Wooster and Abrams check the performance of these two algorithms alongside LRU, LFU and SIZE. The parameters by which the performance is evaluated are user response time, capability to reduce server loads and bandwidth consumption.

3.   Cost based algorithms

The algorithms in this class make use of a cost function based on parameters such as the time since the last access was made, the time at which an object was put into the cache, the time of expiration of the object and so on.

Cao and Irani [102] study cost-aware proxy caching algorithms. They introduce the Greedy-Dual-Size (GDS) cache replacement algorithm. This algorithm integrates locality along with cost and size factors. They mention that trace-driven simulations demonstrate that with the right definition for the cost factor, the Greedy-Dual-Size algorithm does far better than many existing Web cache replacement algorithms in several respects. For example, when compared to such algorithms, it attains high hit ratios and enables superior latency reduction. The Greedy-Dual-Size algorithm is stated to have the capability for bettering the functioning of main-memory caching of Web objects (compare with the results in Markatos [379]).

Greedy-Dual-Size tags a cost with every object and expels the object that has the lowest cost or size. It is also possible to tag a utility function with every object and expel the object that is least useful for diminishing the total latency. This approach is used by the Hybrid cache replacement algorithm discussed by Wooster and Abrams [564] (mentioned earlier).

The Lowest Relative Value (LRV) cache replacement algorithm discussed by Rizzo and Vicisano [467] expels the object that has the lowest utility value. In LRV, the utility of a document is calculated adaptively on the basis of data readily available to a proxy server. Rizzo and Vicisano show that LRV performs better than LRU and can substantially better the performance of a cache that is of modest size.

Scheuermann et al. [492] argue that majority of the cache replacement algorithms do not take into account the large scale of the Web. They discuss the design of delay-conscious cache replacement algorithms that take this fact into consideration by preferentially caching documents that take a long time to get into a cache. They present experimental results concerning a delay-conscious cache replacement algorithm known as LNC-R-W3 (Least Normalized Cost replacement for the Web) that maximizes a performance metric named as *delay-savings ratio* by them. Scheuermann et al. compare the performance of their algorithm with LRU and LRU-Min. LNC-R-W3 uses a rational function of the access frequency, the transfer time cost and the size. In another article [501], Scheuermann and collaborators describe a cache replacement algorithm known as LNC-R-W3-U (LNC-R-W3 with updates) that merges both cache consistency and cache replacement capabilities.

Bolot/Hoscka is a cache replacement algorithm proposed by Bolot and [80]. It uses a weighted rational function of the transfer time cost, the size, and the time of previous access. Size-adjusted LRU (SLRU) developed by Aggarwal et al. [11] arranges objects by the cost to size ratio and picks objects with the most advantageous ratio.

Cohen et al. [132] evaluated server-assisted cache replacement techniques. They represent the utility of caching an object by means of the cost for fetching it, its size, the next request time, and cache prices during the time period between requests. They expel the object of least utility.

Bahn et al. [38] develop a cache replacement algorithm known as Least Unified-Value (LUV). It assesses a Web document on the basis of its cost after normalization by the probability of it being accessed again. Bahn et al. state that this leads to an equitable cache replacement policy. LUV has the ability to adjust to discretionary cost functions of Web documents, as a result of which, it is able to optimize desired quantities such as the hit rate, the byte hit rate, or the delay-savings ratio. LUV makes use of the entire reference history of a document taking into account factors such as the recentness and the frequency of reference, in order to calculate the probability of it being referenced again. Although, it might appear that this could result in significant time and space overheads, surprisingly, LUV may be implemented in an efficient manner with respect to both time as well as space. The time complexity of the algorithm is $O(log_2 n)$, where n is the number of documents in the cache, whereas, the space required to deal with the reference history of a document is only a few bytes. Bahn et al. claim that the LUV algorithm has better performance than prevailing cache replacement algorithms with respect to several performance criteria.

Korupolu and Dahlin [312] discussed a cache replacement scheme known as Hierarchical Greedy Dual (HGD). HGD performs both cache placement and replacement in a collaborative manner in a cache hierarchy.

Before we conclude this chapter, we must note that the performance of cache replacement algorithms depends to a great extent on the nature of Web accesses. Rabinovich and Spatscheck [455] argue that limited progress in developing cache replacement algorithms would not have a substantial impingement on proxy caching.

4.   Further reading

Partl and Dingle [431] compared the efficiency of Web cache replacement algorithms and also discussed the advantages of a shared cached space. They compared four popular cache replacement algorithms along with their own cache replacement algorithm known as STCWS. They mention that their algorithm performed well when compared to the four algorithms studied by them.

Bolot et al. [81] discuss the design of efficient caching schemes for the World Wide Web. They argue that many of the algorithms that were developed for Web caching were initially developed for memory caches and thus were not really designed for Web caches. Such algorithms tend to have some major drawbacks. Bolot et al. develop a cache replacement algorithm that minimizes the document retrieval latency as perceived by the user and takes into account document transfer times and sizes of documents.

Mogul et al. [398] investigate the possible advantages of employing *delta-encoding* and data compression for Web cache replacement policies. Many caching methods replace the contents of documents entirely when caches get updated. This is wasteful because only the differences (viz. the delta's) could be moved. Mogul et al. mention that substantial betterment in the response size and latencies could be obtained for a subset of HTTP content types. They mention that data compression could also be employed profitably. They report that merging both delta-encoding and data compression shows much better results than the individual methods. The combination of delta-encoding and data compression is often referred to as delta-compression. Mogul et al. suggest some extensions to the HTTP protocol in order to incorporate both delta-encoding and data compression.

Belloum and Hertzberger [57] study the impact of one-timer documents (documents that are accessed only once or potentially very few times) on Web caches. They study the impact of one-timer documents on a number of cache replacement polices and mention that several such policies often retain one-timer documents for a long time in a cache. As a result, they propose a method for dealing with one-timer documents. They also evaluate their method and study how it is able to deal with one-timer documents. In another article [58], Belloum and Hertzberger study several cache replacement strategies and compare them by means of trace-driven simulations.

Kangasharju et al. [290] discuss the implementation of optimized cache replacement algorithms in a soft caching system (viz. caching by recoding images to lower resolutions). In order to do this, they look at the algorithms suggested for optimized soft caching and test them by employing real proxies.

It may indeed be worthwhile to partition caches in order to gain some benefits. Murta et al. [404] analyze the performance of partitioned caches for the World Wide Web. They mention that although many different solutions exist for Web caching such as:

- client caching

- server caching

- proxy caching

- hierarchical caching and

- co-operative server caching

a problem that appears for all of them is the question of managing cache space effectively. Murta et al. mention that majority of the caching techniques attempt to maximize either the hit ratio or the byte hit ratio. For this reason they focus on these aspects. They suggest that a cache may be divided into partitions. These partitions are permitted to store groups of documents based on their sizes. Murta et al. contrast their strategy with cache replacement strategies that employ algorithms that are either based on the size of documents or make use of the Least Recently Used (LRU) cache replacement algorithm. They mention that their strategy performs well and betters the performance in terms of the hit ratio as well as the byte hit ratio.

Reddy and Fletcher [462] discuss an intelligent Web caching strategy that makes use of the life histories of documents. They mention that maintaining Web pages in either proxy servers or the browser caches of the clients in a hierarchical manner leads to cache consistency difficulties. Consequently, this necessitates the usage of cache maintenance strategies that are effective and also precise in order to ensure good performance. Reddy and Fletcher argue that many of the prevailing techniques such as the Least Recently Used (LRU) cache replacement technique are completely insufficient for handling the heavy loads on networks anticipated in the coming years. They make use of the life histories of documents in order to maximize cache performance. They use a technique named by them as *damped exponential smoothing*. This technique is used for representing in a precise manner the rate at which files are requested and altered. Reddy and Fletcher show that their strategy which employs the life histories of documents does better to a considerable extent than the LRU cache replacement algorithm. It is stated to achieve this without any loss of efficiency or deterioration of performance. Also refer [460].

In an article related to the above discussion, Reddy and Fletcher [461] compare the performance of a simple adaptive caching agent that makes use of the life histories of documents along with the strategies prevalent at that point of time.

Arlitt et al. [25] assess content management techniques for Web proxy caches. By means of traces of client requests to a Web proxy, they evaluate how various cache replacement policies perform. They introduce an approach for bettering the functioning of a cache while considering several metrics at the same time. They name their technique as *Virtual Caches.*

Gschwind and Hauswirth [221] develop a high performance cache server known as NewsCache for Usenet News (a high traffic news source). They present results of an experimental comparison of several cache replacement strategies.

Dilley et al. [174] discuss improvements to the cache replacement policies of the open source caching software Squid. They describe how they developed two cache replacement policies and enforced them for Squid.

Kelly et al. [300] discuss biased cache replacement policies for Web caches. They mention that based on the needs, it is possible to provide differential quality of service (QoS). For example, different servers may require load reduction to contrasting extents. Kelly et al. present a variation of the Least Frequently Used (LFU) cache replacement algorithm. Their algorithm is receptive to fluctuating levels of server values for cache hits. They mention that on the basis of an assumption concerning server values, their algorithm produces a higher proportion of byte hit ratios for servers that attach more importance or weight for cache hits. They mention that their cache replacement algorithm does more good for servers than either the Least Recently Used (LRU) or the Least Frequently Used (LFU) cache replacement algorithms.

Rochat and Thompson [468] discuss a proxy caching technique based on locating Web objects by taking into account semantic usage. They describe an approach different from that of well-known cache replacement algorithms such as the Least Recently Used (LRU) cache replacement algorithm or the Least Frequently Used (LFU) cache replacement algorithm. They take into consideration characteristics such as object usage, cross-references between documents and geographical location. For their technique, they make use of the following:

- a normalized indexing tree

- an algorithm for getting a better picture of the Web usage patterns

- a data structure for depicting cross-references amongst documents.

Arlitt et al. [26] evaluate the performance of Web proxy cache replacement policies. They study the usefulness of various Web proxy workload characteristics in assisting good cache replacement decisions. They assess workload characteristics such as object size, recency of citation, and frequency of reference. They also discovered long term unwanted secondary effects due to the replacement policies and assessed them. Arlitt et al. conclude from their experiments that higher cache hit rates are obtained by employing size-based replacement policies. Such policies keep numerous small objects in the cache, thereby increasing the likelihood of an object being found in the cache when it is asked for. In order to attain higher byte hit rates, Arlitt et al. suggest that a small number of slightly bigger files should be held in the cache.

Cheng and Kambayashi [123] present a cache replacement algorithm known as LRU-SP. It is an extension to the LRU cache replacement algorithm and takes into account popularity characteristics in addition to size. LRU-SP is built on the Size-adjusted LRU (SLRU) algorithm and another cache replacement algorithm known as Segmented LRU. Cheng and Kambayashi compare the performance of LRU-SP alongside Size-adjusted LRU, Segmented LRU, and the LRV cache replacement algorithm due to Rizzo and Vicisano. They extend their own ideas and discuss cache content management techniques in which contents of caches are distributed among sub-caches. They evaluate their scheme by means of LRU-SP and show that LRU-SP does better than the other three cache replacement algorithms mentioned above.

Jin and Bestavros [273] discuss popularity-aware Greedy-Dual-Size (GDS) algorithms for Web access. They mention that the relative frequency with which objects are sought by the employment of a proxy is rarely taken into account while designing cache replacement algorithms. They state that many cache replacement algorithms often rely on secondary properties that are simpler to obtain, in order to guess popularity characteristics. In their article, they describe:

- an online algorithm for efficiently obtaining popularity information about the Web objects sought by means of a proxy

- a new cache replacement strategy that is an improvement over the Greedy-Dual-Size cache replacement algorithm.

They show that their algorithm performs better than other popularly used algorithms.

Jin and Bestavros [274] describe a Web cache replacement algorithm known as GreedyDual*. This algorithm is a variant of the Greedy-Dual-Size (GDS) cache replacement algorithm. GreedyDual* makes use of metrics that were proposed previously by them. These metrics are used to change the relative value of long-duration popularity when compared to short-duration temporal correlativity of references. They mention that both long-duration popularity and short-duration temporal correlativity of references for Web cache replacement policies have not been well studied. They had shown earlier that Web reference patterns differ considerably in the prevalence of these two sources of temporal locality. Their caching technique is designed to adapt dynamically to the preponderance of these two sources of temporal locality.

Hamilton et al. [234] study the problem of developing cache replacement policies that are either optimal or near-optimal. It is a fact that the objects that happen to be accessed are often accessed with varying frequencies. In addition, they usually have different retrieval costs when they are not found not in the cache, as they may have to be accessed from servers at varying distances and with different retrieval speeds. Hamilton et al. state that if the cache sizes are not too big and there are only a few objects then an optimal replacement policy can be determined by solving a dynamic programming problem.

Psounis and Prabhakar [452] mention that the LRU cache replacement algorithm has been known to perform badly when it is employed in Web caches. This has prompted the aggregated application of measures such as the recency and frequency of use, the size, and the cost of retrieving a document, in order to develop strategies for cache replacement. Despite the fact that these strategies result in considerable betterment in the hit rate and also cause latency diminution, nevertheless, they often require sophisticated data structures. One way to dispense with such complex data structures is to employ a randomized algorithm for approximating them. Psounis and Prabhakar develop a randomized scheme and state that it performs well when contrasted with extant schemes and is also advantageous in some respects.

Starobinski and Tse [511] study probabilistic methods for Web caching. They develop randomized policies for managing Web caches. Their policies require constant time to deal with a hit or a miss. Their analysis involves probabilities and demonstrates that the performance of their algorithms is almost on par with an optimal off-line algorithm.

Vakali [530] discusses a history-based approach for designing cache replacement algorithms, wherein, a record of the history of cached objects is utilized for aiding cache replacement decisions. Vakali describes four cache replacement algorithms HLRU, HSLRU, HMFU and HLFU. These four cache replacement algorithms are history-based variants of the LRU, Segmented LRU, Most Frequently Used (expels most frequently requested objects from the cache) and the LFU cache replacement algorithms. The HLRU, HSLRU, HLFU algorithms are reported to exhibit better hit ratios and byte hit ratios when compared to their counterparts. In another article [531], Vakali discusses the application of the ideas of evolutionary computing to design cache replacement algorithms. Also refer [529].

Williamson and Busari [553] develop a synthetic Web proxy workload generator known as ProWGen for studying the sensitivity of proxy cache replacement policies to chosen Web workload characteristics. By using synthetic workloads generated by ProWGen, they demonstrate the relative sensitivity of three widely used cache replacement algorithms: LRU, LFU-Aging (a variant of LRU), and Greedy-Dual-Size to Zipf slope (see Glossary for a definition of Zipf slope and also refer the chapter on Zipf's law), temporal locality, and correlation between popularity and file sizes. Williamson and Busari also demonstrate the comparative insensitivity of these algorithms to one-timers (documents that are not accessed more than once or potentially few times) and the heavy-tail index (see [7] for more information on heavy-tails). Williamson and Busari also study the variations in the performance of the three cache replacement algorithms.

Cohen et al. [139] state that caches are being populated in advance in order to increase the accessibility of popular Web objects. Web objects are pushed by push-servers to the proxy cache servers by means of a multicast-based distribution or other approaches. Cohen et al. mention that it is not easy to develop scheduling algorithms for push-servers. Such algorithms must find out which Web objects must be broadcast when. Cohen et al. formulate a cache pre-filling push problem and solve it by developing effective algorithms.

Irani [260] studies page replacement algorithms when the pages are of varying sizes. The algorithms have applicability for Web page replacement in Web caching. Irani studies two models for the cost of an algorithm on the basis of a request sequence. The goal of the first model is to minimize the number of page faults, whereas, in the second model the goal is to keep the total number of bits that have been read into the cache to a minimum. Both off-line and randomized algorithms are discussed for the two models.

Chen et al. [120] describe a cluster-based parallel Web server system known as p-Jigsaw (Jigsaw is a Web server developed by the World Wide Web consortium). It relies on cooperative caching to minimize disk accesses. Chen et al. also assess three cluster-aware cache replacement algorithms.

Haverkort et al. [237] describe a class-based LRU cache replacement algorithm that takes into account both size and recentness of objects. Their goal is to get a good mix of both big and small objects in the cache. Consequently, this in turn must help achieve good functioning for both small and big objects. Haverkort et al. claim that the implementation overheads of their algorithm are comparable to the traditional LRU algorithm.

5. Exercises

1 What are cache replacement algorithms? Explain their significance.

2 Mention popular cache replacement algorithms.

3 Investigate different ways of classifying such algorithms.

4 Compare and contrast LRU and LFU.

5 What are key based cache replacement algorithms?

6 What are the benefits of employing size as a criteria when performing cache replacement?

7 What are cost based cache replacement algorithms?

8 Compare and contrast traditional, key based and cost based cache replacement algorithms.

9 Investigate criteria other than size and cost for designing cache replacement algorithms.

Chapter 8

CACHE COHERENCY

Caches help in reducing access latency, however, they have an undesirable secondary effect. They sometimes supply users with Web pages that are not current when compared to the original copies on Web servers from which they came. This means that users are supplied with stale pages. In order to avoid supplying stale Web pages to users, caches have to update Web pages contained within them so that they are very fresh. The problem of maintaining cached Web pages up to date with the master copies is called as *Web cache coherence*. Dingle and Partl [177] argue that coherence techniques meant for use with distributed file system caches may not be adequate for Web caches. They survey a number of techniques for maintaining Web cache coherence and present extensions and modifications to techniques that were prevailing earlier.

1. Cache consistency

The phrase *cache consistency* is often used instead of *cache coherency*. There are at least four well studied techniques for ensuring cache consistency. They include client polling, invalidation callbacks, Time-To-Live (TTL) and If-Modified-Since. Some of these mechanisms were described by Dingle and Partl [177].

Table 8.1. Techniques for ensuring cache consistency

Client polling
Invalidation callbacks
Time-To-Live (TTL)
If-Modified-Since

1.1   Client polling

In client polling, caches put time stamps on every object that is cached and routinely check the time stamp of the cached object with that of the original version that is available at the origin server. This helps to find out if cached objects are up to date with the original at the origin server. If they are not up to date then they are updated by fetching the latest version from the origin server.

An elegant method for detecting changes in files or Web pages is by the application of *hash functions* such as MD5 or SHA-1 (see Glossary). The MD5 hash function produces 128 bit strings when applied to files. If two files are different then the strings produced by MD5 will also be different unless there happens to be a *collision*. A collision is said to occur when MD5 (or for that matter any other hash function) produces the same string for two different files. However, collisions are extremely rare with MD5. It is therefore possible to detect even minor changes to files by employing such hash functions. In addition, they may be computed very rapidly.

1.2   Invalidation callbacks

It is possible to bypass the requirement for periodic verification of inconsistency by clients by entrusting the task of detecting stale objects to the origin server. This approach is employed by the *invalidation callback* technique for ensuring cache consistency. In this case, the server has to maintain records of those proxies that cache its objects. It must interact with these proxies whenever objects get altered. The invalidation callback mechanism allows for the possibility of saving network bandwidth since clients do not have to poll the servers every now and then. However, issues such as scalability, security and privacy crop up due to the requirement that servers need to monitor the caches for every cached object. In addition to this, the servers are burdened with extra work.

1.3   Time-To-Live

The Time-To-Live (TTL) (also refer Glossary) approach fixes life spans for objects. After cessation of the span, objects are considered obsolete and latest versions of the objects are obtained. The primary difficulty with the TTL approach is that it is not easy to fix the life spans of Web objects. In addition, objects that are unlikely to become obsolete very soon must not be updated very often. In other words, their TTL must be kept high. Adaptive TTL is a variation of the TTL approach (see the next section for more details). In this technique, the TTL of an object is made up to date whenever a cache hit takes place.

1.4   If-Modified-Since

If-Modified-Since is another variation of the TTL cache consistency technique. It has been used by the Squid caching software. In this technique, a cache invalidates an object only if its expiry date has arrived and a request for invalidation has been placed with it.

2. Mechanisms for cache coherence

There are two types of cache consistency techniques: strong cache consistency and weak cache consistency.

The main difference between strong cache consistency and weak cache consistency is that in strong cache consistency the cache is forced to ensure the freshness of content served by it by cross-checking with the origin server every time the content is asked for, thereby ensuring that there is no staleness. On the other hand, in weak cache consistency the cache may employ heuristics for checking freshness and need not contact the origin server every time it serves content. Hence, strong cache consistency could turn out to be more expensive for Web caching than weak cache consistency. See [101] for a discussion concerning strong cache consistency techniques.

Table 8.2. Types of cache consistency

Strong cache consistency	Weak cache consistency
Client validation	Adaptive TTL
Server invalidation	Piggyback validation

2.1 Strong cache consistency

Strong cache consistency includes client validation and server invalidation.

2.1.1 Client validation

Client validation is also known as polling-every-time. In client validation, the proxy considers cached objects as being obsolete on every access. It sends an If-Modified-Since header every time the objects are accessed. One major problem with this approach is that it can make the server generate the HTTP response code 304 (see [200]) when objects are not actually modified.

2.1.2 Server invalidation

Liu and Cao [360, 361] describe the server invalidation technique for ensuring strong cache consistency. In this approach, a server sends invalidation messages when it notices that an object has been modified. The messages are sent to clients that interacted with the server and possibly cached the object. This approach could become impractical if numerous clients access a server. The server needs to maintain lists of clients. These lists may themselves become outdated.

Liu and Cao report that the conventional thinking is that the strong cache consistency is too prohibitive for the Web whereas weak cache consistency techniques such as TTL are more suitable. They study the performance of the following three popular cache consistency techniques: adaptive TTL, polling-every-time and invalidation. Their study indicates that invalidation produces slightly less or almost the same volume of network traffic and server workload, and has better client response time when compared to adaptive TTL. On the other hand, they find that polling-every-time has longer response times and also produces more network traffic. They conclude that it is possible to maintain strong cache consistency by means of an invalidation based approach. Compare the discussion in [360, 361] with that in [101].

Gray and Cheriton [216] introduce the concept of *leases*. A lease is a time-based mechanism that enables efficient consistent access to cached data in distributed file systems. Their ideas have been extended for use in Web caching.

Yin et al. [577] discuss the application of volume leases as a means for ensuring cache consistency in networks that are geographically widespread. They contrast two algorithms developed by them with four cache consistency algorithms that were being used previously. They report that their new algorithms help to ensure strong cache consistency but at the same time assure both fault tolerance and also scalability. They state that the volume lease approach works much better than the widely used lease algorithms in existence.

2.2   Weak cache consistency

Weak cache consistency techniques offer an alternative to strong cache consistency techniques.

2.2.1   Adaptive TTL

Adaptive TTL has its origins in the Alex protocol (see Cate [108]). Adaptive TTL regulates the TTL of a document by keeping a close watch of its lifetime. Adaptive TTL uses a useful statistical property of file lifetime distribution, namely, this distribution tends to be bimodal if a file has not been altered for a comparatively long time. The TTL dimension of an object is computed as a fraction of the document's current age. The current age of a document is calculated by subtracting the earlier time of modification of the document from the prevailing time.

Adaptive TTL has been shown by earlier studies (see Cate [108], Gwertzman and Seltzer [229]) to contain the probability of stale documents to within about

5%. Several proxy servers such as CERN httpd (described in Luotonen and Altis [366] and Wessels [548]) make use of adaptive TTL. The Harvest cache system described by Bowman et al. [85] and Chankhunthod et al. [116] also made use of this technique for ensuring cache consistency.

Despite the positive benefits obtained by the use of adaptive TTL, there do exist some shortcomings with it. Dingle and Partl [177] studied various problems with cache coherence techniques that rely on expiration based mechanisms. For example, some users may tolerate stale documents to some extent yet they may have to wait for expiration checks to take place. Users may have no alternative but to reload an entire document by applying the Pragma-No-Cache header (HTTP 1.0) or the HTTP Cache Control header (HTTP 1.1) through their Web browsers in case they feel that the documents are outdated. By the use of adaptive TTL, users may not be fully convinced whether a document is obsolete or otherwise. In addition, they have no simple way to specify the extent of staleness they are willing to cope with. When users discontinue downloading a document, the caches may also follow suit. Thus, we see that are some significant drawbacks with adaptive TTL.

2.2.2 Piggyback validation

This technique was suggested by Krishnamurthy and others (see Cohen et al. [133] and Krishnamurthy and Wills [318, 320, 321]).

The Piggyback Cache Validation (PCV) technique developed by Krishnamurthy and Wills [318, 320] banks on requests from a proxy cache to a server. If a proxy cache has an opportunity to interact with a server it piggybacks a list of cached documents (which may possibly be obsolete) that were fetched earlier from the same server for validation.

Krishnamurthy and Wills [321] describe a Piggyback Server Invalidation (PSI) technique. In PSI, the servers while replying to a proxy piggyback a list of documents that have got altered since the previous access by the proxy. The proxy may increase the lifespan of entries not in the list and also invalidate entries in the list.

Krishnamurthy and Wills [319] also propose a merger of the PCV and PSI techniques for obtaining better results. Among PCV and PSI, the technique most appropriate would be determined by the amount of time that elapsed since the proxy previously asked for invalidation. PSI would be appropriate if this interval is short, whereas, PCV would be preferable if the time interval was long. The reason for this choice is that for short spans, the number of invalidations dispatched by PSI would be comparatively small. On the other hand, for longer intervals the expense for transmitting invalidations would be much more than the expense for seeking validation.

3.   Further reading

Fielding et al. [200] report on the Hypertext Transfer Protocol version 1.1. The article defines the specification of HTTP 1.1 which is an improvement over the earlier HTTP protocol version 1.0.

Padmanabhan and Mogul [423] studied an approach for improving HTTP latency. They state that the HTTP protocol in existence at that point of time (HTTP 1.0) used a distinct TCP connection for every file asked for. They suggest simple alterations to the HTTP protocol so that the additional burden due to such distinct connections is reduced. They show that the latency gets diminished by means of their alterations. The reader may also refer to a report by Padmanabhan [422].

Worrell [566] studies invalidation in large scale Web caches and suggests that a hierarchical caching system may be employed for dealing with the phenomenon of World Wide Wait. Worrell states that a hierarchical scheme gives a chance for trying out unconventional cache consistency approaches. A widely used cache consistency technique makes use of timeouts on a per object basis. The timeout is determined by heuristics. Worrell discusses the application of invalidation protocols for maintaining cache consistency in a hierarchical system of Web caches. Estimates are obtained concerning the number of object revisions. Worrell contrasts the timeout based approach with the invalidation protocol based approach. This is done by looking at factors such as:

- the quantum of network bandwidth utilized,

- the burden on servers

- the fraction of time obsolete data is supplied.

The invalidation protocol was found to substantially diminish the fraction of time cache references are satisfied by supplying obsolete data and is stated to be competitive when compared with the timeout based scheme.

Gwertzman [226] discusses *geographical push-caching* and mentions that various cache consistency protocols were evaluated in order to figure out what would be the most ideal cache consistency protocol. This was done by using a server simulator. It is reported that weak cache consistency protocols were adequate for the Web because of the following reasons:

- they dish out stale data very infrequently (a fraction less than one in a hundredth)

- they do not burden the server much since they add only a small amount of load to the server

- they consume bandwidth essentially tantamount to the base protocol.

Dingle [176] discusses cache consistency in the HTTP 1.1 standard when it was proposed. Dingle performs a critical evaluation of the cache consistency model of HTTP 1.1 and also gives some suggestions to those who are inclined in putting it to practice. Problematic areas concerning the proposal for the standard are also pointed out by Dingle. In order to help those interested in realizing a HTTP 1.1 proxy cache, a model in Java is also described.

Gwertzman and Seltzer [229] discuss cache consistency for the World Wide Web. They mention that many Web caches do not ensure cache consistency to the extent it is advantageous. They conduct a survey and assessment of the prevailing cache consistency mechanisms. They report that a weak cache consistency protocol used by the Alex ftp cache diminished the network bandwidth utilization and load to an extent that was higher than the invalidation mechanisms or the TTL fields. They report that the weak cache consistency protocol could be made to return obsolete Web objects very infrequently (less than one in twenty times).

Rangarajan et al. [459] give a description of a tool known as WCP (Web-Copy). It is meant for simplifying the task of making documents in a Web server up-to-date in a consistent and on-line fashion. Rangarajan et al. mention the necessity of supplying a group of related documents from a Web server in an orderly fashion. They state that either the latest versions of all the documents in the group must be supplied or else outdated versions of all the documents in the group have to be furnished. They stress that Web servers need to deal with this problem in order to ensure that groups of related documents are supplied in a consistent manner. A combination of old versions of some of the documents in the group when provided along with new versions of some other documents in the group may not be appealing to the users in some situations. Their tool WCP ensures that the requirements mentioned above are taken care of and does not call for any modifications to Web servers.

Simonson et al. [504] describe a system meant for enabling references to Web documents in a reliable fashion. The system augments a document's Universal Resource Identifier (URI) with information such as the date and the particulars about the version being used. The system of Simonson et al. is included as a module for the Apache Web server.

Cohen et al. [131] give some suggestions for maintaining TCP connections when persistent HTTP is employed. They recommend that certain particulars (such as URLs that were asked for and also the identities of sender's) which may be contained in the HTTP requests be profitably employed. They rank their approach alongside the one used at that point of time by the Apache Web server. They mention that their approach does far better than other approaches.

Baker and Hartman [41] describe a system known as Gecko. Gecko is a system for facilitating Unix applications access to the Web by means of the

Network File System (NFS) protocol. In Gecko, URLs are translated into file names acceptable to Unix so that Web pages may be accessed without any modifications. Pages are moved from the Gecko server to the clients using NFS as an alternative to HTTP. The cache consistency mechanism of NFS is also used advantageously. Baker and Hartman mention that the use of the NFS protocol in Gecko helped to get a substantially better performance than what would have been got by the mere application of the HTTP protocol.

Dilley [173] discusses the impact of cache consistency on the response time for requests from clients. Responses from the caches are then classified into two categories reckoning on the following circumstances:

- the object requested by the client being obtained from the origin server

- the object requested by the client being serviced from the cache itself.

Dilley states that it was revealed from the investigation of the traces (obtained from the positioned proxy cache servers) that flow of data back and forth from the origin server was the most influential factor that impacted the response time. Hence, Dilley suggests that bettering cache consistency will help diminish the response time and permit a cache to manage or deal with a larger number of requests.

Dilley et al. [175] give a description of a protocol for consistency of distributed objects. Their protocol is known as DOCP (Distributed Object Consistency Protocol). The protocol is meant for bettering the content consistency in proxy cache servers in order to diminish the response times and also the loads on servers. DOCP is an improvement on the Hypertext Transfer Protocol (HTTP). It modifies the normal mode by which the prevailing cache control methods of HTTP work. Proxy servers that make use of the protocol are able to work with non-DOCP proxy servers as well. DOCP makes use of a publish/subscribe paradigm and employs server invalidation in the place of client validation in order to detect modifications to Web objects. DOCP allows for *delta-consistency* in wide area networks (WANs) where it may not be easy to ensure strong cache consistency. In delta-consistency objects are consistent for almost all the time except for a short time period after they have been altered. By means of simulations, Dilley et al. show that DOCP does well when compared to the HTTP cache consistency protocol.

Perret et al. [434] evaluate the performance of the distributed object consistency protocol (DOCP) which was devised by them. They compare the functioning of two protocols for ensuring cache consistency: the Alex adaptive TTL protocol and the Distributed Object Consistency Protocol (DOCP). They study the influence of cache replacement policies and cache consistency protocols on the functioning of caches. They mention that DOCP outperforms the Alex protocol when it comes to discouraging reach to inconsistent objects. DOCP also avoids the requirement of having to communicate or get in touch with the origin server in order to verify the freshness of objects. As a consequence, DOCP not only ensures cache consistency but also ameliorates the response time.

Wills and Mikhailov [555] discuss the consequences of more complete server information on Web caching. They mention that a number of contemporary caching approaches that are based on heuristics lead to an enormous number of needless validations. They believe that it is possible to reprocess cached Web content more fruitfully. They study a more settled proposal for caching Web objects. In their scheme, they treat HTML pages as if they were containers accommodating distinguishable objects possessing disparate features. The servers accumulate information about the state of connectedness between the containers and the enclosed objects. They then piggyback such information on the top of the request/response traffic that is already flowing. Wills and Mikhailov state that their methods ameliorate the performance of cache maintenance techniques substantially.

Barnes and Pandey [53] describe a domain-specific programming language called CacheL. It is meant for specifying tailor-made caching policies. Their language helps cache administrators, servers and end users to produce according to requirements, the way Web objects are cached, replaced and made consistent. A number of policies are often employed by cache administrators for routing requests, for maintaining cache consistency and for cache replacement. Hence, such a language will be beneficial for creating caching policies according to given specifications.

Barnes and Pandey [54] present a caching infrastructure in which cache administrators, servers, and end users can customize how Web objects are cached, replaced, and maintained consistent. The infrastructure is expandable and includes a domain-specific language called CacheL. This language was developed by them (see [53]) for specifying caching policies that can be tailor-made and also varied dynamically. Barnes and Pandey analyze a prototype implementation known as PoliSquid for the Squid caching software. By their analysis, they demonstrate the advantages of their infrastructure for variable coherency policies, localized removal policies, and advance removal of objects from servers.

Spero [509] conducts an analysis of HTTP related performance problems. The Hypertext Transfer Protocol (HTTP) is undoubtedly the most widely used protocol for fetching documents from the World Wide Web. Spero mentions that some of the design characteristics of HTTP do not work well with TCP, thereby resulting in performance related problems and also scalability problems concerning servers. Latency problems are attributed to:

- the use of one TCP connection for every request,
- connection establishment costs, and
- costs due to slow-starts.

Additional latency is also caused since the protocol returns only one object for every request. Since TCP requires that every server must keep state information for all the connections that were closed of late, this could lead to scalability related concerns. It is to be noted that HTTP version 1.1 overcomes some of the shortcomings of the earlier version of HTTP viz. HTTP 1.0 that was used previously.

One of the key features of HTTP 1.1 is the scope for *persistent connections* (see Glossary). This feature is not available in HTTP 1.0. This feature enables a client to fetch several objects from a server by means of only one TCP connection. Mogul [401] studies the utility of persistent HTTP connections. The article reports on the simulations done to study numerous modifications to HTTP. Krishnamurthy et al. [316] pinpoint the fundamental differences between HTTP 1.0 and HTTP 1.1. It is worthwhile to study the shortcomings of the HTTP protocol and come up with suitable alterations and extensions in order to enhance its utility.

Spreitzer and Jansen [510] discuss the problematic aspects of HTTP 1.1. They mention that it is feasible to make some amendments to enable HTTP 1.1 perform better. The aspects of HTTP 1.1 for which they present improvements include the following:

- the development of different application protocols over HTTP

- standardization and also the quality of being protractile

- the functioning or performance in networks

- the close bonding amongst identifiers and protocol stacks, and

- the quality of not permitting or blocking the passage of superimposed traffic across firewalls.

Krishnamurthy and Arlitt [315] study protocol compliance on the Web. They investigate the proportion of Web servers that adhere to the nuances of the HTTP 1.1 protocol. They report that a few servers did not furnish fundamental features such as the HEAD method. They also mention that even well-known servers did not provide for persistent connections. They argue that it would be beneficial to carry out minor modifications to the wordings in the specifications concerning the protocol.

Many extensions have been proposed for the HTTP protocol. One such extension is described by Vingralek et al. [540]. They discuss a system known as Web++ for a fast and dependable HTTP service.

Nottingham [416] discussed mechanisms for regulating object freshness in Web caches. Object freshness relationships are studied and potential methods to optimize them are also developed. This is done on the basis of the network traffic characteristics.

Yin et al. [580] study hierarchical cache consistency in a Wide Area Network (WAN). They look at mechanisms for bettering cache consistency when there could potentially be hundreds of thousands of Web clients. They carry out the following:

- study how workloads impact the scalability of cache consistency mechanisms

- design elementary operators known as split and join for expanding and contracting cache consistency hierarchies

- assess policies based on the two operators for providing fault tolerant and efficient solutions for cache consistency hierarchies

- study the performance of algorithms for ensuring strong cache consistency for several different configurations of hierarchies.

They were able to find out the most beneficial configuration for ensuring strong cache consistency in a WAN. In that configuration, both proxies and servers jointly ensure cache consistency. The two tier hierarchy also adjusts to the patterns of client access. Yin et al. state that the ideal configuration is not difficult to set up.

Yu et al. [584] study a scalable Web cache consistency architecture. Their architecture controls the extent of staleness of Web pages. Their Web cache consistency architecture is essentially a cache invalidation approach rendered scalable by the application of a cache hierarchy, and multicast routing to aid invalidations.

Cao [99] states that conventional cache invalidation techniques are not appropriate for mobile devices because of the mobility of clients and also due to disconnections. A frequently used cache invalidation technique that makes use of invalidation reports (IR) has some shortcomings. For example:

- a client is able to deal with a query only during some time periods (IR intervals) and this induces significant latency

- if a server alters a popular resource, the clients query the server and fetch the data from the server independently, thereby resulting in increased bandwidth consumption.

Cao develops a IR-based cache invalidation algorithm that is able to tackle these two problems and also analyzes its performance.

In a related article (see [100]) Cao develops a proactive cache maintenance approach to deal with problems such as those mentioned above. In this approach, clients smartly prefetch data that will most probably be utilized in the near future. On the basis of a construct known as the *prefetch-access ratio* Cao's technique is able to dynamically optimize either performance or power on the basis of performance needs and usable resources. Cao mentions that the technique is able to show better cache hit rate, throughput, bandwidth usage, and also diminishes query delays as well as power intake.

Duvvuri et al. [187] give an account of a mechanism known as *adaptive leases* for ensuring strong Web cache consistency. They present reasons and arguments that weak cache consistency mechanisms being used by contemporary proxy caches must be made more powerful by supplementing them with strong cache consistency mechanisms. They argue that strong Web cache consistency mechanisms in vogue are not suitable because of the expenses for sustaining them. They highlight their lease approach and also develop analytic models for determining the most favorable time span for leasing. Their empirical results indicate that their method has the following features:

- adds only marginal costs even if the duration of the lease is quite protracted

- does better than the strong Web cache consistency mechanisms in existence

- is not more difficult to put through than the prevailing weak Web cache consistency mechanisms.

Duvvuri et al. also expand the scope of the HTTP protocol in order to integrate the concept of leases. They describe their experience in accommodating their technique for the Apache Web server and also the Squid proxy caching software.

Cohen and Kaplan [136] discuss refreshment policies for Web caches. It is a fact that objects become obsolete after they expire and need to be validated after consultation with either peer caches or the origin server. As a consequence, frequent validation of such objects leads to increased access latency and can also result in wastage of bandwidth. Cohen and Kaplan come up with policies for validating chosen objects in anticipation of their impeding obsolescence. Doing so would make it possible to service a greater number of requests from the clients. This may indeed be done in a decentralized manner. Cohen and Kaplan make use of cache consistency mechanisms that are already widely utilized but at the same time put to good use some discernable characteristics of the patterns of requests, for e.g. recentness. They assess the competitiveness of their techniques by making use of simulations utilizing traces.

Cohen and Kaplan [135] study *age penalty* and its influence on the performance of caches. Caches are often positioned as proxies, reverse proxies, or in a hierarchical fashion and frequently service other caches. The *age* of a cached copy of an object is the time that went by since it was fetched from an origin server. Hence, new cached copies of a particular object can have varying ages and staler copies generally become obsolete more quickly. As a consequence, a proxy cache would incur a higher miss rate if it gets staler objects, perhaps from a reverse proxy cache. In a similar manner, reverse proxy caches that service proxy caches get more requests from them than an origin server would have encountered. Cohen and Kaplan note that the age of content in caches situated at the higher tiers of a hierarchy becomes an important performance determining factor. They study the magnitude of the age penalty for content served by large caches and also content delivery networks.

Yin et al. [579] consider the application of server-driven cache consistency protocols for giant scale dynamic Web workloads. They share the insights they obtained when implementing a server-driven cache consistency protocol for a popular and heavily accessed sports Web site. This site was popular when the sports event was taking place. Yin et al. study the cacheability and scalability aspects of dynamic Web content. They measure the effect of caching dynamic data by means of server-driven cache consistency protocols. They also implemented their cache consistency protocols for the Squid caching software.

4. Exercises

1 What is cache coherence?

2 List the most important techniques for ensuring cache consistency.

3 Explain how client polling works.

4 Explain the functioning of the invalidation callback mechanism for ensuring cache coherence

5 Explain the TTL mechanism for maintaining cache consistency.

6 Investigate how the lifespan of objects is determined in the TTL approach.

7 What is adaptive TTL? Explain how it differs from the normal TTL approach.

8 What is strong cache consistency? How is it different from weak cache consistency? Compare and contrast strong and weak cache consistency.

9 Explain how client validation works.

10 Explain how server invalidation works.

11 Describe the functioning of the piggyback cache validation and the piggyback server invalidation techniques.

12 Mention different HTTP headers used for the purpose of ensuring cache coherence.

III

ASPECTS RELATED TO TRAFFIC

Chapter 9

WEB TRAFFIC CHARACTERISTICS

1. Introduction

It is worthwhile to comprehend the types of workloads generated by users. The efficiency of many caching techniques relies on the temporal characteristics of Web access patterns. In addition, such techniques must make use of suitable policies for the workloads being considered.

2. Studies related to Web traffic characterization

Braun and Claffy [86] undertake a study of Web traffic characterization. They analyze the impact of caching documents from NCSA's Web server. (Note: NCSA is the National Center for Supercomputing Applications). Braun and Claffy exhibit the time series of bandwidth and transaction demands for the server cluster of NCSA's Web server, which has four servers in a single cluster. They split the demands into constituents as per the geographical source of the queries and conduct other investigations. They also study the issue of forwarding queries initially intended for a central server to a cache site that is more sought after than others.

Abrams et al. [6] analyze multimedia traffic data by using a tool named Chitra95 that was developed by them. The tool permits users to perform a variety of functions with collections of trace data including the following:

- querying,

- visualization,

- analysis,

- testing,

- transformation and

- modelling.

The primary application of the tool is for characterizing Web traffic by utilizing a variety of workloads.

Cunha et al. [150] study the distinguishing qualities of traces obtained from Web clients. They undertake this survey in order to comprehend the nature of requests from Web clients for Web objects. In order to do this, they accumulated traces obtained from a real world example. In their study, they examined more than 500,000 requests for Web documents. They organize the outcome of their experiments into data so that it may be used for learning about the tendencies in Web usage. They demonstrate that a number of characteristics of Web usage may be described by the application of power-law distributions, for e.g. the distribution of object sizes, the distribution of requests for Web objects etc. They mention that such power-law distributions may help those desirous of implementing Web caching.

Almeida et al. [20] present for consideration models for temporal and also spatial locality of reference in streams (sequences) of requests reaching Web servers. The phrase *temporal locality* is used to denote repetitive access to particular objects during a time interval. The phrase *spatial locality* denotes access to objects that often necessitate access to related objects. Almeida et al. demonstrate that simple-minded models founded only on document popularity are inadequate for visualizing temporal as well as spatial locality. They formulate a numerical equivalent of a reference stream, which they refer to as the stack distance trace and use this for characterizing temporal locality.

Table 9.1.   Types of locality of reference

Temporal locality
Spatial locality

Arlitt and Williamson [28] describe a workload characterization investigation concerning Web servers. Their workload characterization concentrated on aspects such as the distribution of document types and sizes, the document citations, and the geographical distribution of server requests. Arlitt and Williamson determine ten workload characteristics that are common over the data sets used by them. They also recommend ways to improve performance based on their study of workload characteristics.

Almeida et al. [21] study the effect of geographical and cultural factors on the workload of a proxy server and conclude that such factors indeed have a strong influence.

Abdulla et al. [4] study Web proxy traffic characterization and discover invariants that are valid across a set of ten traces. These traces represent traffic as observed by proxy cache servers and were gathered from varied sources. The request rates also varied from a few requests to thousands of requests per minute. Abdulla et al. note that by considering the characteristics of traffic it is possible to significantly improve the benefits of caching. Compare the results in [4] with [446, 445].

Barford et al. [49] studied the characteristics of changes in Web client access patterns and its implication for caching. It is often unclear how the features of workloads change with time. Barford et al. compare the nature of two Web client workloads belonging to two different periods of time. The examine the similarities and differences in the statistical and distribution related properties across the two sets of data. They notice that the types of distribution most suitable for reporting document size remain the same in both sets of data. They notice that the advantage gained by using size based policies get diminished by the passage of time. They also observed that the opportunities for caching files also got lessened alongside.

Breslau et al. [88, 89] study two topics related to Web caching. The first topic is concerned with the question of whether Web requests from a fixed user community is distributed according to Zipf's law (see the glossary and also refer the chapter on Zipf's law). The second topic is related to earlier studies on the characteristics of Web proxy traces. These studies demonstrate that the hit ratios and temporal locality of traces show some asymptotic features that are uniform across various sets of traces. Breslau et al. seek to establish if such properties are inherent to Web accesses or whether they are merely artificial features of such traces. They find that the two topics mentioned above are actually interrelated. They study page request distribution (as witnessed by the Web proxy caches) by making use of traces from various sources. They find that although this distribution does not follow Zipf's law exactly, it tends to follow a Zipf-like distribution. They also mention that a Zipf-like distribution is adequate for explaining some of the asymptotic properties noticed at Web proxies. They conclude that many of the properties of hit ratios and temporal locality are actually inherent to Web accesses observed by the proxies.

Douglis et al. [180] investigated the rate of change of Web objects and other metrics while conducting a live study of the Web. Their study establishes that the rate of change of Web objects does play a vital role in deciding the performance of Web caching strategies.

Duska et al. [186] studied the locality and sharing characteristics of Web client accesses. They present results concerning the analysis of access traces obtained from seven proxy servers deployed in various locations. They use static analysis and trace-driven simulation to characterize the locality and sharing properties of the accesses. They conclude that caches with many clients show a higher degree of sharing and therefore incur higher hit ratios.

Pitkow [446, 445] presents a summary of characterizations of the World Wide Web and lists some of the steady and unvarying features that were observed at clients, servers and proxies. They are listed below:

- The popularity of files

- The sizes of files

- The properties of Web traffic

- The incidence of self-similarity in traffic

- The periodic nature of traffic

- The popularity characteristics of Web sites (or their servers)

- The lifetimes of documents

- The incidence of broken links at the time of surfing the Web

- The prevalence of redirects

- The quantum of Web page requests per Web site

- The time taken to read a page

- The time taken to suspend a session

Nabe et al. [408] characterize Web traffic on the basis of access log data accumulated at four Web servers. They find that the document size, the time between request arrivals and the access frequency of Web traffic follow *heavy-tail distributions* (refer [7] for more information about heavy-tails). The document size and the time between request arrivals were found to follow *log-normal distributions*, and the access frequency follows the *Pareto distribution* (see any good book on statistics for more particulars about various distributions mentioned here or refer [7]). For the request inter-arrival time, Nabe et al. find that an *exponential distribution* is acceptable when the busiest hours have to be considered. Nabe et al. also study the influence of document caching (at a proxy server) on the Web traffic characteristics. They state that although the traffic volume is actually diminished by document replacement policies, nevertheless, the traffic characteristics are not much impacted.

Arlitt and Jin [27] conduct an elaborate workload characterization investigation concerning a 1998 World Cup Web site. They state that the site experienced over a billion requests during a three month period. On the basis of their observations, they report that although advances in the art of construction of caches for the Web are altering the workloads of Web servers, nonetheless, substantial progress is still indispensable. As part of their study they discover that more sophisticated Web cache consistency mechanisms are needed.

Mahanti and Williamson [368] mention that obtaining a better understanding of Web traffic characteristics is essential for bettering the functioning of the Web. They employ Web proxy workloads from various tiers of a caching hierarchy to study how the workload characteristics vary over the tiers. From their study they observe that:

- a substantial number (nearly 95%) of the documents looked at in the workload are either HTML pages or image files

- the distribution of transfer sizes of documents is heavy-tailed, with the tails becoming heavier on climbing up the hierarchy

- the popularity characteristics of documents does not follow the Zipf distribution exactly

- one-timers account for almost 70% of the documents referred to

- the density of references is more at servers and less at proxy caches

- the density of references diminishes on climbing the cache hierarchy

- the rate at which documents get altered is greater at proxies situated in higher tiers.

Mahanti et al. [367] study temporal locality characteristics existing in the document referencing action seen at Web proxies. They also study the influence of such temporal locality on document caching.

Williamson and Busari [553] develop a synthetic Web proxy workload generator known as ProWGen. They use it for studying the sensitivity of proxy cache replacement policies to chosen Web workload characteristics.

3. Further reading

Judge et al. [279, 281] discuss how the Web traffic due to user requests may be modeled. Sedayao [495] also looks at Web traffic patterns with similar objectives.

Heimlich [239] studies whether *packet trains* are present in the NSFNET national backbone network traffic. By convention, models of packet arrival in communication networks have adopted Poisson arrival patterns. However, some studies indicated that a packet train was probably a much more general model. Heimlich states that protocol realizations may make use of the concept of packet trains and effectuate per train processing instead of per packet processing. This may be beneficial in some situations.

Bray [87] presents some questions involving distinctions based on qualities concerning the Web and also attempts to provide answers to them. Bray tries to get answers that are capable of being expressed as numbers. The numbers resulting from the answers are then used to develop 3-D visualizations of localities in the Web.

Crovella and Bestavros [147] discuss the topic of self-similarity in the World Wide Web. They study self-similarity in the Web by means of experimentally observed distributions from Web client traces and also from data gathered on an individual basis from Web servers. They reason that self-similarity in the Web may be described in terms of the outcomes on file caching and the user predilection during file transfer.

Gribble and Brewer [217] describe the analysis of a large Web client trace. They mention the design related aspects of Internet middleware services. As a result of their analysis, they report that they were able to observe the following characteristics:

- Web clients are heterogeneous in nature

- the presence of diurnal cycles in the client's Web related actions which could be forecast

- significant latency experienced by services when sending data to the clients.

Manley and Seltzer [378] present an analysis of Web servers logs for numerous Web sites. They develop a taxonomy of a variety of Web sites and characterize the patterns by which they were accessed. They state that from their study they observe that the use of CGI (Common Gateway Interface) is not growing, thereby going against the popular perception that the use of CGI is ever increasing. They also state that long latencies are not attributable entirely to the burden on the servers. They demonstrate that permitting numerous persistent connections could indeed be an obstacle to resource consumption. This could be worse than what is got when only one persistent connection is allowed.

Judge et al. [283] study the size of HTTP response packets and discuss how the volume of Web traffic may be calculated. In another article, Judge et al. [282] discuss how HTTP response packets may be sampled in order to forecast the volume of Web traffic.

Pitkow [444] discusses the question of finding out reliably usage data concerning the World Wide Web. Pitkow presents reasons and arguments that server-side sampling offers a much more reliable source of information. This approach is stated to entail neither any modifications to the HTTP protocol nor any compromise of user privacy.

Liu et al. [359] look at the effects of proxy caching on the response time. In their study, they observed that more than 25% of the total time that went by was spent on establishing TCP connections. They also look at the effects of bandwidth restrictions on the response time. They find that contrary to the popular view, a single standalone proxy cache does not diminish the response time on every occasion.

Wills and Mikhailov [556] discuss the characterization of Web resources and server responses in order to obtain a deeper comprehension of the possibilities for employing caching. They state that although there have been many studies concerning characterization of Web resources and even though they have helped in developing superior caching policies and techniques, nevertheless, not much has been done to study the characteristics of resource changes at servers. As a consequence, Wills and Mikhailov study the nature of resource changes at servers and also how the servers send meta-data concerning such resources. They collect statistical data concerning the nature and rate of changes associated with the type of resource. They also gather response header information with every resource fetched from the server. This information is acquired from the server. Wills and Mikhailov mention that their technique of data collection for characterization of Web resources is superior to techniques that were used earlier. (Note: Compare with the discussion in Douglis et al. [180]).

Adler [8] analyzes Apache httpd log files to discover a phenomenon described as the Slashdot Effect. Slashdot.org is a popular high volume Web site providing news on topics of current interest. The effect basically is that Web servers hosting a Web site get high hit ratios due to the hot news being broadcast by that Web site.

Bilchev et al. [77] give a description of a Web cache modelling toolbox. They formulate and implement a Web cache infrastructure model for the investigation of characteristics that are not so easy to obtain from log data. Their model can also be used for assessing caching situations that do not exist in reality. Their model also allows for the study of temporal features. By using real-life log data, they conclude that the popularity of Web pages branches out as we go up the cache hierarchy. They use their model to predict the cache population dynamics in a fictitious scenario of caches that are made deliberately large.

Chen and Mohapatra [122] undertake a characterization study of Web documents. They present a characterization of Web documents based on their types and their environment (e.g. academic, commercial and news). They state that the efficiency of caching can be bettered if caching priorities and TTL preferences are given to some varieties of documents.

Choi and Limb [129] develop a behavioral Web traffic model for aiding the assessment of shared communications networks. Their model is based on Web requests instead of Web pages. Judge [278] discusses how the peak HTTP request rate may be estimated for a set of Web users.

Pirolli and Pitkow [443] attempt to get a better understanding of the surfing patterns of Web users. Such a study is worthwhile because by knowing which documents will be requested in the near future, the caches can offer better service by fetching such documents in advance and storing them. Pirolli and Pitkow make use of Web server logs and look at session durations, the number of clicks per visit etc. They contrast various methods for reckoning surfing patterns.

Foong et al. [201] mention that efficient caching relies on making best use of locality of reference. They suggest that at least four dimensions of locality are exhibited by Web accesses. They utilize a logistic regression model (see [202]) to verify their conjecture.

Understanding Web traffic characteristics may aid the improved functioning of several algorithms employed for implementing caching. Jin and Bestavros [273] state that the relative frequency with which objects are obtained by means of a proxy is often considered sparingly when designing cache replacement algorithms. They mention that several cache replacement algorithms frequently depend on secondary properties (that are simpler to get) for the purpose of guessing popularity characteristics. They describe popularity-aware variants of the Greedy-Dual-Size (GDS) cache replacement algorithm. They describe an online algorithm for obtaining popularity information effectively.

Kelly and Reeves [299] look at ways of determining accurately the optimal sizes for Web caches on the basis of several factors. They devise an algorithm which they claim is a useful tool for measuring temporal locality in Web cache workloads.

Krishnamurthy and Wang [317] suggest that it would be beneficial to find out which sets of clients send a greater proportion of requests to a Web site. They reason that it would help moving content closer to such sets of clients. They introduce the concept of clustering of clients. This basically involves clubbing together clients that are possibly governed by a single entity and are near each other in a topological sense. They develop a network-aware method for clustering of clients.

Bahn et al. [39] conduct a study characterization study of World Wide Web references in Korea. Their analysis includes Web document based analysis, Web server based analysis and international link based analysis. They demonstrate how their analysis may be used for caching.

Bai and Williamson [40] employ trace-driven simulation and artificial workloads to understand how requests arrive at every level of a simple Web proxy cache hierarchy. They mention that a Web cache in the hierarchy reduced both the peak and the mean request arrival rate for their workloads. They study distributions for modeling the requests arrival counts in hierarchical Web caching.

Gupta and Ammar [225] comment that analysis of server logs from multimedia servers, a FTP server, and a Web server indicated that a few files that happened to be responsible for much of the load on a server displayed highly variable popularity behavior. This occurred regardless of the character of content and the protocol employed to fetch such content. Gupta and Ammar note that this may be of significance for caching, server replication, content distribution networks, and multicast where content is dispersed. They study the influence of multimedia popularity on multicast scheduling and develop a new multicast scheduling technique.

4. Exercises

1 Why is it desirable to get a good understanding of Web traffic characteristics.

2 What are the implications of changes in Web client access patterns?

3 Investigate how the rate of change of Web objects influences the design of Web caching techniques.

4 What is Zipf's law? What is a Zipf-like distribution?

Chapter 10

FORECASTING PATTERNS OF ACCESS

1. Introduction

A number of techniques such as cache coherence, cache placement, cache replacement and prefetching (refer the chapter on prefetching) depend to a great extent on the patterns of access by the users. Several techniques have been suggested in order to predict future requests. We discuss some of these in the chapter on prefetching. Such predictions help to ameliorate the exchange of data between proxies and servers. Several techniques rely on the Prediction by Partial Match (PPM) technique (widely used in data compression) for predicting which documents a user might access in the immediate future.

2. Studies related to access pattern prediction

Fan et al. [195] study the capabilities of Web prefetching between low bandwidth clients and proxies. Padmanabhan and Mogul [424] studied the application of prefetching for latency reduction. Palpanas and Mendelzon [429] studied the application of partial match prediction for prefetching.

Web server hints often benefit both caching and prefetching. Cohen et al. [137] study efficient algorithms for predicting requests to Web servers. They propose methods for grouping resources that will in all probability be accessed together, into *volumes*. These are then used to generate hints. Such hints may be tailored as per the intended application viz. prefetching, cache replacement and cache validation. Cohen et al. discuss the theory of optimal volume construction and exhibit some efficient heuristics. Their algorithm predicts accesses to the extent possible but at the same diminishing false predictions and keeps the size of hints within manageable limits. They demonstrate that it is feasible to predict requests with high accuracy and without significant overheads.

3.   Further reading

Bestavros [68] studied the application of speculation to reduce Web server loads and also for diminishing the service time. The servers speculate which documents are likely to be requested by the clients on the basis of statistics available to them. On the basis of the speculation, a server sends the requested document and also other documents that it feels will be requested by the user. Here the speculation is done by the server and not by the client. Hence, server speculation based data dissemination is different from prefetching.

Dias et al. [170] describe a smart Internet caching system that attempts to make best use of the capabilities of both caches and mirrors (refer Glossary for a definition)in order to provide better response times. Their caching system endeavors to characterize Web access patterns. It undertakes to download files even before they are asked for by a client. Dias et al. use both heuristics and probabilities for representing the access patterns. Their system is made up of a caching gateway.

Schechter et al. [491] discuss the application of path profiles for forecasting HTTP requests. They present an algorithm for generating these profiles in an effective manner. They also demonstrate that they can forecast HTTP requests by means of the path profiles with a high probability. As a consequence, dynamic content may be created just before a client asks for it. It is easy to see that accurate forecasts of HTTP requests will diminish the latencies associated with such requests as the servers can take action in anticipation of requests.

Access pattern prediction is also helpful for Web content adaptation. Abdelzaher and Bhatti [2] conduct a study of Web content adaptation for bettering the performance of servers under overload conditions. Clients that attempt to establish a connection with an already overloaded server will often be unable to connect to it. Abdelzaher and Bhatti propose a method for overcoming the overload problem by adjusting handed over content to the existing load situation. They argue that their scheme is a practical one due to the following reasons:

- the possibility for making the process of content adaptation operate with minimal intervention

- savings and other benefits

- the quality of being realizable without the need for alterations to Web servers, Web browsers or Web protocols.

Abdelzaher and Bhatti also develop a software tool for Web content adaptation.

Aubert and Beugnard [31] observe that tuning a Web cache is a non-trivial matter given the fact that the complexities of architectures and the number of parameters are steadily increasing. Taking a clue from this observation, they suggest that Web caches must tune themselves by taking into consideration the prevailing traffic conditions and relevant parameters.

Iyengar et al. [263] analyze and characterize large-scale Web server access patterns. They make use of time-series analysis for characterizing Web server access patterns. They state the advantages of their approach when compared to methods that were used previously. For this, they make use of a real-life example. They also mention that their approach may be used to build new benchmarks for giant-scale highly accessed or popular Web sites.

Aida and Abe [14] describe an address generation algorithm for generating pseudo IP addresses. This may be used for depicting diverse Internet access patterns. Aida and Abe state that the pseudo IP address sequences produced by their algorithm affords reliable cache performance and may be used as a substitute for trace-driven simulation. Their algorithm may be used for simulations dealing with Internet performance, Web caching, DNS etc.

To conclude, there is no doubt about the usefulness of accurate access pattern prediction for techniques such as cache coherence, prefetching, cache validation and cache replacement.

4. Exercises

1 Why is it is important to predict access patterns? What are the benefits of making such predictions?

2 What is PPM? How is it used for access pattern prediction?

3 Mention the applications of prefetching techniques.

4 Investigate various algorithms for predicting requests to Web servers.

IV

COMPLEMENTARY TECHNIQUES

Chapter 11

PREFETCHING

1. Introduction

In the context of Web caching, the term *prefetching* refers to the operation of fetching information from remote Web servers even before it is requested. Objects such as images and hyperlinked pages that are cited in a Web page (say a HTML page) may be fetched well before they are actually called for. It should be noted that a tradeoff occurs. Web objects are prefetched assuming they will be requested in the near future. An accurate selection of such objects would lead to a reduction in the access latency, whereas inaccurate picks would only result in wasted bandwidth.

Prefetching techniques gain significance due to the fact that there are limits on the performance betterment that may be obtained by applying just plain caching (see Abrams et al. [5], Douglis et al. [180] and Kroeger et al. [326]). As noted by Douglis et al. [180], the rate of change of Web objects puts a barrier on the gains that may be obtained by caching. Abrams [5] observed that the maximum cache hit ratio obtainable by employing a proxy cache is limited to about 50% (under their workloads) irrespective of its design. This in effect means that one out of two documents will not be found in the cache. Prefetching is a means to overcome this restriction of plain Web caching strategies (that do not employ it) and often complements such strategies.

2. Prefetching examples

It is easy to visualize the following three prefetching instances: prefetching between Web clients and Web servers, prefetching between Web clients and proxy caches, and prefetching between proxy caches and Web servers.

Figure 11.1.   An illustration of prefetching

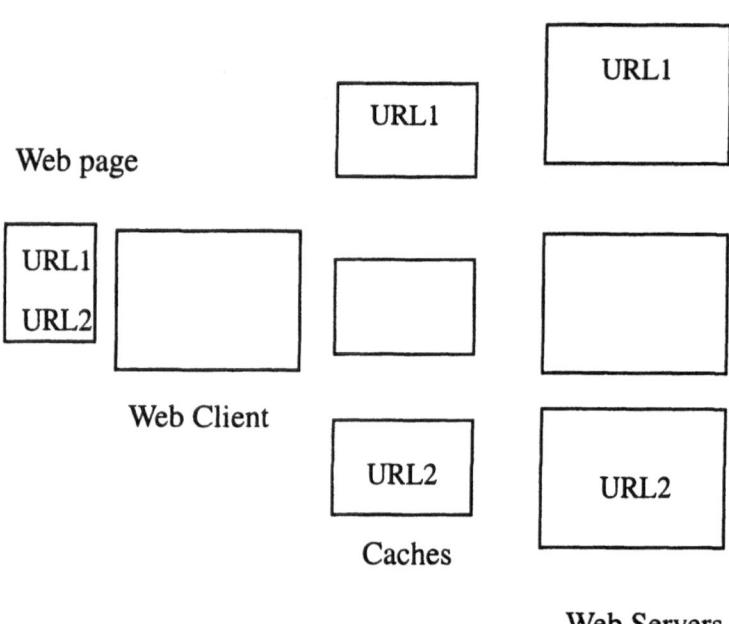

Table 11.1.   Prefetching possibilities

Exist between
Web clients and Web servers
Web clients and proxy caches
Proxy caches and Web servers

2.1   Prefetching between Web clients and Web servers

It would be beneficial to develop an effective strategy for reducing the perceived access latency by anticipating and prefetching files expected to be requested shortly, when a user is browsing a Web page. Padmanabhan and Mogul [424] studied one such strategy. In their scheme, servers analyze requests from several clients and make predictions. As this happens, clients begin prefetching on the basis of the predictions made by the servers. Thus the scheme of Padmanabhan and Mogul is an example of prefetching between clients and servers. As we may expect, the effectiveness of their scheme depends to a large extent

Figure 11.2. Three different prefetching instances

Web Client   Proxy Cache   Web Server

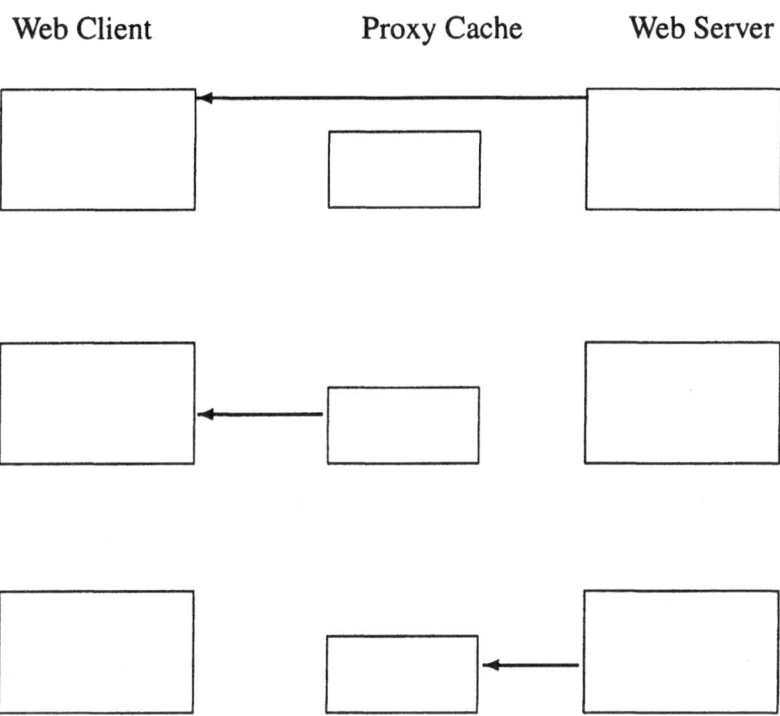

on the accuracy of the predictions. The prediction algorithm used by them is based on an earlier one due to Griffioen and Appleton (refer [424] for details).

Padmanabhan and Mogul assess the efficacy of their scheme by trace-driven simulations over both low and high bandwidth connections. They show that prefetching data from the servers to the clients can reduce the access latency experienced by the clients by a maximum of about 45%. However, this comes at the cost of nearly double the normal network traffic. Despite the fact that their results show that prefetching helps, it is to be noted that there is a reduction in the average access time *only* at the cost of a corresponding increase in the network traffic. This perhaps explains why real-world implementations of the theoretical ideas of prefetching research are hard to come by. However, in many practical applications it may be beneficial to conceal the access latency from the users to the extent possible. In such applications prefetching may turn out to be very useful.

Bestavros and Cunha [72] studied the benefits of a data dissemination scheme that enables data to diffuse from its source to servers that are closer to the end users. Their scheme reduces network traffic and performs load balancing among servers by tapping geographic and temporal locality of reference properties displayed in client access patterns. Bestavros and Cunha present results of log analysis and trace-driven simulations to measure the performance improvement that may be achieved. They conclude that it is better than what might be got by the application of client-based caching. They also view their scheme as one that complements client-based caching instead of supplanting it. The chief idea in their approach is to make good use of the data available at servers concerning client access patterns. Other related papers include [69, 70].

Palpanas and Mendelzon [429] studied the application of partial match prediction for prefetching data. Partial match prediction is a technique often employed by some data compression algorithms (refer any good book on data compression). As mentioned earlier, a good prediction algorithm should limit the number of inaccurate predictions to a minimum. By means of simulations, Palpanas and Mendelzon show that it is possible to obtain a high fraction of accurate predictions. Their experiments suggest that 18% to 23% of the requests can be foretold with 80% to 90% exactness.

Cunha and Jaccoud [151] use an assemblage of Web client traces and study how accurately a user's future Web accesses can be predicted from past accesses. They develop two user models that assist in guessing a user's future Web access. One of their models uses a random walk approximation whereas the other is based on digital signal processing techniques. In addition, they also give suggestions on how to make use of the models for a simple prefetching technique.

Crovella and Barford [146] study the network effects of prefetching. They establish that even in the instance when prefetching bestows no extra traffic, it can have unwelcome effects on performance. They show that immature approaches to prefetching can step-up the burstiness of individual sources and lead to increased average queue sizes in network switches. However, they also show that applications such as Web browsers can stay clear from the unwanted queuing effects of prefetching. For this, they evolve a simple rate-controlled prefetching scheme to downplay the negative effects on the network by minimizing the transmission rate of prefetched documents. Their work indicates that it may be worthwhile to explore new ways of overcoming the pitfalls of prefetching in order to make it practically useful.

2.2   Prefetching between proxy caches and Web servers

Kroeger et al. [326] explore the bounds of Web latency reduction from caching and prefetching. They deduce several bounds on the performance enhancement seen from these techniques. In order to measure these bounds, they use traces of Web proxy behavior observed in the real world. For these traces they noticed that local proxy caching could diminish the latency by a maximum of about 26% whereas prefetching could curtail the latency by at most 57%. On the other hand, a combined caching and prefetching proxy could yield no more than 60% latency reduction. An important observation made by them is that the latency reduction from caching is substantially constricted by the rate of change of objects in the Web (see Douglis [180]). For their work, they assume the presence of a proxy server interposed between the client (viz. the browser) and the Web server. They make the reasonable assumption that communication between the client and the proxy is in general a small component of the total latency whereas the communication between the proxy and the server constitutes a significant fraction of the total event latency. They observe that for the workload studied by them, plain caching provides modest help in diminishing latency whereas prefetching can achieve more than double the improvement obtained by plain caching despite shortcomings.

Kroeger et al. [326] categorize prefetching into two classes: local based and server-hint based. According to them, prefetching algorithms that do not make use of information from a server would be thought of as examples of local prefetching disregarding whether they are used at a client or at a proxy. Such algorithms may utilize local information such as citation patterns for the purpose of prefetching. On the other hand, in server-hint based prefetching, the server makes use of the knowledge it has acquired about the objects requested as well as the patterns of citation from the clients. However, the prefetching has to be accomplished by an agent that is near the client. As we may guess, the complexities involved in this particular strategy make its practical realization a cumbersome effort. One common caution that must be exercised when interpreting results obtained by trace-driven simulations is that they are often heavily dependent on the workload modeled.

Markatos and Chronaki [380] propose a top 10 approach to prefetching, wherein prefetching occurs both at the client and the proxy. Their approach blends the servers knowledge of their most popular documents (their top 10) with client access profiles. The basic idea of Markatos and Chronaki is that Web servers must regularly forward their most popular documents to their clients (which may themselves be Web proxies). These in turn may forward them to their clients (which may also be Web proxies) and so on. Their approach to prefetching is based on the cooperation of the clients and the servers in order to arrive at fruitful prefetch operations. The server side is responsible for sporadically computing a list of its most popular documents (the top 10) and distributing it to its clients. One important point to be noted here is that very few Web servers in existence today make effective use of such statistics. In contrast to other sophisticated prefetching algorithms, the algorithm of Markatos and Chronaki uses an uncomplicated and easy to compute metric. This makes their strategy more practical. In order to evaluate their scheme, they employ trace-driven simulations based on access logs from several servers. Their results indicate that their scheme can predict more than 40% of a client's requests, although stepping-up network traffic by at most 10% in most cases.

Figure 11.3.   Top 10 prefetching approach

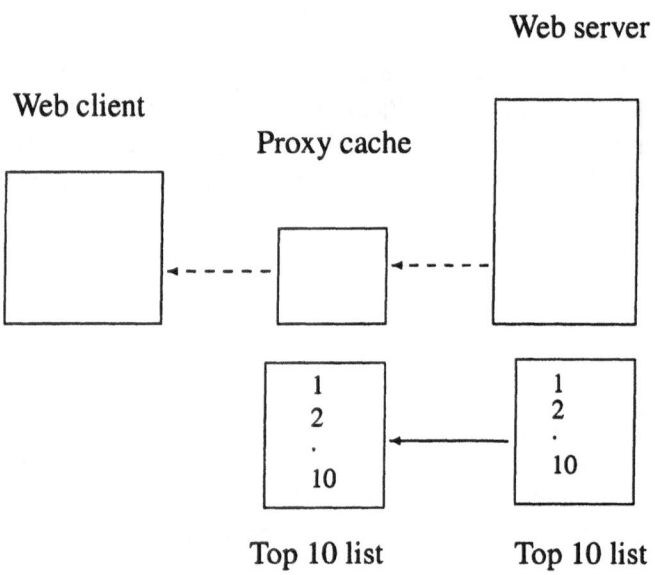

Cohen et al. [133] investigate ways of improving the end-to-end performance of the Web by using server volumes and proxy filters. Their aim is to cut down the user sensed latency and the quantum of TCP connections, and to ameliorate cache coherency and cache replacement while allowing for prefetching of resources. In their scheme, server response messages admit piggybacked information tailor-made for the requesting proxy. The server orders associated resources into volumes and employs a proxy-generated filter to customize the piggyback information. Their scheme can be used without necessitating any changes to the HTTP 1.1 protocol. They exhibit an effective data structure for building server volumes and employing proxy filters. This data structure also helps in volume up keep and piggyback information generation. Their strategy is a good example of prefetching between the proxies and the servers. They establish the strength of their approach by assessing various volume construction and filtering techniques across an assembly of extensive client and server logs. They demonstrate that compounding proxy supplied data with server returned hints provides an efficient model for improving the end-to-end performance of the Web. For more details the reader may refer their article [133] and also the book of Krishnamurthy and Rexford [314].

Chinen and Yamaguchi [128] discuss the design and implementation of an interactive prefetching proxy server called the WWW Collector or WCOL for short. WCOL runs on several widely used UNIX platforms. The prefetching system of Chinen and Yamaguchi collects references to other pages by parsing the HTML of the client's Web page when it is sought and accumulates cited pages (or images as the case may be) for every request by the client. One important benefit of their scheme is that the prefetching mechanism is the onus of the proxy server considering that it is often difficult to incorporate prefetching in browser clients. This is mainly because of the fact that many of them are commercial products for which the source code is rarely available in the public domain. For their system, except for the hit ratio, they did not measure other performance parameters as it was not easy to do.

Figure 11.4. Minimal modifications desired for prefetching

Minimal modifications at client, proxies and servers desired for implementing prefetching

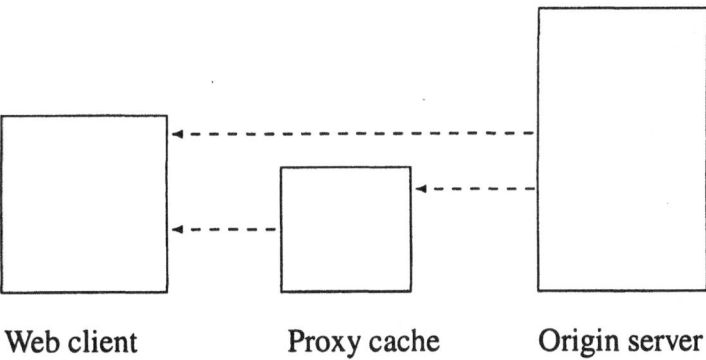

Web client   Proxy cache   Origin server

Gwertzman and Seltzer [227, 228] analyze geographical push-caching (also refer the chapter on flavors of caching). In their scheme, a Web server selectively forwards its documents to caches that are nearest to its clients. Their idea is to make better use of the server's knowledge of the access patterns and disperse data to collaborating servers. They use trace-driven simulations to assess their scheme and show that it reduces bandwidth expenditure and server load to the same extent as Web proxy caching but with a thriftiness in global cache space of nearly two orders of magnitude. Their scheme complements both client caching and proxy caching.

2.3   Prefetching between Web clients and proxy caches

Loon and Bharghavan [363] discuss ways of alleviating latency and bandwidth problems in Web browsing for mobile users. The problems peculiar to this application include low bandwidth availability to end users, long and variable latencies in document access in addition to temporary disconnection. In order to surmount these difficulties, Loon and Bharghavan profile user and group access patterns and use these profiles for prefetching documents. They also filter HTTP requests and responses so as to lower data transmission over problematic links. They stock documents on the basis of the user profiles so that limited Web browsing becomes a reality even during the period of disconnection. A crucial observation to be made here is that prefetching during the duration of inactivity can make good use of the low bandwidth accessible. Loon and Bharghavan discuss the design and implementation of a Web proxy based system that makes use of the ideas mentioned above. As may be seen here, Web caching for mobile devices is even more complex than in ordinary computers. Here prefetching can be used advantageously to improve the user's Web browsing experience.

Figure 11.5.   Prefetching in a mobile device

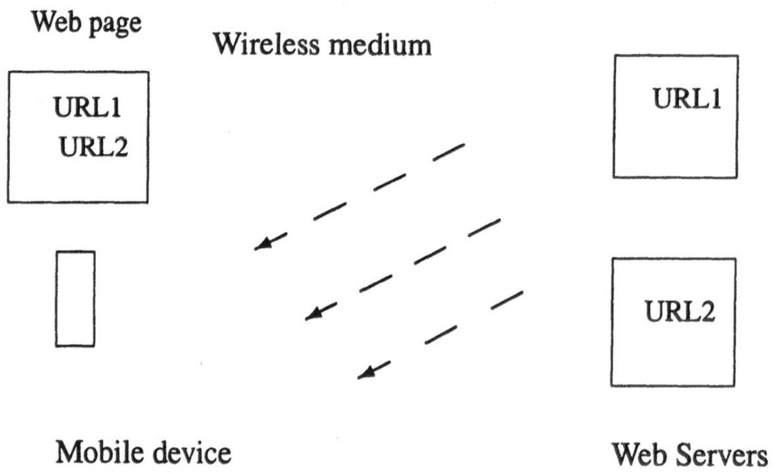

Fan et al. [195], study Web prefetching between low bandwidth clients and proxies. This makes sense due to the fact that a vast majority of users in the world connect to the Web through slow dial-up connections. Their scheme enables Web access latency reduction by prefetching between proxy caches

Table 11.2. Constraints in Web browsing for mobile devices

Limited bandwidth availability at clients
Variable latencies
Temporary diconnection
Power constraints

---

and browsers. It banks on the proxy to forecast which cached documents a user could access next. It makes use of the idle time between user requests to push or pull the documents to the user. Fan et al. assess the strength of their technique at quashing client latency by means of trace-driven simulations. They probe the design of prediction algorithms and look into their performance. Their results show that prefetching when supplemented with a large browser cache and delta-compression (see the chapter on cache replacement for more information on delta-compression) can bring down the client perceived latency by about 23.4%. This diminution is accomplished by using the Prediction by Partial Match (PPM) algorithm (refer any good book on data compression for information on PPM algorithms). However, their approach produces 1% to 15% extra network traffic. As usual, one must be judicious when understanding such results due to the fact that they often depend to a great extent on the workload modeled.

Figure 11.6. A low bandwidth client

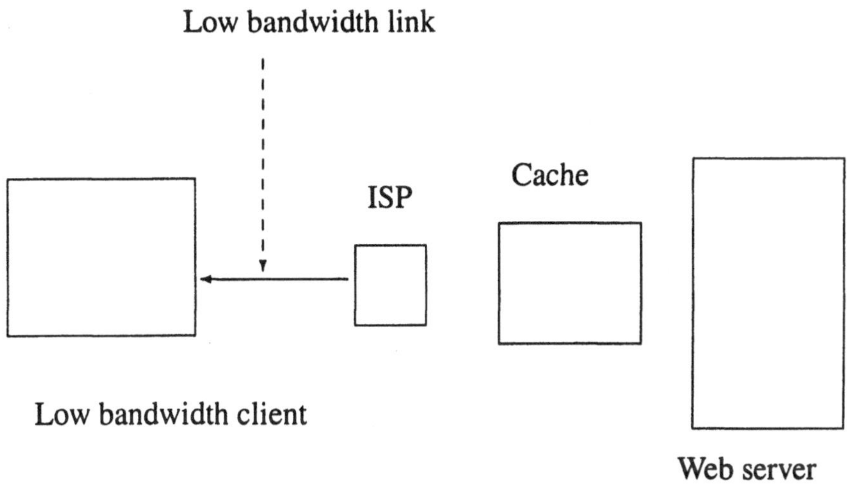

Cohen and Kaplan [134] study the factors conducive to user perceived latency and describe the use of prefetching as a means to overcome it. Their analysis shows that DNS query times, TCP connection set up, and start-of-session holdups at HTTP servers often bestow more to the latency than transmission time. This is so particularly for clients with high bandwidth connections. Cohen and Kaplan offer simple methods to handle these factors. They accomplish this by pre-resolving host names (viz. DNS prefetching), prefetching TCP connections in anticipation of the actual HTTP requests and also by sending blank HTTP HEAD requests to Web servers. The application of their technique at Web browsers or proxies does not necessitate protocol modifications or solicit cooperation from other components in the system. They suggest ways to make their solution amenable for curbing the likely burden to Web proxies and Web servers. They also mention that their approach complements other prefetching and caching techniques. For example, prefetched TCP connections may be used for cache validation, noticing and discarding outdated links, pursuing redirected links and also for prefetching meta-data. However, the benefits must be weighed carefully against the overheads. Krishnamurthy and Rexford [314] mention the tradeoffs in prefetching.

3.   DNS prefetching

Domain Name System prefetching (DNS prefetching) comprises performing the domain name to address translation in anticipation of the actual request. An important point to be noted is that the access latency will not be substantial if the local DNS has a cached copy of a Web server's IP address. However, it could be significant if other DNS servers have to be accessed in order to service a particular request.

It is very much possible that DNS lookups are faster for some servers than others. Wills and Shang [560] by virtue of their experiments argue that the DNS lookup technique was quicker for popular Web servers when compared with random Web servers. They report that the functioning of the DNS lookup technique was more favorable for popular Web servers in terms of various factors.

Danzig et al. [158] undertake a study of Domain Name System (DNS) related traffic and examine the performance of the DNS. They study the efficiency of caching domain names and reason that a profound change in the stipulation and effectuation of name servers is necessary. This is also essential because several million computers in the world enforce the DNS and a huge amount of DNS traffic is heading to a small number of root name servers.

LeFebvre and Craig [342] study reverse DNS lookups for Web servers. Such lookups are required when a Web server needs to know the domain name of one of its clients. It must therefore execute a lookup in the Domain Name

Figure 11.7. DNS prefetching

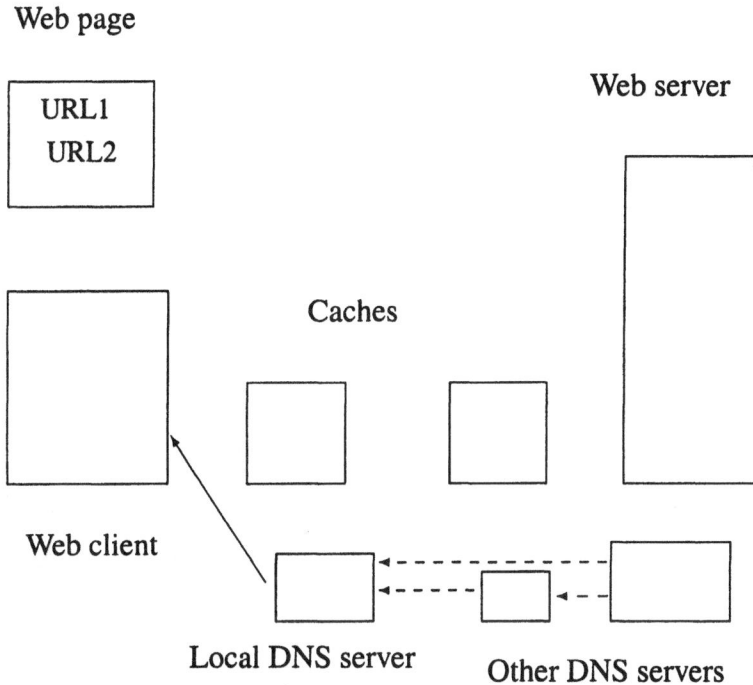

System's reverse domain. Such lookups can not only be time consuming but may also have undesirable effects on the Web server's response to its clients. This therefore necessitates a system for executing reverse DNS lookups rapidly. LeFebvre and Craig develop such a system and name it as Rapid DNS. It is a client/server system that functions as an intermediary between a Web server and a DNS server. It allows for caching of outcomes and also restricts Web server lookups to data present in its cache. This enables a substantial betterment in the response time for instances when awareness of a host name is not vital for the functioning of a Web server.

Huitema and Weerahandi [248] report on the results of some measurements related to the Internet. They comment that domain name resolution through the common gethostbyname() interface took more than 2 seconds in 29% of their tests. They attribute this to the flat structure of the domain name space, especially in the case of the most popular domains. They observe that this structure diminishes the benefits of caching. They also note that it centralizes the onus of resolving names for the entire Internet on a tiny set of servers which find it difficult to cope with.

Figure 11.8.   Reverse DNS lookups

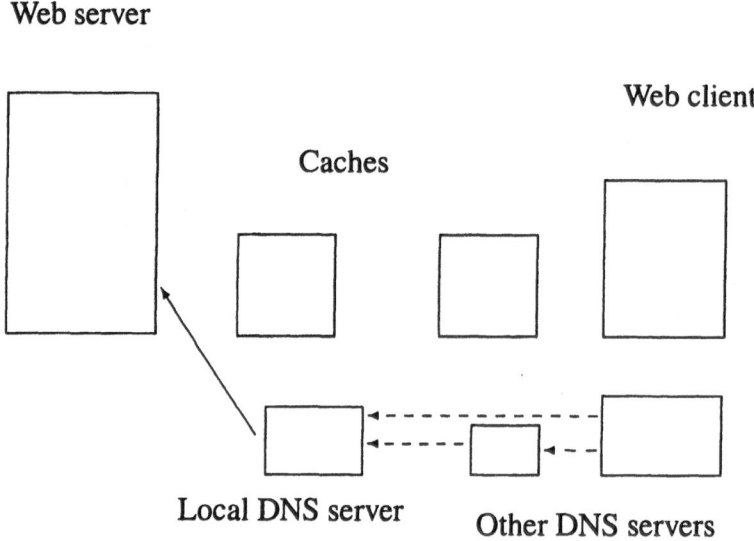

Jung et al. [287] present an elaborate analysis of traces of DNS and related TCP traffic accumulated on the Internet links of two universities. Their analysis shows how clients at these establishments interact with the wide-area DNS system. Their study deals with performance aspects and the existence of failures and also analyzes the efficiency of DNS caching.

4.   Other prefetching schemes

Jiang and Kleinrock [270] study an adaptive prefetching scheme. In their scheme, files that are very likely to be requested in the near future are downloaded based on the access history and also the network conditions. They use two modules: a prefetch module and a threshold module. The prefetch module estimates the likelihood of a file being sought in the near future. The threshold module calculates the prefetch threshold for each associated server. The access probability is compared with the prefetch threshold. Jiang and Kleinrock present a prediction algorithm for Web browsing. They demonstrate the usefulness of their algorithm by means of simulations. They mention the importance of being adaptive to the user's behavior and to the network conditions. In another article (see [271]), they study the application of their adaptive prefetching scheme for Web prefetching in a mobile environment.

Prefetching has also been studied by Duchamp (see [185] and [344]). Safranov [484, 485] presents a page rank backed prefetching method for accesses to Web page clusters. In this scheme, pages related to a requested Web page are ranked. The ranking is then used to decide which pages need to be prefetched. An empirical evaluation of the prefetching process was done by employing real world server logs. The scheme is stated to be better than random prefetching in the case of clustered access.

Kokku et al. [309] discuss the performance of a non-interfering Web system christened NPS. They mention that their system can be set up without any alterations to browsers, servers, the network or to the HTTP protocol. NPS abstains from the requirement of thresholds or magic numbers often used (for e.g. by Jiang and Kleinrock [270, 271]) to restrain the undesirable effects of prefetching. Kokku et al. demonstrate that prefetching using NPS cuts down response time by about 25%. They do this by employing trace-driven simulations. NPS makes use of a congestion control protocol named TCP-Nice. The protocol finds use in other applications (see [536] and also [309]).

Venkataramani et al. [537] study the possible gains from the application of prefetching for content distribution. They distinguish between short-run prefetching and long-run prefetching. In short-run prefetching, caches use the access history of late to predict and prefetch objects expected to be summoned in the near future. On the other hand, long-run prefetching relies on long-run steady state object access rates and update frequencies to discover objects for replication to content distribution locations. Long-run prefetching is more suitable for large proxies and content distribution networks (CDNs). Venkataramani et al. note that although long-run prefetching boosts network and disk space utilization it could assist in bettering the hit rate. They employ trace-driven simulations and analytical frameworks to test various algorithms for picking out Web objects for long-run prefetching. They point out that substantial gains can be got at moderate costs by concentrating on long-lasting Web objects. This occurs in spite of the fact that the Web's Zipf-like (see the Glossary and refer the chapter on Zipf's law) access patterns do not make it easy to prefetch an adequate number of Web objects to significantly ameliorate hit rates.

Dikaiakos [172] studied the difficulty of picking Web content in the context of a periodic push strategy that employed satellite links to distribute information to global Web caches. The principal idea in that strategy is to prefetch preferred resources by means of satellite so as to avoid choking already clogged terrestrial connections. A model is employed to show that the Web-content selection problem can be cast as one needing combinatorial optimization. Further, it is established that this problem is an integer programming problem belonging to the complexity class NP-Complete and therefore solvable by well-known approximation algorithms. Further results are presented in [171].

Jung et al. [286] study Web caching with cumulative prefetching in the context of multimedia data transfer. This study is useful because transferring multimedia data needing long-lasting connections with sequential data transmissions frequently breaks down across wide area networks (WANs). Repeated endeavors to get large Web objects through proxy caches would ravage network resources with no success assured. Jung et al. offer on-demand cumulative prefetching to increase the utility of proxy caches and for more effective accessibility of large multimedia files. Their analysis establishes that their scheme of on-demand cumulative prefetching can be accomplished without too many runs and with nominal supplementary bandwidth. In their analysis, they compute parameters such as byte hit ratio and bandwidth costs. However, they do not estimate user perceived latency. Their results suggest that on-demand prefetching can be efficiently realized by employing a cumulative approach. Another advantage of their scheme is that cumulative prefetching may be merged with rate-controlled prefetching. Doing so will diminish the queuing time lag in networks often ascribable to prefetching.

5.   Further reading

Mockapetris and Dunlap [397] discuss the development of the Domain Name System (DNS) and examine the ideas that went into the preliminary design of the DNS in 1983. They note the achievements and the drawbacks and try to foresee its growth.

Banâtre et al. [45, 46] describe ETEL. ETEL is a newspaper-based distributed information system. ETEL is a subset of the Web and provides an assurance of the relevancy of the information due to temperance by an editor. It makes use of predictive prefetching.

Wang and Crowcroft [544] study the application of prefetching for the Web. They look at tradeoffs in prefetching and infer that only in instances when the traffic is not heavy or the prefetching efficiency is substantial, statistical prefetching might not diminish perceived delay. Wang and Crowcroft describe the implementation of deterministic prefetching in a hot list manager.

Inoue et al. [258] discuss a caching technique for a satellite network which was intended for serving consumers in different parts of the world. Their system makes use of prefetching. An agent chooses the prefetching actions that must be carried out and also determines the time intervals for prefetching.

Jacobson and Cao [264] discuss the potential and limits of Web prefetching between low-bandwidth clients and proxies. The basic idea is to make use of the idle time between Web requests to predict future requests from the clients and also push documents to the client. A 256 KB buffer is used for pre-pushing, resulting in a latency reduction of about 20% at the client.

Prefetching may also be beneficial for rendering the bandwidth utilization patterns smooth. Maltzahn et al. [377] mention that huge HTTP traffic variations occur within a single day. As a consequence, they come up with the idea of *bandwidth smoothing*. The idea is to prefetch resources during off-peak hours so that bandwidth requirements during peak hours get reduced. Doing so could actually better the hit rate. Maltzahn et al. make use of machine learning techniques in order to implement bandwidth smoothing. In another article, Maltzahn et al. [375] conduct a feasibility study of their bandwidth smoothing technique. They show that it is feasible to prefetch Web content during off-peak periods when the bandwidth requirements are less. They assess the benefits of employing the bandwidth smoothing technique.

Figure 11.9. Prefetching during peak hours

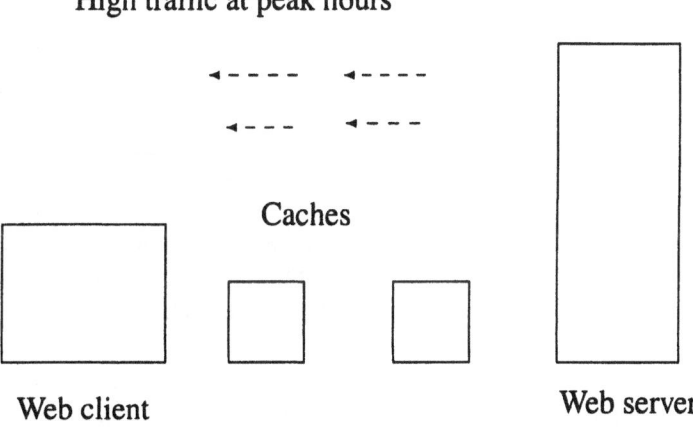

High traffic at peak hours

Caches

Web client   Web server

Prefetching might actually worsen the traffic

Swaminathan and Raghavan [513] present a prefetching technique by characterizing the browsing behavior of Web clients. By applying their technique, they demonstrate betterment in the client cache hit ratio in the presence of dynamic URLs (the contents of the URLs keep changing every few minutes or during every visit). Such dynamic URLs are not beneficial for caching techniques that deal only with static data.

Cao[100] describes a proactive power-aware cache maintenance technique in which clients prefetch data that is most likely to be used in the immediate future. This prefetching is carried out in an intelligent manner. Cao makes use of a *prefetch-access ratio* to dynamically optimize either performance or power on the basis of the requirements. Cao's technique is stated to improve

Figure 11.10.   Prefetching at off-peak hours might lead to bandwidth smoothing

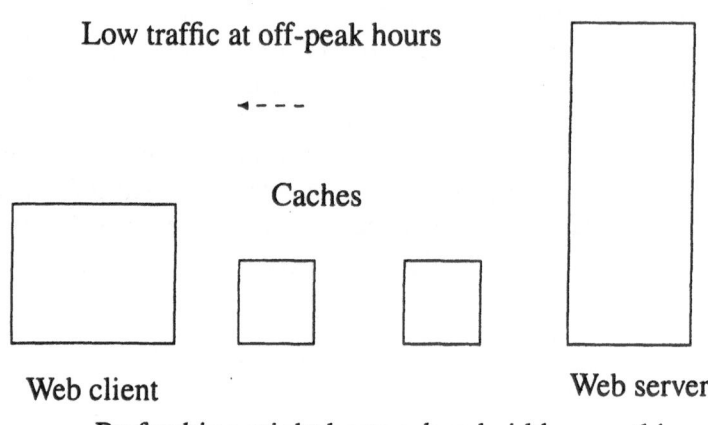

Low traffic at off-peak hours

Caches

Web client   Web server

Prefetching might bestow bandwidth smoothing

cache hit rate, throughput, bandwidth usage, and cuts down query delays and power usage (see the chapter on measuring performance for definitions of terms mentioned here).

Chang and Chen [115] develop a cache replacement algorithm that combines the benefits of both caching and prefetching. Web caching makes use of the temporal locality of Web objects, on the other hand Web prefetching makes use of the spatial locality of Web objects. The merger of these two techniques could result in the worsening of their performance if a careful approach is not followed. Chang and Chen develop a normalized profit function to assess the profit that could accrue due to the process of caching an object on the basis of a prefetching rule. By using profit functions, Chang and Chen develop a cache replacement algorithm known as IWCP (integration of caching and prefetching). They state that their algorithm does well when compared to other algorithms.

Gitzenis and Bambos [213] demonstrate the advantages of power-controlled data prefetching and caching in wireless packet networks. The objective here is to keep the total delay and power cost to a minimum by carefully selecting the data item to be fetched and by choosing the appropriate power level.

Wu and Chen [569] discuss the prediction of Web page accesses by the analysis of proxy server logs. They represent user access patterns as sequences of successive Web page accesses. They identify sequences that occur repeatedly and arrange them in the form of an index. By using this index they develop a technique for predicting user requests. They also come up with a framework for prefetching Web pages.

Hou et al. [243] study prefetching in hierarchical caching. They mention that users who are located close to the leaf level of a caching hierarchy encounter a higher miss rate (see Glossary for definitions) and delayed response time than users who are at higher levels. Therefore a technique must be developed to overcome this shortcoming. Hou et al. develop a freshness and retrieval threshold based cache prefetching technique for palliating the bias against users near the leaf level of a caching hierarchy.

In a series of articles [573, 574, 575, 576] Yang and collaborators discuss the application of data mining for Web logs in order to aid caching and prefetching. They state that mining Web logs is beneficial for both the techniques. Also refer [82].

Figure 11.11. Prefetching in a hierarchical caching system

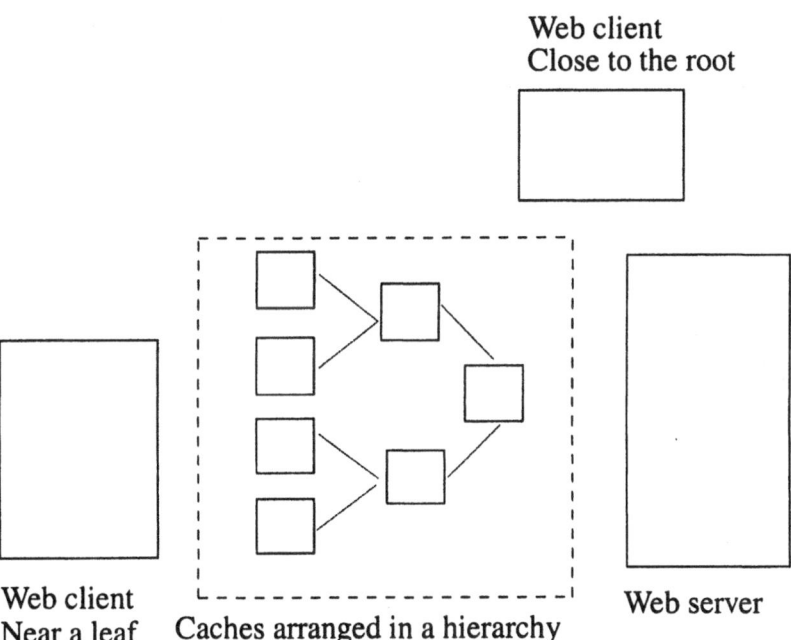

6. Exercises

1 Explain the concept of prefetching. How does it differ from plain Web caching strategies?

2 Investigate how the rate of change of Web objects puts a restriction on the gains from plain Web caching strategies. Show how prefetching can be of help here.

3 Study partial match prediction algorithms. Explore their applications in data compression and prefetching.

4 Study the negative effects of prefetching. List ways of overcoming them.

5 Experiment with the source code for WCOL. Investigate the complexity of porting WCOL on to your favorite OS platform.

Chapter 12

LOAD BALANCING

1. Introduction

Load balancing is a well studied topic and as a result there are numerous articles on the subject. There are at least two good books [83, 311] on load balancing which may be referred to by the reader. Since load balancing is a technique that complements Web caching, therefore, a brief mention is made in this chapter. Consequently, the discussion about load balancing here is not broad in scope or content and has been included for the sake of completeness.

2. Studies related to load balancing

Wessels [548] directs efforts towards the undermentioned issues while studying caching strategies for the Web:

- the evolution of a single-process, non-blocking proxy server for less than normal system load

- the sustenance of current and precise cache data by inducing the least possible network burden

- a preliminary sketch indicating the plan for economical algorithms for cache maintenance.

Wessels also mentions software tools for Web caching. The software is intended to provide faster response times to clients and also to simultaneously inflict lower loads on servers. A model is contemplated as a result of which server sites come forth with callbacks to sites that preserve cached copies of the information available on the servers. Wessels also gives an account of a cache negotiation protocol. The protocol is intended for equipping content providers with the capability for controlling the mode and the duration of dispersion of their content in caches that are far-flung.

Kong and Ghosal [310] describe a technique known as *pseudo-serving* in which users themselves play a key role. This technique is intended for overcoming network congestion when *flash-crowds* exist. In such a situation numerous users in different locations attempt to fetch identical groups of files from a server within a short time span. In pseudo-serving, a user is able to fetch files from servers even in a flash-crowd situation since the user possesses a file for a short duration and services at most two other users in that interval.

Grimm et al. [218] consider the problem of load and network traffic balancing in large scale cache meshes. They describe the lessons learned by them while sustaining the cache hierarchies within the German broadband research network (DFN). About ten distributed cache servers were used as the foundation for a large scale cache hierarchy by them. Grimm et al. tried various mesh designs and evaluated their performance. Their basic aim was to ameliorate the load and traffic balance amongst the caches. They mention that during the course of their modifications, they also attempted to increase the utility of the entire cache mesh. They believe that cache mesh designers may gain some useful insight as a result of their experience.

Bunt et al. [93] study the means for attaining load balance and efficient caching in Web servers that are bunched together as a cluster (viz. several servers are made to function as a single unit for better performance). They study policies for allotting requests in such servers. They assess diverse load distribution policies as regards their capability for attaining good balance, in addition to their effect on the efficiency of per-server caching. For this, they make use of trace-driven simulation and employ two commercial Web servers capable of handling a few million requests a day. They infer from their experiments that the use of current state data is crucial for obtaining good load balance only when the attainable per-request bandwidth is weakly determined by the network or the clients. They mention that it is possible to obtain both good cache behavior and load balancing simultaneously. However, they state that this necessitates the use of policies that take into consideration both these goals.

Conti et al. [142] discuss an approach that makes use of quality of service (QoS) as the basis for distributing load amongst replicated Web servers.

Cardellini et al. [105] mention that the use of traditional algorithms for distributed systems are not suitable for dispatching requests between servers within a cluster. They state the need for DNS dispatching algorithms that are more suited for clusters of Web servers. They develop algorithms that make use of state estimation in order to provide a scalable system. Casalicchio and Colajanni [107] describe client-aware dispatching algorithms for Web clusters that offer multiple services. In their schemes, Web switches make use of Layer 7 (L7) (application layer) information for dispatching client requests amongst servers within a cluster.

Laoutaris et al. [336] develop a simple load balancing algorithm based on their ideas for designing meta algorithms (see the discussion in the chapter on caching architectures). They state that their algorithm is capable of balancing load efficiently and may also be an answer to the filtering effect in hierarchical Web caches noted by Williamson (see [554]).

3. Further reading

It is possible to achieve load balance in subtle ways. Since considerable HTTP traffic variations can occur within the span of a day, it is worthwhile to consider prefetching resources during time periods when the bandwidth needs are not much. Maltzahn et al. [377] discuss this idea of *bandwidth smoothing*. They study the practicality of their technique [375] and demonstrate that it is feasible to prefetch Web content during off-peak periods when the bandwidth requirements are not substantial. They accomplish this without any loss of cache consistency.

Chapter 13

REPLICATION

1. Introduction

Replication is the process of duplicating (mirroring) the contents of origin servers in multiple locations in order to enable quicker access to replicas of the original site. Replication has the same goal as Web caching i.e bringing content closer to the end user. However, it operates in a different fashion when compared to Web caching. Both replication and Web caching are complementary techniques. Now-a-days many commercial service providers offer content distribution services. The networks created with the objective of distributing content are known as Content Distribution Networks (CDNs). The coverage related to replication and Content Distribution in this chapter will not be substantial since many books on such topics go into more details. For example, refer [455, 538].

2. Studies related to replication

Gwertzman [226] studies autonomous replication in wide-area networks (WANs) and brings in the concept of *geographical push-caching*. This caching technique is described in more detail in the chapter on various flavors of Web caching.

Baentsch et al. [35] look at the advantages and shortcomings of both caching and replication for the World Wide Web. They study the behavior of a proxy server for both caching and replication strategies by considering several parameters such as:

- the degree of replication,
- document popularity,
- the hit rates and

- the error rates.

Kermarrec et al. [302, 303] develop a framework for consistent, replicated Web objects. They suggest that it would be preferable to use different caching and replication techniques for distinct Web pages based on their features. They put forward for consideration a framework in which dissimilar techniques could be chosen for distinct Web pages.

Makpangou et al. [370] describe a replicated directory service known as Relais for replicated caches that are weakly consistent. It was designed to better the performance of Web caching within an organization. Relais agglomerates a set of distributed caches and mirrors and makes use of a replication protocol to create an impression of a single consistent cache. The cost of keeping the directories consistent is controlled because of employing a weak cache consistency protocol. Relais was built by using the Squid caching software.

Rabinovich [456] discusses issues related to Web content replication and studies the difficulties that spring up in *dynamic replication*. In dynamic replication, object replicas are produced, altered or moved to appropriate Web hosts by adapting to the patterns of use.

Russell and Hopkins [482] analyze log files produced by the UK National Web Cache (JANET) (currently defunct) and also by numerous origin FTP sites. They infer that a FTP proxy cache with particulars about mirror sites could substantially reduce the amount of data that needs to be sent over networks that are already overburdened. They describe the design and implementation of a caching FTP server known as CFTP.

Bharat and Broder [73] conducted a study of host pairs with replicated content. Their basic objective was to get a better picture of mirroring on the Web. They employed about 179 million URLs during a Web crawl performed in 1998. Their article presents data about the extent of mirroring in the Web. They state that knowing and comprehending the nature or meaning of mirroring on the Web can be of great help for preventing superfluous procurement of information and may also be used to make up for broken links.

Byers et al. [95] discuss the employment of tornado codes to speed up the progress of downloads when gaining access to multiple mirror sites. They develop a feedback-free protocol that has its origins in erasure codes. They mention that their protocol can provide excellent download speeds at the cost of transmitting a modest number of extra packets into the network. They also state that their solution is scalable and may similarly be used in conjunction with wireless networks or satellite networks.

Kangasharju et al. [293] discuss how copies of objects may be traced by making use of the Domain Name System (DNS). They devise an application known as the Location Data System (LDS). This system permits a random host to get the IP addresses of servers that hold a particular URL. LDS is a modification of the Domain Name System (DNS) and necessitates only marginal alterations to the domain name servers. Kangasharju et al. give suggestions for applying their ideas for Web caching as well as for mirrored servers. They mention that LDS works well when used for sites that are not fully mirrored when compared to what is got by the application of LDS for caching. They also look at how a host may utilize location data so as to fetch requested objects in a smart manner.

It is often desirable to understand how mirror sites perform in practice. Myers et al. [407] study the performance characteristics of mirror servers on the Internet. Mirror sites are frequently used to improve the availability of the contents of Web sites so that users may access the content quickly. However, in order to get the best performance, the mirror which responds most quickly will have to be identified by the Web clients. Myers et al. report their experiments in fetching documents from servers that happened to mirror various Web sites. They report that close to optimal performance may be obtained by focusing only on a fraction of the servers instead of looking at all the mirrors of a Web site.

Vingralek et al. [540] describe the design of a system for a fast and dependable HTTP service. Their system known as Web++ ensures a high degree of reliability by dynamically replicating Web data amongst several Web servers. Web++ picks a server that is not only reachable but also most likely to furnish the best possible response time. Web++ also ensures that data is delivered if there are one or more live servers possessing the data that is being sought. In case the failure of a server is noticed, the requests from the Web clients are met by some other server that is in working condition. This occurs in a transparent manner, thereby saving the end users the trouble of configuration. Vingralek et al. state that Web++ does not necessitate any modifications to Web browsers. Web++ is therefore an extension of the Hypertext Transfer Protocol (HTTP). Vingralek et al. report that Web++ betters the client response time on the average by at least 36.6% and often by about 59%.

Pierre et al. [438] studied differentiated strategies for replicating Web documents. They argue that no single caching or replication policy can effectively deal with documents of all categories. They suggest that every document may be replicated by the application of a policy that is appropriate for it. They conducted some simulations to see how such policies performed. They state the performance was found to be good. They also mention that their results indicate that it is possible to construct adaptive replicated Web documents that are able to choose the policy most advantageous for them.

Rodriguez et al. [472] discuss parallel access for mirror sites. They mention that although mirroring of Web sites is becoming increasingly common, nonetheless, the task of identifying the most appropriate mirror is not a trivial one. They develop a technique by means of which Web clients may get in touch with many mirror sites in parallel and start retrieving documents from them.

The Web clients may do this in order to overcome the difficulties associated with selecting the most suitable mirror site. In the technique of Rodriguez et al. the Web clients link with many mirror sites by means of unicast TCP. They then fetch various portions of the documents from several mirror sites and at the same time make use of the provisions for adjusting to the state of circumstances in the network. Rodriguez et al. mention that their technique offers speeds which are as good as the quickest server in existence.

Rodriguez and Sibal [473] discuss an architecture known as SPREAD. It incorporates client validation, server invalidation, and also makes use of replication. It is meant for spreading and managing Web content.

Tang et al. [515] studied how globally replicated services may be supported by a Domain Name System (DNS) variant that is cognizant of routing metrics.

Jamin et al. [267] discuss constrained mirror placement in the Internet. Mirror sites are often used for shortening the response time and also for reducing the burden on Web servers. Jamin et al. study the benefits of having more mirror sites when various placement algorithms are used. They assume the highly probable scenario that mirrors can be placed only in designated locations.

Pierre et al. [442, 441] discuss self-replicating Web documents. They also offer a platform known as Globule for self-replicating Web documents. Their platform deals with various facets of replication such as:

- the development of kinship between servers,

- the production and annihilation of replicas,

- choosing the most suitable replication approaches, on a document by document basis,

- maintenance of consistency and also

- re-routing clients to the replicas and so on.

Although, Globule is meant for Web documents, it could also be used with documents that are stream-oriented. Pierre et al. also incorporate Globule as a module for the Apache Web server.

Wills et al. [559] suggest the bundling of a group of objects associated with a Web page into a single object for access by clients. They argue that this helps to ensure more effective content delivery.

Qiu et al. [453] discuss proper positioning strategies for Web server replicas in order to ameliorate the performance of Content Distribution Networks (CDNs) (see Glossary for definitions). Such networks replicate data amongst servers positioned in various locations in the Internet. Such replication ensures much better performance than centrally located origin servers. There has been considerable research effort in discovering strategies for effective re-routing of requests to the most suitable replicas. This was done in order to diminish the latency and also for the purpose of distributing load uniformly among servers. Nevertheless, placement strategies for Web server replicas in order to obtain more acceptable performance from Content Distribution Networks have not been well studied. Qiu et al. describe numerous placement algorithms that make use of particulars such as the latency and the request rates so as to arrive at the correct assessment concerning placement of replicated servers. They mention that the performance of CDNs is affected to a great extent by the way in which the replicated servers are placed within the Content Distribution Network (CDN). Qiu et al. also study the influence of factors such as the network topography and the absence of adequate information concerning client workloads, on the placement algorithms.

Andrews et al. [22] discuss client assignment in a distributed system of content servers. They develop a system known as Webmapper for clustering IP addresses and allotting each cluster to an optimal content server, and also analyze its performance.

Guo et al. [224] describe a probe-based server selection protocol for networks furnishing differentiated services. They attempt to combine quality of service (QoS) techniques and server replication. These two techniques can complement each other since the former provides differentiated services to users while the latter offers load balancing amongst a group of servers. In order to achieve the merger of the two techniques, we should pick a server from a set of replicas so that it lives up to the QoS requirements of a user. Guo et al. develop a probe-based protocol to detect network resources and make reservations for requests in networks that support differentiated services. They also contrast the functioning of five heuristics for server selection.

3. Further reading

Novikov and Hamilton [417] describe a software application known as FTP Mirror Tracker. This is intended to empower transparent re-routing to the closest anonymous FTP mirror sites. This re-routing is carried out under the command of the user. The re-routing is accomplished in two ways:

- by utilizing a Web cache server, and

- by sending HTTP requests to the FTP Mirror Tracker.

Bahn et al. [37] state that a huge proportion of Web objects such as image files of banners, buttons and logos are replicated wastefully all over the Web. Web caching systems often tend to treat replicas as different objects mainly because they possess distinct URLs. Bahn et al. describe a simple and effective approach for dealing with replicated objects for Web proxy caches. They make use of MD5 checksums along with sizes of objects to deal with replicas. They state their scheme substantially ameliorates the cache hit rate and the byte hit rate by getting rid of superfluous objects from the cache.

V

PRACTICAL ASPECTS

Chapter 14

FAULT TOLERANCE IN CACHING SYSTEMS

1. Introduction

Many caching products that are otherwise good in several aspects often ignore the important aspect of fault tolerance. It is desirable to know how caching systems get influenced in case of failure of one or more caches or in the event of failure of a cache server. Many organizations that intend to deploy a caching system often wish to understand how it will affect the existing set up. To answer this question one needs to probe what happens in the event of a cache failure. Now-a-days many commercial caching solutions provide mechanisms for fail over.

2. Fault tolerant Web caching solutions

Some systems with multiple cache units provide capability for clustering in case more than one unit is deployed. Clustering is often used alongside the round-robin DNS scheme. When requests move between all the units listed in the DNS record, every unit could broadcast sporadically to the rest of the cluster that it is operational. In the event of failure of an unit within a cluster, no information may be broadcast that it is in working order. In such a situation, another unit within the same cluster acts on its behalf. Although, products may overcome some failures, it may not be easy for them to surmount all types of failure.

It may be feasible to redirect traffic around a cache that failed by means of specialized hardware. Some products make use of a hardware element (such as a switch) that helps to bypass a cache that is not working.

It would surely be desirable to develop fault tolerant solutions that have a fairly inconspicuous effect on the user. For example, it should be ensured that a breakdown does not hinder usage for long intervals of time.

It may often be feasible to balance load across a caching system. Network components such as L4 switches (see Glossary for a definition of L4) may be used for this purpose (see Barish and Obraczka [52]). Many commercial products come with switches that are able to keep a watch on caching appliances and divert traffic in the event of breakdowns. In addition to their application for fault tolerance, such switches may also provide the ability for load balancing.

Although L4 switches may be beneficial for complex set ups, nonetheless, they may be prohibitive in applications which require too many such switches. Therefore a trade off occurs here. L4 switches can assist in routing traffic to the most accessible cache server in a smart manner. In the event of a cache failure a switch does not direct further requests unless it comes alive again. L4 switches possess features that make it easy to use them for other purposes such as maintenance checks without interrupting service.

Several commercial Web caching products employ WCCP (see the chapter on inter-cache communication for more on WCCP). All Web related traffic going through a specialized Cisco router that has the ability to use WCCP is forwarded to a cache that is also WCCP-capable. In the event of a cache failure WCCP avoids forwarding any further requests to the cache unless it becomes operational once again.

It has to be emphasized that coming up with a fault tolerant system is not a trivial task. For example, in a system with a large number of caches, it may not be possible to give an assurance that a request would be sent to a cache having the object being sought. In order to deal with this problem, L4 switches keep a note of the cache that serviced a particular request. WCCP-enabled caching solutions may make use of hashing to route requests to appropriate caches. It may also be possible to use protocols such as ICP in case no switches happen to be employed in a caching solution. Caches may send multicast requests to ICP-capable servers. If no response is received within a pre-specified time span, such caches may download the desired object directly from the origin server. They may also do this in case all caches report cache misses. In the event of a cache hit, the desired object may be got from the cache with the best response time. As described earlier, ICP is helpful for hierarchical caching systems. While developing fault tolerant solutions for caching, one must consider ease of deployment and also the flexibility. ICP has many features that satisfy this requirement.

3.   Exercises

1 Why is it desirable to develop caching techniques that are fault tolerant?

2 Investigate how a network gets affected in the event of failure of one or more caches.

3 Describe commonly used mechanisms for developing a fault tolerant caching system.

4 Explore publicly available caching products and find out whether they guarantee a fault tolerant environment. Come up with ideas for making them fault tolerant.

5 Explain the role of network components in providing a fault tolerant caching system.

6 Explain the role of protocols such as WCCP and ICP in creating a fault tolerant environment for the purpose of Web caching.

7 Investigate the costs and benefits of setting up a fault tolerant caching system.

8 Study how the efficiency of a system of Web caches gets affected by the implementation of a fault tolerant approach.

Chapter 15

CACHING FOR LIBRARIES, ISPS AND OTHERS

1. Introduction

Caching is especially important for organizations such as libraries and Internet Service Providers (ISPs). This is due to the fact that they store large volumes of information accessed by users.

2. Web caching for libraries

In case of libraries, the information to be downloaded is often common to the users. Such information could include information from specialized research databases. The contents of journals and magazines may be accessed by users several times and they may be downloaded from Web sites. Libraries often provide Internet access to their users to download information from such databases. Web caching can benefit such users because it can improve response times and avoids the need for paying for unnecessary bandwidth expenditures. Very often in libraries, a large number of users access the same set of Web pages repeatedly.

Libraries are often an important part of both commercial organizations and non-commercial organizations (such as universities). Such organizations may have branches in geographically distant locations. They often subscribe to journals that may be downloaded from the Web. If they are charged on the basis of the number of minutes of access and if the content downloaded is of a repetitive nature then obviously Web caching will be of great help to save them the cost of access. However, there may be some copyright or licensing restrictions that could inhibit organizations from employing Web caching. A cache makes a local copy and this may infringe such restrictions. On the contrary, much of the information in the Web is provided free of charge even if copyright restrictions apply (for e.g. research papers for use by individuals).

3.   Web caching for ISPs and others

Internet Service Providers (ISPs) offer Internet access to their consumers for a fee. Very often a large number of users (perhaps belonging to a single organization) utilize the services of ISPs. The subscribers of an ISP often access Web content that is shared by them for e.g the latest news. As a consequence, ISPs can improve the response times significantly by making use of Web caching. However, copyright and other restrictions may prevent them from reaping the benefits of Web caching. Huston [251] describes the deployment of proxy caches in Internet Service Provider (ISP) networks.

Commercial organization owning Web sites can benefit from Web caching in many ways. For example, all users within such organizations often have common interests when they search for content in the Web. They may be looking for information about a particular product or process. If companies have a large number of Internet users then caching is definitely helpful to avoid wastage of bandwidth and to improve the response times and the productivity of the users. Commercial organizations often have dedicated high speed links for their own use and have branches in geographically distant places. They may employ streaming media or Webcasts to exchange information between various branches. Caching is definitely helpful for building scalable intranets. Companies may also display the latest developments on their Web sites for their customers. They often use dynamic content and can benefit from Web server accelerators and the Active Cache technique. Companies often subscribe to the services of commercial Content Distribution Networks (CDNs) in order to speed up access to their Web sites. CDNs mirror the content of their customers in servers located in many parts of the world. They helps the customers of the companies to obtain speedy access to the company's Web sites.

Gschwind and Hauswirth [221] design a high performance cache server known as NewsCache for Usenet News (a high traffic news source). The cache server is intended to save network bandwidth, computing power, disk storage, and be harmonious with existing standards. Gschwind and Hauswirth describe the results of an experimental assessment of NewsCache.

Sun et al. [512] study the consequences of Web caching on network planning. They observe that using a properly designed Web cache with a 50% hit rate is more efficient than doubling the bandwidth of an ISP's access link to the Internet, in order to diminish the retrieval latency. Hence, about half of the bandwidth of the access link may be reduced by employing Web caching without forsaking retrieval latency. They state that caching will therefore be beneficial for ISPs, enterprises and universities that intend to link their intranets with the Web.

Chapter 16

BUILDING CACHE FRIENDLY WEB SITES

1. Introduction

Due to the benefits accrued by the application of Web caching, it is desirable to build Web sites that are cache friendly. The Cache Now campaign (see http://vancouver-webpages.com/CacheNow/) has provided some guidelines for achieving this. Some measures that may be taken to make Web sites cache friendly are listed below.

2. Cache friendly practices

- If possible enter into an existing cache hierarchy. Such hierarchies can be at the institution of the users, the regional tier, the national tier or the global tier.

- Try to make use of Web browsers that patronize a proxy cache.

- Encourage the use of Web browsers that make effective use of a local cache.

- Promote the usage of LAN servers within the organization.

- Allow for joint usage of links to Web objects that users may have in common, such as applets and graphics.

- Stay clear from unwanted CGI (Common Gateway Interface) scripts.

- Whenever practical attempt to make CGI scripts cacheable.

- Try to use Java or Javascript as alternatives to CGI for validating forms.

- Be cautious while using server side scripts.

- Make use of cookies only when they are unavoidable. Cookies and dynamic data slow down Web servers considerably (see the chapter on caching dynamic data).

- Try to keep dynamically generated data within reasonable limits for e.g. dynamic URLs.

- Employ Active Cache or Web server accelerators (see the chapter on caching dynamic data for more particulars about these techniques) to speed up the processing of dynamic data. This helps to deal with dynamic data that appears to be inherently uncacheable.

- Use streaming media or multimedia objects judiciously. Make use of appropriate protocols and caching strategies for dealing with such data. For example, in multimedia applications the Real Time Streaming Protocol (RTSP) might be a better choice than HTTP (see [314]).

- Do not make use of secure servers for securing objects that do not have to be secure.

- Restrict the use of cache unfriendly policies such as the use of cache bursting for counting the number of hits of a Web page.

- Make optimal use of the space available for the purpose of caching. For example, some Web browsers allow the users to specify the space that may be allotted for use by the browser's cache.

- Make references to objects in a uniform fashion.

- Allow caches to possess copies of Web pages and images that do not change frequently. Employ suitable cache replacement policies.

- Try to make caches identify Web pages that are being updated on a regular basis and adopt special caching techniques for dealing with such pages

- Try to control the use of dynamic URLs

- Try to adopt supplementary approaches that may assist caching such as replication, load balancing, prefetching (see the respective chapters for more information).

3.   Exercises

1 What is a cache friendly Web site? What are the benefits of developing a cache friendly Web site.

2 Make a list of cache friendly practices. Investigate how such practices would affect the organization that implements it.

3 What is cache busting?

4 List some cache unfriendly practices and mention how they may be avoided.

Chapter 17

CACHING AT THE GLOBAL LEVEL

1. Introduction

The practice of Web caching is growing not only in organizations but also at the regional, national and the international levels. There have been many attempts to create a global cache network. Some projects such as the National Lab for Applied Network Research (NLANR), JANET etc. contributed to this effort. Other campaigns such as the CacheNow campaign (see `http://vancouver-webpages.com/CacheNow/`) raised the general awareness of Web caching, in order to facilitate wide spread deployment of caches across the globe.

2. Caching projects at the global level

Given below is a list of some caching projects at the national or international levels. See the CacheNow home page (`http://vancouver-webpages.com/CacheNow/`) for links.

Table 17.1. Some caching projects at the national or international levels

---

NLANR
DESIRE
Japan Cache Project
CHOICE project in Europe
SingNet in Singapore
w3cache in Poland
Le Projet Renater-Cache in France
SWITCH caching service in Switzerland
JANET (currently defunct)

NLANR stands for National Laboratory for Applied Network Research. DE-SIRE stands for Development of a European Service for Information on Research and Education.

Figure 17.1.   Different tiers of a global cache hierarchy

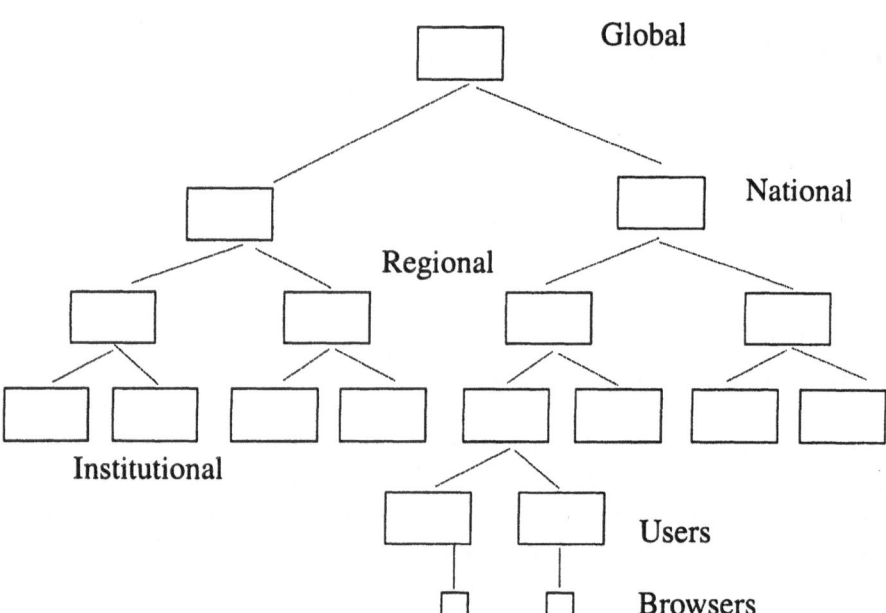

Neal [411] describes the positioning of the Harvest cache software in New Zealand. One important reason for the rapid assimilation of Web caching techniques all throughout New Zealand was primarily because of the high cost of network bandwidth. Because of this, New Zealand was among the earliest countries in the world to take up Web caching techniques. The article by Neal reports on the positioning of the Harvest Web caching software not only in New Zealand but also in several other countries in the world. The article also presents a survey of Web cache users in New Zealand.

Smith [506] discusses the national Web cache JANET (currently defunct) for the United Kingdom. Various aspects of the project including the software, the hardware, the network environment and the history of the project are presented in the article.

Wessels [549] sketches the development of the NLANR cache hierarchy and also mentions the configuration challenges that were encountered at the global scale while maintaining it. Wessels describes the establishment related constraints and the prerequisites for setting up and calibrating a cache for optimal performance when it was meant to be a member of the global cache hierarchy.

Wessels also gives a brief description of the firsthand knowledge that was gained as a result of maintaining the caches.

Inoue et al. [258] discuss an adaptive Web caching technique for a satellite network serving various countries in the world with the hub being located in Japan. They use a Web caching technique that incorporated prefetching. An agent is employed to periodically coerce the caching system to disperse documents throughout the network so that they may be cached. Documents are also prefetched whenever needed. The agent decides the prefetching plan of action. Various factors influence the agent's decisions for reorganization of the caches. These include the following:

- hit ratios

- network bandwidth utilization, and

- the patterns of access.

These factors necessitate that the caching system be adaptive. The agent takes care of auxiliary activities that have to be performed. These include, for example, refreshing the cache by replacing pages by the application of the Least Recently Used (LRU) cache replacement algorithm and also deciding the time intervals for prefetching.

Nabeshima [409] reports on the Japan cache project. The idea of a domain cache is brought in to deal with accesses related to a single domain name. The Japan cache project maintains a cache server for serving the public for access to Web servers in the Japan (jp) domain. Various experiments were conducted as part of the project. Some of these included the following:

- prefetching during off-peak hours

- management of cache coherence between servers

- maintenance of a replication server as a HTTP server.

It was found that although domain caching is efficient, prefetching could not be carried out expeditiously due to problems in guessing user accesses.

Lee et al. [339] report on the costs and benefits of a cache hierarchy in Korea, while Krashakov and Shchur [313] report on the state of Web caching in Russia in 1998. Cormack [144] describes the experience gained as a result of maintaining a cache at the institutional tier.

3.   Further reading

Bekker et al. [56] analyze the practicality, effectiveness and user friendliness of Web caching servers in the context of the DESIRE caching project. They conclude on the basis of their study that there will be situations in which the consumers may have to circumvent the default caching behavior.

Gauthier [211] discusses the long term viability of large scale Web caches. The report studied the impact of caching for the Internet backbone. Factors such as improvements in the CPU speeds, disk density and speed, router speed and the growth of the backbone were taken into consideration.

4.   Exercises

1 Why is it desirable to deploy caches at the regional, national and international levels.

2 List some important caching projects at such levels.

3 Why is it necessary that there should be awareness of caching at a global scale?

VI

ASPECTS RELATED TO PERFORMANCE

Chapter 18

MEASURING PERFORMANCE

1. Introduction

In order to ascertain the efficacy of a Web caching solution, it is necessary to measure its performance. Therefore, it is desirable to have some standards or benchmarks against which the performance of a particular Web caching solution may be evaluated. Such benchmarks may help in choosing the most suitable Web caching solution for the problem at hand. It is very much possible that a particular structure may be beneficial for certain applications while other applications may require some other alternatives. Some organizations may opt for proxy based caching solutions. They may try to overcome the problem of configuring Web browsers by forcing the use of browsers that provide for auto-configuration. Large organizations may make use of network components such as routers and switches. They may also employ transparent caching. Some organizations may prefer highly scalable solutions anticipating future needs. Organizations whose Web sites contain highly dynamic content may employ Active Cache or may use Web server accelerators. Needless to say, the subject of measurement of performance is restricted not just to finding the efficiency of a given Web caching solution but also encompasses evaluation of the performance of cache replacement algorithms, cache consistency protocols, the role of fundamental protocols such as HTTP and TCP and so on.

2. Parameters for measuring Web performance

As we may see from the examples mentioned above, the needs are highly varied. Some common metrics that are used to quantify the performance of Web caching solutions include the following: hit ratio, byte hit ratio, response time, bandwidth saved etc.

Performance of Web caching solutions may be quantified by measuring parameters such as those listed below:

- price

- throughput (e.g. the number of HTTP requests per second generated by users, the rate at which a product delivers cache hits etc.)

- cache hit ratio (the ratio of the number of requests met in the cache to the total number of requests)

- byte hit ratio (the fraction of the number of bytes served by the cache divided by the total number of bytes sent to its clients)

- the number of minutes until the first cache hit/miss after a breakdown

- the cache age (the time after which the cache becomes full)

- hit ratio/price (e.g. hits/ second per thousand dollars)

- downtime (e.g. time to recover from power outages or cache failures).

Good benchmarks often help in designing better solutions. Two well known free benchmarks for evaluating the performance of Web caching solutions are the Wisconsin Proxy Benchmark (WPB) (see Almeida and Cao [16]) and the Web Polygraph (see http://www.web-polygraph.org).

Table 18.1.   Benchmarks for evaluating Web caching systems

Wisconsin Proxy benchmark
Web Polygraph

3.   The Wisconsin Proxy Benchmark

Almeida and Cao [16] describe the Wisconsin Proxy Benchmark (WPB) version 1.0. WPB is a benchmark meant for comparing the performance of proxy servers and for predicting how they would perform in the real world. A group of computers supporting Web browsers is connected to the Web proxy that is to be tested. The proxy in turn is connected to a group of Web servers. The client processes are made to execute the client codes in the benchmark instead of running a browser. Similarly, the server processes are made to execute server codes instead of the Web server. The client is designed so that it is able to send HTTP requests to the proxy. A limited variety of requests types are permitted and this excludes persistent HTTP connections supported by HTTP 1.1. The file size distributions that were used for the server program at the time of testing were not realistic although, more realistic distributions could have been chosen. More realistic files sizes were contemplated for inclusion in future versions of the benchmark.

Almeida and Cao measure the performance of four different proxy servers using their benchmark. They study the influence of additional disk arms on the performance of the proxy. They conclude that merely adding extra disk arms may not yield improvement in the performance for every application although the disk arms may appear to be the bottleneck restricting proxy throughput. They also find that the benefits of caching proxies gets eroded if low bandwidth modem connections are used by clients. Many benchmarks do have some shortcomings and WPB is no exception. For example, WPB version 1.0 does not support DNS lookups, persistent HTTP connections, spatial locality in Web accesses, some HTTP request types and so on. Hence, the Wisconsin Proxy benchmark is detached from reality to an appreciable extent.

Figure 18.1. Setup supported by the Wisconsin Proxy Benchmark

Web proxy

Web clients

Web servers

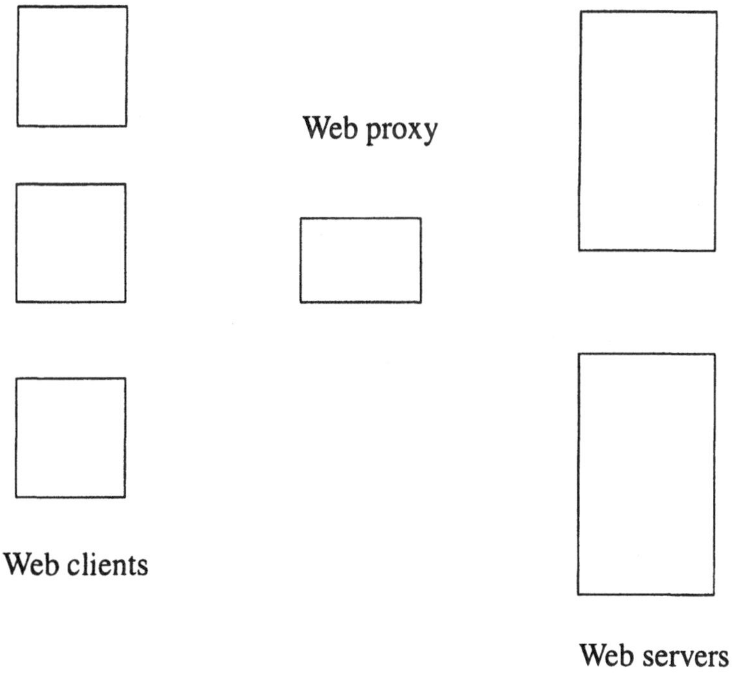

4. Web Polygraph

Web Polygraph is a tool for measuring performance that was initially developed at the National Laboratory for Applied Network research (NLANR). It is used for evaluating the performance of HTTP intermediaries such as proxy caches, server accelerators for origin servers, switches (L4 and L7), content filters etc. It is a tool for generating Web traffic and for simulating Web clients and servers. It can also produce workloads for modeling Web access patterns. It can be used to produce various workloads for simulating models of content popularity. Even Zipf-like workloads can be created by Web Polygraph (see the chapter on Zipf's law and refer to Breslau et al. [88, 89]). Web Polygraph can simulate concurrent requests from a set of clients to a set of servers. Some of the features available in Web Polygraph version 2.8.0 (available at the time of this writing) include the following (also refer [478]) :

- support for secure http (viz. https)

- support for HTTP authentication

- support for Internet Protocol version 6 (IPv6)

- possibility for adjusting the load on the basis of real-time measurements such as response times, throughput etc.

- pragmatic traffic generation (HTTP and SSL)

- standard workloads that may be used immediately

- ability to simulate network packet losses and delays

- ability to support several HTTP request methods

- capabilities for DNS lookups

- capability for specifying the percentage of HTTP 1.0 and HTTP 1.1 requests and responses

- support for persistent connections

- ability to simulate aborted requests

- support for various content types

- support for various file size distributions

- ability to simulate object popularities

Thus, we see that Web Polygraph is a very useful tool for evaluating the performance of Web intermediaries.

5. Factors often overlooked while evaluating performance

As Web caching itself is a relatively new discipline, techniques for measuring the efficiency and usefulness of Web caching solutions have been evolving slowly. In Web caching, theory has advanced much faster than practice.

Given below is a list of parameters often used for evaluating the performance of a Web caching solution.

Table 18.2. Parameters often used for evaluating the performance of Web caching systems

Price
Throughput
Hit ratio
Byte hit ratio
Cache age
Hit ratio/price
Downtime

While quantifying the performance of caching solutions we must not ignore aspects such as aborted requests, cookies, DNS lookup latencies, client side latencies, server side latencies, different popularity characteristics among servers, the type of content, network packet losses etc. It may so happen that many of these parameters are often interrelated. For example, hit ratio is affected by inadequate disk space in a cache server, by deficiencies in the object placement/replacement policies, by network overload and so on. Maximizing a single parameter alone may not suffice.

Table 18.3. Some factors often overlooked while evaluating the performance of Web caching solutions

Aborted requests
Dynamic content
Presence of cookies
DNS lookup latencies
Client side latencies
Server side latencies
Popularity characteristics of servers
The type of content (e.g. multimedia data) and the size of objects
Packet losses
The interaction between various parameters

6.   Further reading

Glassman [214] discusses the performance of a caching relay for the World Wide Web. The distribution of requests for Web pages is characterized and this is employed to evaluate how this impacts the functioning of the cache.

Sedayao [494] examines the consequences of running the Mosaic Web (one of the earliest Web browsers) by looking at packet traces, analyzing log files, and by simulating a HTTP proxy server. Sedayo also gives some suggestions for enhancing performance and for optimizing the consumption of network resources on the basis of the features of HTTP requests and other characteristics.

Arlitt and Williamson [29] study the influence of several replacement, threshold and partitioning policies on the performance of a Web server by means of trace-driven simulations.

André de Jong et al. [168] report on the costs and benefits of running caching services. Their article gives a description of their analysis of the cost effectiveness of different alternatives in order to see whether the benefits outweigh the costs. This was done by them for the SURFnet Web caching mesh. The SURFnet caching mesh with which they experimented contained about 20 child caches for every parent cache in the mesh. They conclude that the advantages of caching outweigh the costs of deploying it (at all tiers of the mesh) and also bring about a considerable diminution of the perceived latency.

Graham-Cumming [215] studies the incoming and outgoing Web related traffic for several commercial enterprises over a period of one year. This study lead to some helpful guidelines for network administrators to keep the Internet access costs within reasonable limits and also to avoid legal problems.

Iyengar et al. [261] study the performance of Web servers under high loads. Effective performance of Web servers is an important need for Web sites that deal with a large number of requests. Iyengar et al. note that Web servers perform dismally when there are requests for dynamic Web pages. They mention that the performance of a Web server gets improved if its rejects a greater fraction of requests when it functions at optimal or near optimal capacity.

Maltzahn and Richardson [376] compare the performance of two well-known Web proxies: CERN's httpd and Squid under bulky workloads in real world applications. They observed that although these two Web proxies were designed in a different manner, their performance however was essentially the same. The two popular Web proxies were assessed on the basis of resource usage and their dependence on the load conditions.

In another article, Maltzahn et al. [373] discuss performance related issues of enterprise level Web proxies. They look at two popular Web proxies, CERN's httpd and Squid and mention that httpd did better than other Web proxies with the exception of a version of Squid that was current at that point of time.

Nielsen et al. [414] study the consequences on network performance due to HTTP 1.1, Cascading Style Sheets (CSS) and Portable Network Graphics (PNG) images. They report on their study of the effect of persistent connections, pipelining and document compression at the link level on both client and server HTTP realizations. They report that their experiments indicate that HTTP 1.1 is meeting the design objectives that were set for it. They mention that paying attention to implementation particulars is crucial for realizing the advantages of the HTTP 1.1 protocol.

Afonso et al. [9] discuss quality of service (QoS) in Web caching. They argue that in order to understand the effects of changes of architectures in a Web caching system, standards of caching server QoS must be defined. They develop many tools for quantifying the QoS in Web caching systems. They study the QoS of two representative examples: cache servers of a university, and a national network.

Liedtke et al. [355] describe a server architecture for designing LAN servers with good performance. Servers often have to deal with a large number of clients and serve dynamic Web pages, graphics and video. Since servers could become bottlenecks if they are not efficient therefore it becomes essential to design servers that have high performance. Liedtke et al. develop a sample server system known as Lava based on their architecture.

Niclausse et al. [413] discuss a caching policy for the World Wide Web. Their caching policy takes into consideration factors such as:

- network latency,

- document size,

- access frequencies for documents and

- the time since the cache was accessed previously.

By means of trace-driven simulations, Niclausse et al. demonstrate that their policy is superior when compared to many other policies when it was assessed in terms of metrics such as the hit ratio, the byte hit ratio and so on.

Barford and Crovella [50] study the production of typical Web workloads for measuring the performance of servers and networks. Such a study should help in knowing how servers and networks behave when workloads vary. Barford and Crovella develop a tool for Web workload production. Their tool known as SURGE (Scalable URL Reference Generator) produces references tallying with the experimentally observed values of the following:

- server file size distribution

- request size distribution

- relative file popularity

- embedded file references

- the temporal locality of reference

- intervals during which individual users are idle.

Barford and Crovella report that their tool SURGE makes use of servers in a different style when compared to other Web server benchmarks.

Feldman [197] talks about continuous online extraction of HTTP traces from packet traces. In order to understand the problems related to Web performance, it may become essential to resort to monitoring the packets of information being sent between various components of a network such as the clients and the servers. Feldman describes a software that works with a tool known as the PacketScope monitor. The software is used for continuous online extraction of HTTP traces from packet traces. It is said to have performed well in retracing elaborate logs of several million downloads from the Web.

Hine et al. [240] discuss how to merge the knowledge acquired about the behavior of Web clients along with resource dependencies in order to better the performance of the Web. They investigate two approaches for achieving this:

- merging knowledge acquired about the behavior of Web clients along with resource dependencies, in order to diminish the access latency by prefetching chosen Web documents

- utilizing knowledge dependencies in order to affect cache replacement related resolutions.

They mention that were able to observe the extent of betterment in the performance in both approaches by means of simulations.

Marshall and Roadknight [382] discuss the possibility of associating cache performance with user behavior. They develop a simple model of independent users as a result of analyzing user traces. The model may be used for forecasting precisely the cache performance for a large set of user groups. Their model looks at caches as an agglomeration of independent users and views each user as a tiny cache.

Miera et al. [385] exhibit an outline for assessing the performance of proxy cache hierarchies. They realized their framework for the Squid proxy cache. Their technique may be looked at as a technique for picking a good hierarchy set up from numerous alternatives.

Banga and Druschel [48] look at the pitfalls during the process of evaluating the capacity of Web server by the use of artificial workloads. They assess a method for producing Web traffic that can be bursty and also has peak loads that exceed the capacity of a Web server. Their technique also models losses and delays that are characteristic of WANs.

There cannot be any doubt about the importance of measuring the performance of commercial and also non-commercial caching products available for use. It will be beneficial to come up with a methodology for assessing performance. Rousskov et al. [481] report on the results of a comparison of the performance of Web caching products. The reader may also refer http://www.measurement-factory.com for more recent evaluations.

Saraiya and Vasudevan [488] discuss the subject of measuring the performance of network caches. They suggest that the performance of network caches must be gauged with respect to the end consumer response time advantages. They also suggest that attributes such as:

- network and server delays,

- access patterns of the Web clients, and

- the features of the content being accessed

should be taken into consideration while measuring the performance of network caches. With these objectives in mind, Saraiya and Vasudevan come up with a technique that is suitable for assessing the performance of network caches.

Barford and Crovella [51] measure Web performance in the wide area. Their project uses infrastructure distributed across the Internet. They use a Web traffic generator to produce typical Web workloads.

Kurcewicz et al. [330] describe a filtering algorithm for proxy caches. They mention that proxies often attempt to cache as many objects as possible in order to improve the hit ratio. This is achievable only if there is adequate disk space. One important point to be noted here is that merely attempting to improve hit ratios may not help in getting high performance from the proxy cache. Disks often become the chief obstacle for cache servers. The presence of substantial burden on disks could result in decreased proxy cache efficiency. Due to these reasons, Kurcewicz et al. suggest the incorporation of filtering algorithms for Web caches. Objects that are potential candidates for being requested in the future are filtered by the application of the filtering algorithm. Their technique is said to achieve high hit ratios while at the same time maintaining disk load at substantially low levels.

Pierre and Makpangou [440] describe the working of a distributed Web cache system assessment tool known as Saperlipopette!. This tool is meant to benefit decision making when designing large Web cache systems. Typical questions concerning the design a large scale caching system such as the ideal number of caches to be employed, the right choices concerning their sizes etc. may be answered by using the tool.

Chan and Woo [112] give a description of a practical method for achieving maximum efficiency in Web transfer. They study a technique known as *cache-*

based compaction for diminishing the latency of Web browsing over a low-speed link. Their technique involves a trade-off between computation and bandwidth. Their main idea is that objects can be coded in an extremely economical form if objects having the same characteristics that were transported previously could be used as references. They present:

- an effective algorithm for picking out objects having the same or similar characteristics as references

- an encoding/decoding algorithm that diminishes the size of a Web object by making use of the similitude or likeness with the reference objects.

Chan and Woo test the efficacy of their technique by means of experiments.

Davison [162] describes an architecture known as Simultaneous Proxy Evaluation (SPE). It is meant for assessing the performance of multiple Web proxies concurrently. In SPE, requests for Web objects are replicated and sent to every participating Web proxy. The SPE architecture was designed in order to overcome the difficulties associated with test conditions that are not realistic enough, and also with obsolete or unsuitable workloads. SPE may also be used with proxies that employ prefetching. Several parameters such as

- the hit ratio,

- the byte hit ratio,

- cache coherence and

- access latencies

may be evaluated by employing SPE.

Davison [163] conducts a survey of proxy cache evaluation techniques and outlines an expanse of proxy cache evaluation methods on the basis of the origin of the workloads employed and also the type of algorithms used. Davison then tries to fit the surveyed work into the expanse.

Davison [164] argues that Web traffic logs that are routinely used for assessing the performance of Web proxy caches are not a perfect source of support for drawing conclusions as they have some serious shortcomings. Davison then lists some of these shortcomings and how they may be overcome by using logs that are more perfect and complete in many respects. By using logs that contain more complete content, Davison studies the supplementary perception available and how it could be beneficial for proxies, especially those that employ prefetching.

Krishnamurthy and Wills [319] attempt to obtain a clearer understanding of the interaction between proxy cache coherency and replacement policies by means of trace-driven simulations. They conclude that a major cost factor for caches that are comparatively small is the cache replacement policy, whereas for caches that are big the cache coherency policy becomes the paramount cost factor.

Maltzahn et al. [374] explore different techniques for diminishing the disk I/O of Web proxy cache servers. The most crucial constriction affecting the performance of proxy cache servers is probably disk I/O. Maltzahn et al. mention that design modifications in the architecture of the prevailing version of the Squid caching proxy could drastically diminish the disk I/O, thereby improving performance significantly. They observe that it is possible to develop methods of diminishing disk I/O by adopting the following approaches:

- retain the locality of the HTTP requests and at the same time map them into cache references

- employ virtual memory in the place of files for objects that are not big when compared to the system page size.

They state that an assessment of these two methods showed that they diminished disk I/O by about 50% to 70%.

It often becomes crucial to comprehend the performance related aspects of Web servers especially during *mirroring* (see Glossary). Mirroring is undertaken in order to improve the response time for end consumers. Myers et al. [407] study the performance related features of mirror servers.

Nakamura et al. [410] describe a system known as ENMA for measuring the performance of Web servers. It is intended to help understand the behavior of Web servers that may be seen from outside. ENMA uses packet monitoring to help comprehend the behavior of Web servers. ENMA is able to measure the time taken for establishment of connections, the number of concurrent connections etc.

It is beneficial to study the architecture of Web servers in order to extract good performance from them. Pai et al. [427] study an efficient and portable Web server known as Flash. They report an architecture known as the asymmetric multi-process event-driven architecture. They study this architecture by means of the Flash Web server. They contrast the architecture of Flash with that of two widely used Web servers: Apache and Zeus. They report that Flash performs at least 50% better than prevailing Web servers.

It is desirable to assess the performance of various cache consistency protocols. Perret et al. [434] contrast the performance of the Distributed Object Consistency Protocol (DOCP) which was developed by them along with a previously existing cache consistency protocol (refer the chapter on cache coherence for more particulars on cache consistency aspects).

It may be worthwhile to build environments for comparing the performance of various algorithms used for Web caching. Zhang et al. [588] describe

WebCASE, a simulation environment for experiments related to Web caching. They state that the Perl programming language with excellent facilities for processing text is a good pick for studying Web caching. Their simulation environment is known as the Web Caching Algorithm Simulation Environment or WebCASE for short. It was developed using Perl and is meant for studying the performance of algorithms related to Web caching. It could be a useful aid for developing new algorithms. WebCASE has a graphical interface for displaying the run time execution or behavior of Web caching algorithms. Also refer [587].

Bhatti et al. [75] study the consolidation of user-perceived quality into Web server design. They present the results of experiments designed for estimating the tolerance of users to the quality of service (QoS). They perform their study in the context of e-commerce. They suggest that incorporating user needs for quality of service should be salutary to all the beneficiaries.

Bianchini and Carrera [76] conduct an analytical modeling and simulation based assessment of a cluster-based network server. They try to identify the benefits of locality-conscious request distribution within the cluster.

Feldman [198] describes a tool called as BLT (Bi-layer tracing) for drawing out or fetching traces by means of packet monitoring. It is meant for both the HTTP layer and also the TCP layer. Feldman mentions that BLT puts forward for consideration a lot more valuable choice when compared to logs procured from Web proxies, Web servers or the clients. This is attributed to the preciseness of the time stamps and the particulars obtained as a result of giving careful consideration to different protocol layers. It is also ascribed to the non-encroaching style of data accumulation obtained through the use of BLT. The tool is stated to have been used for a number of Web performance related investigations.

Kelly and Reeves [299] describe two approaches for finding incisively the optimal storage capacity for Web caches on the basis of factors such as the anticipated workload, memory and network bandwidth costs. In the first approach, they look at compromises between memory and bandwidth in an idealized setting. The second approach is used when the workload at a single cache is expressed in terms of an explicit sequence of requests and the cache makes use of any cache replacement policy that is based on the Least Recently Used (LRU) cache replacement algorithm. Kelly and Reeves use an effective algorithm for estimating the performance of the cache accurately. They mention that their algorithm offers a handy tool capable of reckoning temporal locality in Web cache workloads.

Wills and Shang [560] study the contribution of Domain Name System (DNS) lookup costs to Web object retrieval. There are several factors that affect the functioning of Web servers and Web clients. The time or effort involved in DNS lookup is one of the them. Wills and Shang comment that by their experiments they are able to conclude that the DNS lookup technique performed well (lookups are faster) for Web servers that happen to be visited often when compared to random Web servers. They also report that the performance of the DNS lookup technique was more advantageous for popular Web servers in terms of local cache hit ratios, and also for authoritative and non-local, and non-authoritative response times.

The issue of *scalability* must not be ignored while discussing the performance of caching solutions. Jung and Chon [284] discuss a new approach for scalable storage of large Web objects. Likewise, it would not be prudent to ignore *reliability* issues. Kalyanakrishnan et al. [289] report a case study on the reliability of Internet hosts from the perspective of end consumers. Little et al. [358] discuss the construction of reliable Web applications by making use of atomic actions.

Rabinovich and Aggarwal [457] describe RaDaR, a scalable architecture for a global Web hosting service. Web hosting services are currently expanding very rapidly. As a consequence, several million Web objects may have to be housed in several thousand Web servers all over the globe. Once the magnitude of the problem of Web hosting services gets bigger, it becomes more tricky to provide good performance. Rabinovich and Aggarwal study the difficulties due to the huge scale of the problem. They describe an architecture for Web hosting services that does not contain any troublesome nodes that could become a hindrance for assuring good performance. They mention that their architecture shows good scalability and also assures better performance than existing architectures.

Almeida et al. [19] analyze the impact of Web robots on the performance of Web caching systems and argue that they result in a higher miss ratio in server-side caches. They argue that caching policies must treat HTTP requests from robots in a way different from that of normal HTTP requests from humans.

Lu et al. [365] discuss a control-theory based approach for differentiated caching services. They state that not much effort has been directed to provide differentiated caching services. They develop an architecture for differentiated content caching and explain how ideas from control theory could be utilized to provide differentiated caching services. They implement their differentiated caching services technique for the Squid proxy cache and remark that differentiation helps to attain better functioning for premium content. Squid is used by many ISPs and hence they can contemplate offering differentiated caching services.

Murta and Almeida [405] introduce the concept of performance maps to help the comprehension of the behavior of policies that are employed for Web caching. They study two metrics that are commonly used for evaluating cache replacement algorithms: hit ratio and byte hit ratio and describe an analytical model that links these two metrics. They mention that the relation between the hit ratio and the byte hit ratio is a function of the mean size of the cache server responses and the mean size of the hit responses. Understanding the relation between these metrics is very useful in understanding many algorithms related to Web caching. Based on the analytical model, they bring forth the concept of performance maps. This concept helps to understand the functioning of Web cache replacement algorithms and helps in their design. Performance maps also lead to a clearer understanding of the tradeoffs between the hit ratio and the byte hit ratio.

Shriver et al. [503] discuss storage management for Web proxies. They state that Web proxies in existence today make use of antiquated file systems. Such file systems were designed several years ago for workload demands and needs quite unlike that of a present day Web proxy cache. Shriver et al. not only characterize Web proxy workload but also discuss the design of a light-weight file system known as Hummingbird. Their experiments using trace-driven simulations show that Hummingbird's throughput is almost 8 times more than a version of Squid that ran on the high performance XFS file system.

Du and Subhlok [184] assess the performance of cooperative Web caching by using the Web Polygraph tool. They compare several cooperative cache hierarchies built using Squid proxy cache servers. They also make use of a proxy cache log analysis tool known as Squeezer to obtain statistics about cache cooperation.

7.   Exercises

1 Explain the benefits of measuring performance in the context of Web .

2 Name two important measuring tools used for rating Web caching systems.

3 What is WPB? Mention the parameters by which WPB performs an evaluation. Which parameters does it ignore?

4 On what parameters does Web Polygraph evaluate a Web caching system?

5 What is byte hit ratio? How is it different from the normal hit ratio?

6 Name some important parameters against which Web caching systems can be evaluated.

7 Investigate whether any of these parameters are interrelated.

Chapter 19

ZIPF'S LAW AND ITS ROLE IN WEB CACHING

1. Zipf's law for Web accesses

It is an interesting problem to ascertain if the relative frequency with which Web pages are requested follows any discernable pattern. Some early studies gave evidence that this is indeed so and that Zipf's law is followed by such requests. Zipf's law for Web accesses states that the relative frequency of a request for the i'th most popular Web page is proportional to $1/i$. Zipf's law is a power-law relationship between the frequency of citation of an item (viz. its popularity) and its relative rank among the cited items based on the frequency of citation. Zipf's law is named after G. K. Zipf [591].

Zipf's law for Web accesses If f denotes the popularity of an item and i denotes its relative rank then f and i are related as follows:

$$f = c/i^{\beta} \tag{19.1}$$

where c is a constant and β is between 0 and 1. If β equals 1 then the popularity distribution is said to follow Zipf's law exactly. If β is greater than 0 and less than 1 the popularity distribution is said to be Zipf-like.

The term *Zipf slope* is used to denote the slope of the Zipf-like popularity profile in a given Web workload. A steeper slope generally means that a significant proportion of requests are interested in a minuscule percentage of Web content. A steeper Zipf slope is therefore likely to be beneficial for Web caching.

2. Zipf's law and its implications

Huberman et al. [246] discuss strong regularities in Web surfing. They mention that a model was utilized to study the patterns of Web surfing behavior.

This model is stated to have explained the Zipf-like distributions of hits noticed at Web sites.

Breslau et al. [88] discuss the implications of Zipf's law for Web caching. They show that if one assumes that the references in the Web access streams (sequences of requests) are independent and the reference probability of the documents follow Zipf's law then the observed properties follow from Zipf's law. They study cache replacement algorithms and observe that the algorithm suggested by Zipf's law gives the best performance.

Breslau et al. [89] address two concerns. The first is whether Web requests from a fixed user community are distributed according to Zipf's law. The second is related to a number of previous studies on the characteristics of Web proxy traces which have shown that the hit ratios and temporal locality of the traces display some asymptotic properties that are uniform across the different sets of traces. The question here is whether they are simply an artificial feature of the traces.

Padmanabhan and Qiu [425] studied the content and access dynamics of a busy Web site. They concentrated on the server side unlike conventional approaches that often look at client accesses as seen by the proxies. Padmanabhan and Qiu study the dynamics of both the server content and the client accesses to the server. They report that:

- files do not change much when they are altered

- a minor fraction of the files get altered again and again

- the popularity of files displays a Zipf-like distribution.

Serpanos et al. [499] discuss the application of Zipf's law to aid efficient caching of Web objects. By means of their results, a Web cache can determine the distribution of the utilization of Web objects that it must cache, on the basis of the noticed utilization patterns of Web objects. Serpanos et al. state that multimedia caches can benefit from this application of Zipf's law as proper cache sizes may be chosen to enable desired hit ratios.

Doyle et al. [182] mention that although object popularity distributions in the Web tend to be Zipf-like, nonetheless, caches do not take in requests for the most popular objects in a balanced manner. They refer to this effect as the *trickle-down effect*. They use artificial traffic patterns (i.e. synthetic workloads) to exemplify the trickle-down effect and to study its influence on the constituents of a content delivery architecture. They concentrate on the implications of this effect for request distribution strategies in server clusters.

Xie and David O'Hallaron [570] study locality in search engine queries and its implications for caching. For this purpose, they make use of two real world search engine traces. Their analysis shows that:

- queries exhibit substantial locality

- the frequency of the queries displays a Zipf distribution

- queries that are popular may be cached either at the servers or at the proxies

- queries that are not popular should be cached at the user end and this includes queries that are made up of several words

- in case caching must be accomplished at the user end, it may be sufficient to cache such data for a period of just a few hours in order to take care of the temporal locality of queries

- caching at the servers or the proxies should be done for a longer duration viz. a few days

- it may be a good idea to prefetch data taking into account the list of words supplied by a user.

3.   Exercises

1 What is Zipf's law?

2 Why is Zipf's law studied in the context of Web caching?

VII

GLOSSARY

Chapter 20

GLOSSARY

GLOSSARY

Address   A numerical quantity that unambiguously distinguishes a system or some element of a system.

Application   A specific function furnished to an end consumer in a network. Typical applications include file transfer, browsing etc.

Application layer   A protocol layer that implements an application. It is the seventh layer of the ISO/OSI reference model. It is concerned with application related functions.

Area   An administratively delineated branch of an autonomous system.

Autonomous system   A group of hosts and routers working subordinate to the command of an administrative domain.

Backbone   A network that links routers usually stationed in different locations in the world. It is a specific routing area to which all other areas link up.

BGP   Border Gateway Protocol. A routing protocol used for enabling routing between autonomous systems.

Border Gateway Protocol   See BGP.

Broadcast   Transmitted information meant for every system on a subnetwork. The conversational usage of this word is used to denote transmission of information.

Browser   The word browser is often used as a short form for the phrase *Web browser* throughout this book. A Web browser is an executable for viewing Web content. Popular Web browsers include Netscape Navigator and Microsoft Internet Explorer. Web browsers are basically Web clients used for obtaining Web content from Web servers and displaying them in a human readable form.

Browser client   See Browser.

Browsing   The process of viewing Web content using a Web browser.

Byte hit ratio   It is the ratio of the number of bytes served by a Web component from its cache to the aggregate number of bytes served by it.

Cache   Memory that is set aside as a specialized storage meant for being constantly updated. Caches are used to speed up data transfers. The word cache is often used as a short form for the phrase *Web cache* throughout this book. Sometimes the word cache is also used to denote a proxy cache or a browser cache depending on the context. In the verb form, the word cache is used to refer to the process of saving data for future consumption.

Cacheable   Something that can be cached.

Cache hierarchy   An organization of caches that involves the placement of caches at different tiers.

Cache hit   A request that can be fulfilled by a cache by means of a response that has been cached by it. This is in contrast to a cache miss.

Cache miss   A request that cannot be fulfilled by a cache by means of responses that have been cached by it. This is in contrast to a cache hit.

Caching   The process of saving information for future consumption. It is often used as an abbreviation for the phrase *Web caching* throughout this book. A somewhat deeper meaning for caching in the context of this book is the process of bringing copies of Web objects closer to the end consumers in order to enable quicker access to them.

Caching proxy   A Web proxy that is meant to be used for the purpose of caching.

CDN   Content Delivery Network. It is an intermediary between content suppliers or content providers and end consumers.

Content Delivery Network   See CDN.

Cookie   It is a HTTP header element meant for signalling that content must be personalized. Cookies are placed by HTTP servers in browsers so that they may be used as a reference when requests are made in the future. Cookies can be used to perform many useful functions.

Destination   A system which receives a message or for which the message was destined.

DNS   Domain Name System. It is a database that is online and is meant to be used for converting a domain name into its IP address.

DNS Server   A server used for enforcing the Domain Name System.

Document   Throughout this book, the term document is used to refer to an assemblage of Web objects that are exhibited as an undivided unit on a browser.

Domain   A constituent of the DNS namespace.

Domain Name System   See DNS.

Dynamic object   An object that is brought into existence by a server every time whenever there is a request for this object. This is contrast to a static object which may be fetched from a file whenever needed. Dynamic objects are harder to cache than static objects.

FTP   File Transfer Protocol. A protocol for accessing files from remote FTP servers. FTP allows files to be uploaded to remote FTP servers, permits files to be downloaded from such servers and supports miscellaneous operations.

File Transfer Protocol   See FTP.

Hashing   The process of employing a hash function for translating entities in a set to entities in another set.

Hash function   A function employed for the purpose of hashing. Popular hash functions include MD5 and SHA-1. These functions output strings of length 128 bits and 160 bits respectively.

Hit   See Cache hit.

Hit ratio   The ratio of the number of requests serviced by a component from its cache to the total number of incoming requests at that component. It is sometimes referred to as the hit rate.

Host   An equipment that is coupled to the Internet and possesses a unique IP address for the purpose of identification.

HTML   Hypertext Markup Language. A language used for representing documents on the Web.

HTTP   HTTP Hypertext Transfer Protocol. An application layer protocol used for browsing the World Wide Web. The current version is HTTP 1.1. Earlier versions include HTTP 1.0 and HTTP 0.9.

Hyperlink   A citation in a HTML Web page that is used to indicate an object in the World Wide Web. This is achieved by the use of an URL Virtually all browsers allow display of an object referred to by a hyperlink by just a mouse click on the hyperlink.

Hypertext Markup Language   See HTML.

Hypertext Transfer Protocol   See HTTP.

ICMP   Internet Content Message Protocol. A protocol often used for diagnosing problems within a network. It allows control messages to be exchanged regarding packet flows, host accessibility, congestion and so on. It operates alongside the Internet Protocol.

IETF   Internet Engineering Task Force. A standards organization concerned with standards for the Internet. It is well known for reports known as RFCs. RFC stands for Request For Comments.

Internet   The International data communication network based on the Internet Protocol. It is basically a collection of networks that are linked together by means of the TCP/IP set of protocols.

IP   Internet Protocol. The fundamental protocol used by the Internet. It is used for linking data networks with the Internet.

Internetwork   A huge communications network that comprises manifold interconnected subnetworks.

Internet Protocol   See IP.

Internet Service Provider   See ISP.

IP address   An identifier used to denote a host that is a constituent of the Internet. Hosts often have a minimum of one unique 32-bit IP address in order to enable easy access.

ISP   Internet Service Provider. A provider of Internet related services to the general public.

Layer 4   See L4.

L4   Layer 4. It is the fourth layer in the ISO/OSI reference model. It is the transport layer and is concerned with data transport related functions.

L4 switch   A switch that makes use of Layer 4 (the transport layer) information for decision making at the time of forwarding information. Typical information used for decision making at the time of forwarding includes IP addresses of either the origin or the destination, TCP port numbers and so on.

L5   Layer 5. It is the fifth layer in the ISO/OSI reference model. It is the session layer and is concerned with application related functions.

L5 switch   A switch that makes use of Layer 5 (the session layer) information for decision making at the time of forwarding information.

Latency   The time interval between the time a client sends a request and the time it receives a response. The phrase *access latency* is often used throughout the book to denote latency.

MD5   A hash function that translates a random string of characters into a 128 bit quantity. MD5 has a very low probability of transforming two different random strings into the same quantity. Such an occurrence is known as a collision. Hash functions such as MD5 have many useful applications. See also SHA-1.

Mirror   A copy of an origin server that has been replicated either completely or only partially.

Mirror site   Mirror Web site. A Web site that has exactly the same content of a particular Web site except for the fact that it makes use of distinguishable URLs.

Mirroring   The process of making and sustaining a mirror.

Multicast   Transmitted information intended for a group of systems. IP multicast is used to send datagrams (packets of information) to many hosts on the Internet. Compare with unicast.

Object   Also referred to as Web object or resource throughout this book. It is a slice of data recognizable by means of a URL. A single JPEG image is an example of an object. A HTML Web page may often be composed of multiple Web objects.

Origin server   An origin server is a definitive source of Web content. It is a Web server in which the Web content (viz. the collection of Web objects) dwells. Content suppliers or content providers station Web content in the origin servers so that the end consumers may utilize the content.

Persistent HTTP   See persistent HTTP connection.

Persistent HTTP connection   A characteristic in HTTP that enables a client to fetch several objects from a server by means of only one TCP connection. Persistent connections are supported by version 1.1 of HTTP but not by earlier versions.

Ping   A command available in almost all operating systems for originating an ICMP echo request and reply interchange. It is routinely used to test whether a system is alive and functional.

Prefetching   It is the process of fetching information prior to the actual request. As an illustration if a user visits a HTML Web page, the Web objects represented by the hyperlinks in the Web page may be fetched even before they are really asked for.

Proxy   An utility meant for supplying a cache to be used jointly by a group of clients. The proxy behaves like a Web server for its clients and functions like a client for the origin servers. We use the term proxy to denote the phrase *Web proxy* throughout this book. Compare with Reverse proxy.

Proxy cache   See Caching proxy.

Reliable Transport   It is the obligation of a few transport protocols to guarantee that data is handed over to the intended destination without either errors or any duplication. For example, reliable multicast is the same as plain multicast except that reliability is also assured alongside.

Replication   The process of making and sustaining a replica of a resource.

Reverse proxy   A mediator that acts on behalf of the origin server. It works just like a proxy except that it is under the command of the content supplier and is not controlled by the end consumer.

Reverse proxy caching   See Reverse proxy.

Router   A system that works as a mediator between the points where messages originate and their intended destinations.

Routing   It is the operation of interchanging network topography data so that routers may come to a decision about how to send messages accordingly. The word routing is also often used colloquially to denote forwarding.

Server   An application that services requests received from other applications which are also referred to as clients and normally run on some other hosts. The term server is often used as a short form for the phrase *Web server* throughout this book, although, the word could mean different things depending on the context. For example, it could be used to denote a DNS server or a Web server.

Static object   A Web object that can be retrieved from a file without any alteration for many requests. Compare with Dynamic object.

SHA-1   A hash function that translates a random string of characters into a 160 bit quantity. Compare with MD5.

Source   A system that sends a message.

Switch   A switch is basically a network component. It is an appliance for sending data obtained from an inbound network connection to an outbound network connection. Switches may be designed to make use of information available at different layers of the ISO/OSI reference model for the purpose of forwarding data. As a consequence, there exist L4 switches, L5 switches etc.

TCP   TCP Transmission Control Protocol. A transport layer protocol employed by the Web for handing over requests from the clients to the servers. TCP is often used along with the Internet Protocol to derive greater advantage.

TTL   Time-To-Live. It is a field used to denote the amount of time an object can be considered to be valid or in existence.

Transmission Control Protocol   See TCP.

Transparent cache   A cache that intercepts communication between the clients and the servers. The reason for using the word *transparent* is due to the fact that with such caches there is no need for configuring clients in order to make use of them. In other words, they are transparent to the clients.

Transparent caching   Caching that involves the use of a transparent cache.

Transport Layer   It is the fourth layer of the ISO/OSI reference model. It is concerned with data transport related functions. It is also known as Layer 4 or L4.

Uncacheable   Something that cannot be cached.

Unicast   Communication intended for only one system. This is in contrast to multicast, wherein the communication is intended for several systems.

URL   Uniform Resource Locator. A string of characters used for recognizing the location of an object in a network.

Web   The word Web is widely used as an abbreviation for the *World Wide Web*. See WWW.

Web browser   See Browser.

Web browsing   See Browsing.

Web cache   See Cache.

Web caching   See Caching.

Web proxy   See Proxy.

Web site   An aggregation of Web objects that are in the possession of a specific content provider.

WWW   World Wide Web. The World Wide Web is a subset of the Internet that is accessible to the public.

Zipf's law   A power-law relationship between the frequency of citation of an item (viz. its popularity) and its relative rank among the cited items based on the frequency of citation. If f denotes the popularity of an item and i denotes its relative rank then Zipf's law states that

$$f = c/i^\beta \qquad (20.1)$$

where c is a constant and β is between 0 and 1. If β equals 1 then the popularity distribution is said to follow Zipf's law exactly. If β is greater than 0 and less than 1 the popularity distribution is said to be Zipf-like.

Zipf slope   The *Zipf slope* denotes the slope of the Zipf-like popularity profile in a given Web workload. A steeper slope generally denotes that a high proportion of requests are focused on a small portion of Web content.

Appendix A
Useful Web sites

- ACM (includes digital library for their publications)
  `http://www.acm.org`
- Apache (the most popular Web server)
  `http://www.apache.org`
- Brian Davison's Web caching and content delivery resources
  `http://www.web-caching.com`
- Cacheability engine
  `http://www.mnot/net/cacheability/`
- CacheNow campaign (also lists caching projects)
  `http://vancouver-webpages.com/CacheNow/`
- CERN (source of httpd)
  `http://www.w3.org/hypertext/WWW/Daemon/Status.html`
- Cisco (originator of Web Cache Communication Protocol)
  `http://www.cisco.com`
- Collection of computer science bibliographies
  `http://liinwww.ira.uka.de/bibliography/index.html`
- DBLP Computer science bibliography
  `http://dblp.uni-trier.de`
- Directory of computer science journals
  `http://elib.cs.sfu.ca/collections/CMPT/cs-journals/`
- Duane Wessels' Web site (includes list of commercial products, tools etc.)
  `http://www.web-cache.com`
- IEEE (includes digital library for their publications)
  `http://www.ieee.org`
- International Web content caching and distribution workshops
  `http://www.iwcw.org`

- Internet Engineering Task Force (IETF) (includes definitive documents known as RFCs)
  `http://www.ietf.org`
- IRcache project
  `http://www.ircache.net`
- Network Bibliography (includes list of articles on computer networking)
  `http://www.cs.columbia.edu/~hgs/netbib/`
- NLANR (National Laboratory for Applied Network Research)
  `http://www.nlanr.net`
- Pei Cao's Web site for Active Cache and Wisconsin Proxy Benchmark (WPB)
  `http://www.cs.wisc.edu/~cao`
- ResearchIndex (includes research articles and their citations)
  `http://www.researchindex.com`
- Scirus (articles on Web caching and other subjects)
  `http://www.scirus.com`
- Squid proxy cache (popular open source software for proxy caching)
  `http://www.squid-cache.org`
- Tools for performance testing and protocol compliance
  `http://www.measurement-factory.com`
- Web Polygraph (free benchmark tool)
  `http://www.web-polygraph.org`
- WebBib project
  `http://www.cs.wpi.edu/~webbib`
- WCOL (open source proxy server for caching and prefetching)
  `http://shika.aist-nara.ac.jp/products/wcol/wcol.html`

Appendix B
The ISO/OSI seven layer reference model

The International Standards Organization/Open Systems Interconnection model [166] is a helpful model for visualizing networking complexity by means of layers with distinct capabilities. Although, the Internet does not map accurately into the seven distinct layers of this model (due to the merger of some of the layers), nonetheless, the ISO/OSI seven layer reference model is beneficial.

- **The physical layer:** Also known as Layer 1 or L1. This layer is concerned with the physical medium used for networking e.g. copper. It deals with cabling and interface specifications. 10Base-T is an example of Layer 1 specification.

- **The data link layer:** Also known as Layer 2 or L2. This layer is concerned with addressing hosts within a physical network. Protocols such as Ethernet, Frame Relay, Asynchronous Transfer Mode (ATM) and Synchronous Optical Network (SONET) are examples of Layer 2 protocols. Protocols such as Cable Modem, DSL and the Point to Point Protocol (PPP) work across both Layer 1 and Layer 2.

- **The network layer:** Also known as Layer 3 or L3. The objective of this layer is to route data between hosts in the form of datagrams (packets) and also to supply a global address for each host in the Internet. The Internet Protocol (IP) is an example of a Layer 3 protocol.

- **The transport layer:** Also known as Layer 4 or L4. This layer provides an addressing mechanism that enables data to be addressed and handed over to separate applications on a host. The Transmission Control Protocol (TCP), the User Datagram Protocol (UDP) and the Internet Control Message Protocol (ICMP) are examples of Layer 4 protocols.

- **The session layer:** Also known as Layer 5 or L5. For the Internet, the breakup between layers L5, L6 and L7 is seldom applied. This layer helps to maintain sessions.

- **The presentation layer:** Also known as Layer 6 or L6. Applications residing in the application layer are given the means to translate between different data formats through this layer.

- **The application layer:** Also known as Layer 7 or L7. End-user applications dwell in this layer. Protocols such as HTTP, FTP, Gopher, Telnet, NFS, DNS, Simple Mail Transfer Protocol (SMTP, Network News Transfer Protocol (NNTP) are examples of protocols that work across L5 to L7. Application-layer protocols are often enforced as part of the application software such as Web browsers.

The ISO/OSI seven layer reference model

Chapter 21

REFERENCES

References

[1] Laura Abba, Marina Buzzi, and Massimo Ianigro. Introducing transparent Web caching in a local area network. In *Proc. of Intl. CMG Conference*, pages 99–110, 2000.

[2] Tarek F. Abdelzaher and Nina Bhatti. Web content adaptation to improve server overload behavior. In *Proceedings of the 8th International WWW Conference*, Toronto, Canada, May 1999. http://www8.org/w8-papers/4c-server/web/web.pdf.

[3] G. Abdulla. *Analysis and Modeling of World Wide Web traffic*. PhD thesis, Virginia Polytechnic Institute and State Univ., VA, USA, 1998.

[4] G. Abdulla, E. A. Fox, M. Abrams, and S. Williams. WWW proxy traffic characterization with application to caching. Technical Report TR-97-03, Dept. of Comp. Sci., Virginia Tech., USA, 1997.

[5] Marc Abrams, Charles R. Standridge, Ghaleb Abdulla, Stephen Williams, and Edward A. Fox. Caching proxies: limitations and potentials. In *Proceedings of the 4th International WWW Conference*, Boston, MA, December 1995. http://www.w3.org/pub/Conferences/WWW4/Papers/155/.

[6] Marc Abrams, Stephen Williams, Ghaleb Abdulla, Shashin Patel, Randy Ribler, and Edward A. Fox. Multimedia traffic analysis using Chitra95. In *Proceedings of the Multimedia '95 conference*, November 1995. http://www.cs.vt.edu/~chitra/docs/95multimediaAWAFPR/95multimediaAWAFPR.html.

[7] R. Adler, R. Feldman, and M. S. Taqqu, editors. *A Practical Guide To Heavy Tails: Statistical Techniques and Applications*. Birkhauser, Boston, MA, 1998.

[8] Stephen Adler. The slashdot effect – an analysis of three Internet publications. http://ssadler.phy.bnl.gov/adler/SDE/SlashDotEffect.html, 1999.

[9] Manuel Afonso, Alexandre Santos, and Vasco Freitas. QoS in Web caching. *Computer Networks And ISDN Systems*, 30(22-23):2093–2102, November 1998. http://www.elsevier.nl/cas/tree/store/comnet/sub/1998/30/22-23/2061.pdf.

[10] A. Aggarwal and M. Rabinovich. Performance of replication schemes on the Internet. Technical Report HA6177000-981030-01-TM, AT & T Labs, 1998.

[11] C. Aggarwal, J. L. Wolf, and P. S. Yu. Caching on the World Wide Web. *IEEE Trans. on Knowledge and Data Engg.*, 11(1):95–107, January 1999.

[12] C. Aggarwal and Philip S. Yu. On disk caching of Web objects in proxy servers. In *Proc. of CIKM*, pages 238–245, 1997.

[13] Woo Hyun Ahn, Woo Jin Kim, and Daeyeon Park. Content-aware cooperative caching for cluster-based Web servers. *Jour. of Systems and Software*, 69(1–2):75–86, 2004.

[14] Masaki Aida and Tetsuya Abe. Pseudo-address generation algorithm of packet destinations for Internet performance simulation. In *Proceedings of IEEE Infocom*, Anchorage, Alaska, April 2001.

[15] D. W. Albrecht, I. Zuckerman, and A. E. Nicholson. Pre-sending documents on the WWW: A comparative study. In *Proceedings of the 16th International Joint Conference on Artificial Intelligence*, pages 1274–1279, 1999.

[16] Jussara Almeida and Pei Cao. Measuring proxy performance with the Wisconsin proxy benchmark. *Computer Networks and ISDN Systems*, 30(22-23):2179–2192, November 1998. http://www.elsevier.nl/cas/tree/store/comnet/sub/1998/30/22-23/2053.pdf.

[17] Jussara Almeida, Derek Eager, Michael Ferris, and Mary Vernon. Provisioning content distribution networks for streaming media. In *Proceedings of IEEE Infocom*, New York, June 2002.

[18] Jussara Almeida, Jeffrey Krueger, Derek Eager, and Mary Vernon. Analysis of educational media server workloads. In *Proceedings of NOSSDAV*, Port Jefferson, New York, June 2001.

[19] V. Almeida, D. Menasce, R. Riedi, F. Peligrinelli, R. Fonseca, and W. Meira Jr. Analyzing the impact of robots on performance of Web caching systems. In *Proceedings of the 6th International Web Caching and Content Delivery Workshop*, Boston, MA, June 2001.

[20] Virgílio Almeida, Azer Bestavros, Mark Crovella, and Adriana de Oliveira. Characterizing reference locality in the WWW. In *Proceedings of the IEEE Conference on Parallel and Distributed Information Systems (PDIS)*, pages 92–103, Miami Beach, FL, December 1996. http://cs-www.bu.edu/faculty/best/res/papers/pdis96.ps.

[21] Virgílio F. Almeida, Márcio G. Cesário, Rodrigo C. Fonseca, Wagner Meira, Jr, and Cristina D. Murta. The influence of geographical and cultural issues on the cache proxy server workload. *Computer Networks and ISDN Systems*, 30(1-7):601–603, April 1998. http://www.elsevier.nl/cas/tree/store/comnet/sub/1998/30/1-7/1909.pdf.

[22] Matthew Andrews, Bruce Shepherd, Aravind Srinivasan, Peter Winkler, and Francis Zane. Clustering and server selection using passive monitoring. In *Proceedings of IEEE Infocom*, New York, June 2002.

[23] M. Arlitt, R. Friedrich, and T. Jin. Workload characterization of a Web proxy in a cable modem environment. Technical Report HPL-1999-48, Hewlett Packard Labs, 1999.

[24] M. Arlitt and C. Williamson. Web server workload characterization: The search for invariants. In *Proceedings of the ACM SIGMETRICS Conference*, pages 126–137, 1996.

[25] Martin Arlitt, Ludmilla Cherkasova, John Dilley, Rich Friedrich, and Tai Jin. Evaluating content management techniques for Web proxy caches. In *Proceedings of the Workshop on Internet Server Performance (WISP99)*, May 1999. http://www.cc.gatech.edu/fac/Ellen.Zegura/wisp99/papers/arlitt.ps.

[26] Martin Arlitt, Rich Friedrich, and Tai Jin. Performance evaluation of Web proxy cache replacement policies. *Performance Evaluation*, 39(1):149–164, February 2000.

[27] Martin Arlitt and Tai Jin. A workload characterization study of the 1998 World cup Web site. *IEEE Network*, 14(3), May 2000.

[28] Martin Arlitt and Carey Williamson. Internet Web servers: Workload characterization and performance implications. *IEEE/ACM Transactions on Networking*, 5(5):631–645, October 1997.

[29] Martin F. Arlitt and Carey L. Williamson. Trace-driven simulation of document caching strategies for Internet Web servers, September 1996. http://www.cs.usask.ca/faculty/carey/papers/webcaching.ps.

[30] Takuya Asaka, Hiroyoshi Miwa, and Yoshiaki Tanaka. Hash-based query caching method for distributed Web caching in wide area networks. *IEICE Transactions on Communications*, E82-B(6):907–913, June 1999.

[31] Olivier Aubert and Antoine Beugnard. Towards a fine-grained adaptivity in Web caches. In *Proceedings of the 4th International Web Caching Workshop*, April 1999. http://www.ircache.net/Cache/Workshop99/Papers/aubert-0.ps.gz.

[32] Michael Baentsch. Introducing application-level replication and naming into today's Web. In *Proceedings of the 5th International WWW Conference*, May 1996. http://www5conf.inria.fr/fich_html/papers/P3/Overview.html.

[33] Michael Baentsch, L. Baum, G. Molter, S. Rothkugel, and P. Sturm. Enhancing the Web infrastructure – from caching to replication. *IEEE Internet Computing*, 1(2):18–27, March 1997.

[34] Michael Baentsch, L. Baum, G. Molter, S. Rothkugel, and P. Sturm. World-Wide Web caching – the application level view of the Internet. *IEEE Communications Magazine*, 35(6), June 1997.

[35] Michael Baentsch, A. Lauer, L. Baum, G. Molter, S. Rothkugel, and P. Sturm. Quantifying the overall impact of caching and replication in the Web. Technical report, SFB 501, February 1997. http://www.uni-kl.de/AG-Nehmer/Projekte/GeneSys/Papers/tr0297.ps.gz.

[36] Aline Baggio and Guillaume Pierre. Oléron: supporting information sharing in large-scale mobile environments. In *Proceedings of the ERSADS '97 seminar*, Zinal, Switzerland, March 1997.

[37] Hyokyung Bahn, Hyunsook Lee, Sam Noh, Sang Lyul Min, and Kern Koh. Replica-aware caching for Web proxies. *Computer Communications*, 25(3):183–188, February 2002.

[38] Hyokyung Bahn, Sam Noh, Kern Koh, and Sang Lyul Min. Using full reference history for efficient document replacement in Web caches. In *Proceedings of 2nd USENIX Symposium on Internet Technologies and Systems*, Boulder, Colorado, October 1999.

[39] Hyokyung Bahn, Yong H. Shin, and Kern Koh. A characterization study of World Wide Web references in Korea: Analysis and caching implications. In *Proc. of WebNet*, pages 47–52, 2001.

[40] Guangwei Bai and Carey L. Williamson. Workload characterization in Web caching hierarchies. In *Proc. of MASCOTS*, pages 13–22, 2002.

[41] Scott Baker and John H. Hartman. The Gecko NFS Web proxy. In *Proceedings of the 8th International WWW Conference*, Toronto, Canada, May 1999. http://www.cs. arizona.edu/http/html/people/jhh/papers/gecko_www8_final.%ps.

[42] Scott M. Baker and Bongki Moon. Distributed cooperative Web servers. *Computer Networks and ISDN Systems*, 31(11-16):1215–1229, May 1999. http://www.elsevier. nl/cas/tree/store/comnet/sub/1999/31/11-16/2137.pdf%.

[43] A. Bakre and B. R. Badrinath. I-TCP: Indirect TCP for mobile hosts. In *Proceedings of the 15th International Conference on Distributed Computing Systems*, pages 136–143, 1995.

[44] H. Balakrishnan, V. N. Padmanabhan, S. Seshan, and R.H. Katz. A comparison of mechanisms for improving TCP performance over wireless links. In *Proceedings of the ACM SIGCOMM Conference*, pages 256–269, 1996.

[45] Michel Banâtre, Valérie Issarny, and Frédéric Leleu. ETEL: A newspaper-based distributed informations system. In *Proceedings of the 7th ACM SIGOPS European Workshop*, September 1996. http://www.irisa.fr/solidor/doc/ps96/etel.ps.gz.

[46] Michel Banâtre, Valérie Issarny, Frédéric Leleu, and Boris Charpiot. Providing quality of service over the Web: A newspaper-based approach. In *Proceedings of the 6th International WWW Conference*, April 1997. http://www.irisa.fr/solidor/doc/ ps97/www6/www6.html.

[47] G. Banga, F. Douglis, and M. Rabinovich. Optimistic deltas for WWW latency reduction. In *Proceedings of the 1997 Usenix Technical Conference*, pages 289–303, 1997.

[48] Gaurav Banga and Peter Druschel. Measuring the capacity of a Web server under realistic loads. *World Wide Web*, 2(1–2):69–83, January 1999.

[49] Paul Barford, Azer Bestavros, Adam Bradley, and Mark E. Crovella. Changes in Web client access patterns: Characteristics and caching implications. *World Wide Web (special issue on Characterization and Performance Evaluation)*, 2(1–2):15–28, 1999. http: //cs-www.bu.edu/faculty/crovella/paper-archive/traces98.ps.

[50] Paul Barford and Mark Crovella. Generating representative Web workloads for network and server performance evaluation. In *Proceedings of the SIGMETRICS '98 conference*, pages 151–160, June 1998. http://cs-www.bu.edu/faculty/crovella/ paper-archive/sigm98-surge.ps.

[51] Paul Barford and Mark E. Crovella. Measuring Web performance in the wide area. *Performance Evaluation Review*, August 1999. http://www.cs.bu.edu/faculty/crovella/paper-archive/wawm-per.ps.

[52] G. Barish and K. Obraczka. World Wide Web caching: Trends and techniques. *IEEE Communications Magazine*, pages 178–185, May 2000.

[53] J. Fritz Barnes and Raju Pandey. CacheL: Language support for customizable caching policies. In *Proceedings of the 4th International Web Caching Workshop*, April 1999. http://www.ircache.net/Cache/Workshop99/Papers/barnes-final.ps.gz.

[54] Julie Barnes and R. Pandey. Providing dynamic and customizable caching policies. In *Proceedings of the 2nd USENIX Symposium on Internet Technologies and Systems*, Boulder, Colorado, October 1999.

[55] Michael Bauer and Ruya Tang. On the applicability of predictive caching to improve Web server performance. In *Proc. of Intl. Conf. on Internet Computing*, pages 111–116, 2002.

[56] H. J. Bekker, Ingrid Melve, and T. Verschuren. Survey on caching requirements and specifications for prototype. DESIRE European project deliverable D4.1. http://www.ruu.nl/~henny/desire/survey.html.

[57] A. Belloum and L.O. Hertzberger. Dealing with one-timer documents in Web caching. In *Proceedings of the EUROMICRO'98 Conference*, Vastega, Sweden, August 1998.

[58] A. Belloum and L.O. Hertzberger. Replacement strategies in Web caching. In *Proceedings of the ISIC/CIRA/ISAS'98 Conference*, Gaithersburg, Maryland, September 1998.

[59] A. Belloum, L.O. Hertzberger, and H. Muller. Scalable federation of Web cache servers. *World Wide Web*, 4(4), December 2001.

[60] A. S. Z. Belloum, E. C. Kaletas, A. W. van Halderen, H. Afsarmanesh, L. O. Hertzberger, and A. J. H. Peddemors. A scalable Web server architecture. *World Wide Web*, 5(1), March 2002.

[61] T. Berners-Lee and D. Connolly. Hypertext Markup Language 2.0. RFC 1866, 1995. http://www.ietf.org/rfc/rfc1866.txt.

[62] T. Berners-Lee, R. Fielding, and H. Nielsen. Hypertext Transfer Protocol, HTTP/1.0. RFC 1945, 1996. http://www.ietf.org/rfc/rfc1945.txt.

[63] T. Berners-Lee, L. Masinter, and M. McCahill. Uniform Resource Locators (url). RFC 1738, 1994. http://www.ietf.org/rfc/rfc1738.txt.

[64] A. Bestavros and S. Mehrotra. DNS-based client clustering and characterization. Technical Report BUCS-TR-2001-012, Boston University, 2001.

[65] Azer Bestavros. Demand-based data-dissemination in distributed multimedia systems. In *Proceedings of the ACM/IASTED/ISMM International Conference on Distributed Multimedia Systems and Applications*, Stanford, CA, August 1995. http://www.cs.bu.edu/fac/best/res/papers/ismm95.ps.

[66] Azer Bestavros. Demand-based document dissemination to reduce traffic and balance load in distributed information systems. In *Proceedings of SPDP'95: The 7th IEEE Symposium on Parallel and Distributed Processing*, San Anotonio, Texas, October 1995.

[67] Azer Bestavros. Information dissemination and speculative service: Two candidate functionalities for the middleware infrastructure. In *Proceedings of the SIGCOMM'95 Workshop on Middleware*, Cambridge, MA, August 1995.

[68] Azer Bestavros. Using speculation to reduce server load and service time on the WWW. In *Proceedings of the 4th ACM International Conference on Information and Knowledge Management*, pages 403–410, Baltimore, MD, November 1995. http://cs-www.bu.edu/faculty/best/res/papers/cikm95.ps.

[69] Azer Bestavros. Speculative data dissemination and service to reduce server load, network traffic and service time for distributed information systems. In *Proceedings of the 1996 International Conference on Data Engineering (ICDE-96)*, pages 180–189, New Orleans, Louisiana, March 1996. http://www.cs.bu.edu/fac/best/res/papers/icde96.ps.

[70] Azer Bestavros. WWW traffic reduction and load balancing through server-based caching. *IEEE Concurrency*, 5(1), 1997. http://computer.org/concurrency/pd1997/p1056abs.htm.

[71] Azer Bestavros, Robert L. Carter, Mark E. Crovella, Carlos R. Cunha, Abdelsalam Heddaya, and Sulaiman A. Mirdad. Application-level document caching in the Internet. In *Proceedings of the 2nd International Workshop in Distributed and Networked Environments (IEEE SDNE '95)*, Whistler, British Columbia, June 1995. http://cs-www.bu.edu/faculty/best/res/papers/sdne95.ps.

[72] Azer Bestavros and Carlos Cunha. Server-initiated document dissemination for the WWW. *IEEE Data Engineering Bulletin*, September 1996. http://www.cs.bu.edu/fac/best/res/papers/debull96.ps.

[73] Krishna Bharat and Andrei Broder. Mirror, mirror on the Web: A study of host pairs with replicated content. *Computer Networks and ISDN Systems*, 31(11-16):1579–1590, May 1999. http://www.elsevier.nl/cas/tree/store/comnet/sub/1999/31/11-16/2147.pdf.

[74] Samrat Bhattacharjee, Ken Calvert, and Ellen W. Zegura. Self-organizing wide-area network caches. In *Proceedings of the INFOCOM '98 conference*, April 1998.

[75] Nina Bhatti, Anna Bouch, and Allan Kuchinsky. Integrating user-perceived quality into Web server design. *Computer Networks*, 33(1-6):1–16, June 2000. http://www.elsevier.nl/gej-ng/10/15/22/48/25/27/article.pdf.

[76] R. Bianchini and E. V. Carrera. Analytical and experimental evaluation of cluster-based network servers. *World Wide Web*, 3(4):215–229, December 2000.

[77] George Bilchev, Chris Roadknight, Ian Marshall, and Sverrir Olafsson. WWW cache modelling toolbox. In *Proceedings of the 4th International Web Caching Workshop*, April 1999. http://www.ircache.net/Cache/Workshop99/Papers/bilchev-final.ps.gz.

[78] A. Biliris, C. Cranor, F. Douglis, M. Rabinovich, S. Sibal, O. Spatscheck, and W. Sturm. CDN brokering. In *Proceedings of the 6th International Workshop on Web Caching and Content Distribution*, 2001.

[79] Burton Bloom. Space time trade–offs in hash coding with allowable errors. *Comm. of the ACM*, 13(7):422–426, July 1970.

[80] J. C. Bolot and Philipp Hoschka. Performance engineering of the World Wide Web: Application to dimensioning and cache design. *Computer Networks*, 28(7–11):1397–1405, May 1996.

[81] Jean-Chrysostom Bolot, S. M. Lambot, and A. Simonian. Design of efficient caching schemes for the World Wide Web. In *Proceedings of the 15th International Teletraffic Congress (ITC-15)*, June 1997. ftp://ftp-sop.inria.fr/rodeo/bolot/97.ITC.ps.Z.

[82] Francesco Bonchi, Fosca Giannotti, Cristian Gozzi, Giuseppe Manco, Mirco Nanni, Dino Pedreschi, Chiara Renso, and Salvatore Ruggieri. Web log data warehousing and mining for intelligent Web caching. *Data Knowl. Eng.*, 39(2):165–189, 2001.

[83] T. Bourke. *Server Load Balancing*. O'Reilly and Associates, 2001.

[84] Vincent Bouthors and Olivier Dedieu. Pharos, a collaborative infrastructure for Web knowledge sharing. Rapport de Recherche RR-3679, INRIA, May 1999.

[85] C. Mic Bowman, Peter Danzig, Darren R. Hardy, Udi Manber, and M. Schwartz. The Harvest information discovery and access system. *Computer Networks and ISDN Systems*, 28(1–2):119–125, December 1995.

[86] H. Braun and Kimberly Claffy. Web traffic characterization: an assessment of the impact of caching documents from NCSA's Web server. *Computer Networks*, 28(1–2):37–51, December 1995.

[87] Tim Bray. Measuring the Web. In *Proceedings of the 5th International WWW Conference*, pages 993–1005, May 1996. http://www5conf.inria.fr/fich_html/papers/P9/Overview.html.

[88] L. Breslau, P. Cao, L. Fan, G. Phillips, and S. Shenker. On the implications of Zipf's law for Web caching. In *Proceedings of the 3rd International Web Caching Workshop, Manchester, England*, June 1999.

[89] Lee Breslau, Pei Cao, Li Fan, Graham Phillips, and Scott Shenker. Web caching and Zipf-like distributions: Evidence and implications. In *Proceedings of the INFOCOM '99 conference*, March 1999. http://www.cs.wisc.edu/~cao/papers/zipf-like.ps.gz.

[90] Brian E. Brewington and George Cybenko. How dynamic is the Web? *Computer Networks*, 33(1-6):257–276, June 2000. http://www.elsevier.nl/gej-ng/10/15/22/48/25/43/article.pdf.

[91] C. Brooks, M. Mazer, S. Meeks, and J. Miller. Application–specific proxy servers as http stream transducers. In *Proceedings of the 4th World Wide Web Conference*, pages 539–548, 1995.

[92] S. Buchholz and A. Schill. Web caching in a pervasive computing world. In *Proceedings of the 6th World Multiconference on Systemics, Cybernetics and Informatics*, Orlando, FL, July 2002.

[93] Richard B. Bunt, Derek L. Eager, Gregory M. Oster, and Carey L. Williamson. Achieving load balance and effective caching in clustered Web servers. In *Proceedings of the 4th International Web Caching Workshop*, April 1999. http://www.ircache.net/Cache/Workshop99/Papers/bunt-final.ps.gz.

[94] Mudashiru Busari and Carey L. Williamson. Simulation evaluation of a heterogeneous Web proxy caching hierarchy. In *Proc. of MASCOTS*, pages 379–388, 2001.

[95] John Byers, Michael Luby, and Michael Mitzenmacher. Accessing multiple mirror sites in parallel: Using tornado codes to speed up downloads. In *Proceedings of the INFOCOM '99 conference*, March 1999. http://www.cs.bu.edu/fac/byers/pubs/mirrors.ps.

[96] R. Caceres, P. B. Danzig, S. Jamin, and D. Mitzel. Characteristics of Wide–area TCP/IP conversations. In *Proceedings of ACM SIGCOMM '91, Zurich, Switzerland*, September 1991.

[97] R. Caceres, F. Douglis, A. Feldman, G. Glass, and M. Rabinovich. Web proxy caching: The devil is in the details. *ACM Performance Evaluation Review*, 26(3):11–15, December 1998.

[98] R. Caceres and L. Iftode. Improving the performance of reliable transport protocols in mobile computing environments. *IEEE Journal on Selected Areas in Communication*, 13:850–857, 1995.

[99] Guohong Cao. A scalable low-latency cache invalidation strategy for mobile environments. In *Proceedings of Mobicom*, pages 200–209, Boston, MA, August 2000.

[100] Guohong Cao. Proactive power-aware cache management for mobile computing systems. *IEEE Transactions on Computers*, 51(6):608–621, 2002.

[101] L. Y. Cao and M. Tamer Özsu. Evaluation of strong consistency Web caching techniques. *World Wide Web*, 5(2):95–124, 2002.

[102] Pei Cao and Sandy Irani. Cost-aware WWW proxy caching algorithms. In *Proceedings of the 1997 Usenix Symposium on Internet Technologies and Systems (USITS-97)*, pages 193–206, Monterey, CA, December 1997. http://www.cs.wisc.edu/~cao/papers/gd-size.ps.Z.

[103] Pei Cao, Jin Zhang, and Kevin Beach. Active cache: caching dynamic contents on the Web. *Distributed Systems Engineering*, 6(1):43–50, 1999.

[104] V. Cardellini, M. Colajanni, and P. S. Yu. Dynamic load balancing on Web-server systems. *IEEE Internet Computing*, 3:28–39, 1999.

[105] V. Cardellini, M. Colajanni, and Philip S. Yu. DNS dispatching algorithms with state estimators for scalable web-server clusters. *World Wide Web*, 2(3):101–113, July 1999.

[106] R. L. Carter and M. E. Crovella. Server selection using bandwidth probing in wide-area networks. In *Proceedings of INFOCOM*, pages 1014–1021, 1997.

[107] Emiliano Casalicchio and Michele Colajanni. A client-aware dispatching algorithm for Web clusters providing multiple services. In *Proceedings of the 10th International WWW Conference*, Hong Kong, May 2001. http://www10.org/cdrom/papers/pdf/p434.pdf.

[108] Vincent Cate. Alex – a global file system. In *Proceedings of the USENIX File System Workshop*, pages 1–11, Ann Arbor, Michigan, May 1992. http://ankara.bcc.bilkent.edu.tr/prv/ftp/INFO/Internet/Alex/usenix.wofs92.ps.

[109] Steve J. Caughey, David B. Ingham, and Mark C. Little. Flexible open caching for the Web. *Computer Networks and ISDN Systems*, 29(8-13):1007–1017, 1997. http://w3objects.ncl.ac.uk/pubs/focw/.

[110] Jim Challenger, Arun Iyengar, and Paul Danzig. A scalable system for consistently caching dynamic Web data. In *Proceedings of IEEE INFOCOM'99*, March 1999. http://www.research.ibm.com/people/i/iyengar/infocom2.ps.

[111] Jim Challenger, Arun Iyengar, Karen Witting, Cameron Ferstat, and Paul Reed. A publishing system for efficiently creating dynamic Web data. In *Proceedings of IEEE INFOCOM'2000*, March 2000. http://www.research.ibm.com/people/i/iyengar/infocom2000.ps.

[112] Mun Choon Chan and Thomas Woo. Cache-based compaction: A new technique for optimizing Web transfer. In *Proceedings of the INFOCOM '99 conference*, March 1999.

[113] Bharat Chandra, Mike Dahlin, Lei Gao, Amjad-Ali Khoja, Amol Nayate, Asim Razzaq, and Anil Sewani. Resource management for scalable disconnected access to Web services. In *Proceedings of the 10th International WWW Conference*, Hong Kong, May 2001. http://www10.org/cdrom/papers/pdf/p432.pdf.

[114] Girish Chandranmenon and George Varghese. Reducing Web latency using reference point caching. In *Proceedings of IEEE Infocom*, Anchorage, Alaska, April 2001.

[115] Cheng-Yue Chang and Ming-Syan Chen. A new cache replacement algorithm for the integration of Web caching and prefetching. In *Proc. of CIKM*, pages 632–634, 2002.

[116] Anawat Chankhunthod, Peter Danzig, Chuck Neerdaels, Michael F. Schwartz, and Kurt J. Worrell. A hierarchical Internet object cache. In *Proceedings of the 1996 Usenix Technical Conference*, San Diego, CA, January 1996. http://catarina.usc.edu/danzig/cache.ps.

[117] Y. Chawathe, S. McCanne, and E. Brewer. RMX: Reliable Multicast in heterogeneous networks. In *Proceedings of INFOCOM*, pages 795–804, 2000.

[118] H. Che, Y. Tung, and Z. Wang. Hierarchical Web caching systems: Modeling, design, and experimental results. *IEEE Journal on Selected Areas in Communication*, 20(7), September 2002.

[119] Hao Che, Zhijung Wang, and Ye Tung. Analysis and design of hierarchical Web caching systems. In *Proceedings of IEEE Infocom*, Anchorage, Alaska, April 2001.

[120] Ge Chen, Cho-Li Wang, and Francis C. M. Lau. p-Jigsaw: a cluster-based Web server with cooperative caching support. *Concurrency and Computation: Practice and Experience*, 15(7–8):681–705, 2003.

[121] Songqing Chen, Bo Shen, Susie Wee, and Xiaodong Zhang. Adaptive and lazy segmentation based proxy caching for streaming media delivery. In *Proceedings of ACM NOSSDAV*, Monterey, California, June 2003.

[122] Xiangping Chen and Prasant Mohapatra. Lifetime behavior and its impact on Web caching. In *Proceedings of the IEEE Workshop on Internet Applications*, San Jose, CA, July 1999.

[123] Kai Cheng and Yahiko Kambayashi. LRU-SP: A size-adjusted and popularity-aware LRU replacement algorithm for Web caching. In *Proc. of COMPSAC*, pages 48–53, 2000.

[124] Kai Cheng and Yahiko Kambayashi. Multicache-based content management for Web caching. In *Proc. of WISE*, pages 42–49, 2000.

[125] Cho-Yu Chiang, Yingjie Li, Ming T. Liu, and Mervin E. Muller. On request forwarding for the dynamic Web caching hierarchies. In *Proceedings of the 20th International Conference on Distributed Computing Systems (ICDCS)*, April 2000. http://www. cis.ohio-state.edu/~chiang/cnp/icdcs2000.ps.gz.

[126] Cho-Yu Chiang, Ming T. Liu, and Mervin E. Muller. Caching Neighborhood Protocol: A foundation for building dynamic Web caching hierarchies with proxy servers. In *Proc. of ICPP*, pages 516–523, 1999.

[127] Cho-Yu Chiang, Mikihiro Ueno, Ming T. Liu, and Mervin E. Muller. Modeling Web caching schemes for performance studies. In *Proc. of ICPP*, pages 243–250, 2000.

[128] Ken-Ichi Chinen and Suguru Yamaguchi. An interactive prefetching proxy server for improvement of WWW latency. In *Proceedings of the INET '97 conference*, June 1997.

[129] H. Choi and J. O. Limb. A behavioral model of Web traffic. In *Proceedings of ICNP*, Toronto, Canada, November 1999.

[130] K. Claffy, G. Miller, and K. Thompson. The nature of the beast: recent traffic measurements from an Internet backbone. In *Proceedings of INET Conference*, 1998.

[131] E. Cohen, Haim Kaplan, and Jeffrey Oldham. Managing TCP connections under persistent HTTP. *Computer Networks*, 31(11–16):1709–1723, May 1999.

[132] E. Cohen, B. Krishnamurthy, and J. Rexford. Evaluating server–assisted cache replacement in the Web. In *Proceedings of the European Symposium on Algorithms*, 1998.

[133] E. Cohen, B. Krishnamurthy, and Jennifer Rexford. Improving end-to-end performance of the Web using server volumes and proxy filters. *ACM Computer Communication Review*, 28(4):241–253, September 1998.

[134] Edith Cohen and Haim Kaplan. Prefetching the means for document transfer: A new approach for reducing Web latency. In *Proceedings of IEEE INFOCOM'2000*, pages 854–863, March 2000. http://www.research.att.com/~edith/Papers/prefetch. ps.

[135] Edith Cohen and Haim Kaplan. The age penalty and it's effect on cache performance. In *Proceedings of the USENIX Symposium on Internet Technologies and Systems*, San Francisco, CA, March 2001.

[136] Edith Cohen and Haim Kaplan. Refreshment policies for Web content caches. In *Proceedings of the IEEE Infocom conference*, April 2001. http://infocom.ucsd.edu/papers/155-3676306719.ps.

[137] Edith Cohen, Balachander Krishnamurthy, and Jennifer Rexford. Efficient algorithms for predicting requests to Web servers. In *Proceedings of the INFOCOM '99 conference*, March 1999. http://www.research.att.com/~edith/Papers/inf99-submit.ps.Z.

[138] R. Cohen and S. Ramanathan. Using proxies to enhance TCP performance over hybrid fiber coaxial networks. Technical Report HPL-97-81, Hewlett–Packard Labs., 1997.

[139] Reuven Cohen, Liran Katzir, and Danny Raz. Scheduling algorithms for a cache pre-filling content distribution network. In *Proceedings of IEEE Infocom*, New York, June 2002.

[140] M. Colajanni, P. S. Yu, and V. Cardellini. Dynamic load balancing in geographically distributed heterogeneous Web servers. In *Proceedings of the 18th IEEE International Conference on Distributed Computing Systems*, 1998.

[141] M. Colajanni, P. S. Yu, and D. M. Dias. Analysis of task assignment policies in scalable distributed Web-server systems. In *Proceedings of the 18th IEEE International Conference on Parallel and Distributed Information Systems*, number 9, pages 585–600, 1998.

[142] Marco Conti, Enrico Gregori, and Fabio Panzieri. Load distribution among replicated Web servers: A QoS-based approach. In *Proceedings of the Workshop on Internet Server Performance (WISP99)*, May 1999. http://www.cc.gatech.edu/fac/Ellen.Zegura/wisp99/papers/conti.ps.

[143] I. Cooper and J. Dilley. Known HTTP proxy/caching problems. RFC 3143, June 2001. http://www.ietf.org/rfc/rfc3143.txt.

[144] A. Cormack. Experience with installing and running an institutional cache. In *Proceedings of the 3rd International Web Caching Workshop*, 1998.

[145] M. E. Crovella and A. Bestavros. Explaining World Wide Web traffic self–similarity. Technical Report 1995-015, Computer Science Department, Boston University, 1995.

[146] Mark Crovella and Paul Barford. The network effects of prefetching. In *Proceedings of IEEE Infocom'98*, pages 1232–1239, 1998.

[147] Mark Crovella and A. Bestavros. Self-similarity in World Wide Web traffic: Evidence and possible causes. *IEEE/ACM Transactions on Networking*, 5(6):835–846, December 1997.

[148] Mark Crovella and Robert Carter. Dynamic server selection in the Internet. In *Proceedings of the Third IEEE Workshop on the Architecture and Implementation of High Performance Communication Subsystems (HPCS '95)*, August 1995.

[149] C. R. Cunha. *Trace analysis and its applications to performance enhancements of distributed information systems*. PhD thesis, Boston Univ., MA, USA, 1997.

[150] Carlos R. Cunha, Azer Bestavros, and Mark E. Crovella. Characteristics of WWW client-based traces. Technical Report BU-CS-95-010, Computer Science Department, Boston University, MA, USA, July 1995. http://www.cs.bu.edu/techreports/95-010-www-client-traces.ps.Z.

[151] Carlos R. Cunha and Carlos F. B. Jaccoud. Determining WWW user's next access and its application to pre-fetching. In *Proceedings of the Second IEEE Symposium on Computers and Communications (ISCC '97)*, pages 6–11, July 1997.

[152] Massimiliano Curcio, Stefano Leonardi, and Andrea Vitaletti. An experimental study of prefetching and caching algorithms for the World Wide Web. In *Proc. of ALENEX*, pages 71–85, 2002.

[153] K. M. Curewitz, P. Krishnan, and J. S. Vitter. Practical prefetching via data compression. In *Proceedings of the ACM SIGMOD International Conference on Management of Data*, pages 257–266, 1993.

[154] M. Dahlin. Interpreting stale load information. *IEEE Transactions on Parallel and Distributed Systems*, 11:1033–1047, 2000.

[155] Michael Dahlin, Thomas Anderson, D. A. Patterson, and Rwo-Hsi Wang. Cooperative caching: Using remote client memory to improve file system performance. In *Proceedings of the First Symp. on Operating Systems Design and Implementation*, pages 267–280, 1994.

[156] Asit Dan and Dinkar Sitaraman. Multimedia caching strategies for heterogeneous application and server environments. *Multimedia Tools and Applications*, 4(3):279–312, May 1997.

[157] Peter Danzig. NetCache architecture and deployment. *Computer Networks and ISDN Systems*, 30(22-23):2081–2091, November 1998. http://www.elsevier.nl/cas/tree/store/comnet/sub/1998/30/22-23/2056.pdf.

[158] Peter Danzig, K. Obraczka, and A. Kumar. An analysis of wide-area name server traffic: a study of the Internet domain name system. In *Proceedings of ACM SIGCOMM Symposium on Communications Architectures and Protocols*, pages 281–292, Baltimore, Maryland, August 1992.

[159] Peter Danzig and Karl L. Swartz. Transparent, scalable, fail-safe Web caching. Technical Report TR3033, Network Appliance, Inc., 1999. http://www.netapp.com/technology/level3/3033.html.

[160] Peter B. Danzig, Richard S. Hall, and Michael F. Schwartz. A case for caching file objects inside internetworks. In *Proceedings of the ACM SIGCOMM '93 Conference*, San Francisco, CA., September 1993. ftp://ftp.cs.colorado.edu/pub/cs/techreports/schwartz/FTP.Caching-PS/.

[161] Anindya Datta, Kaushik Dutta, Krithi Ramamritham, Helen M. Thomas, and Debra E. VanderMeer. Dynamic content acceleration: A caching solution to enable scalable dynamic Web page generation. In *Proc. of SIGMOD Conf.*, 2001.

[162] Brian D. Davison. Simultaneous proxy evaluation. In *Proceedings of the 4th International Web Caching Workshop*, April 1999. http://www.ircache.net/Cache/Workshop99/Papers/davison1-final.ps.gz.

[163] Brian D. Davison. A survey of proxy cache evaluation techniques. In *Proceedings of the 4th International Web Caching Workshop*, April 1999. http://www.ircache.net/Cache/Workshop99/Papers/davison2-final.ps.gz.

[164] Brian D. Davison. Web traffic logs: An imperfect resource for evaluation. In *Proceedings of th INET'99 Conference*, June 1999. http://www.isoc.org/inet99/proceedings/4n/4n_1.htm.

[165] Brian D. Davison. A Web caching primer. *IEEE Internet Computing*, 5(4):38–45, 2001.

[166] J. D. Day and H. Zimmermann. The OSI reference model. In *Proceedings of the IEEE*, number 71, pages 1334–1340, 1983.

[167] André de Jong, Henny Bekker, and Ingrid Melve. Web caching meshes: Hit or miss? In *Proceedings of the INET '98 conference*, July 1998. http://www.isoc.org/inet98/proceedings/1k/1k_1.htm.

[168] André de Jong, Ton Verschuren, Henny Bekker, and Ingrid Melve. Report on the costs and benefits of operating caching services. DESIRE European project deliverable D4.2, 1997. http://www.surfnet.nl/surfnet/projects/desire/deliver/WP4/D4-2.html.

[169] Pavan Deolasee, Amol Katkar, Ankur Panchbudhe, Krithi Ramamritham, and Prashant Shenoy. Adaptive push-pull: Disseminating dynamic Web data. In *Proceedings of the 10th International WWW Conference*, Hong Kong, May 2001. http://www10.org/cdrom/papers/pdf/p269.pdf.

[170] Gihan V. Dias, Graham Cope, and Ravi Wijayaratne. A smart Internet caching system. In *Proceedings of the INET'96 Conference*, June 1996. http://info.isoc.org/isoc/whatis/conferences/inet/96/proceedings/a4/a4_3.htm.

[171] Marios D. Dikaiakos. Utility and quality–of–service models for periodic prefetching of WWW resources. In *Proc. of the 9th International WWW Conference, Amsterdam*, May 2000.

[172] Marios D. Dikaiakos and Athena Stassopoulou. Content selection strategies for the periodic prefetching of WWW resources via satellite. *Computer Communications*, 24(1), 2001.

[173] John Dilley. The effect of consistency on cache response time. Technical Report HPL-1999-107, Hewlett-Packard Laboratories, September 1999. http://www.hpl.hp.com/techreports/1999/HPL-1999-107.html.

[174] John Dilley, Martin Arlitt, and Stephane Perret. Enhancement and validation of the Squid cache replacement policy. In *Proceedings of the 4th International Web Caching Workshop*, April 1999. http://www.ircache.net/Cache/Workshop99/Papers/dilley-0.ps.gz.

[175] John Dilley, Martin Arlitt, Stéphane Perret, and Tai Jin. The distributed object consistency protocol. Technical Report HPL-1999-109, Hewlett-Packard Laboratories, September 1999. http://www.hpl.hp.com/techreports/1999/HPL-1999-109.html.

[176] Adam Dingle. Cache consistency in the HTTP 1.1 proposed standard. In *Proceedings of the ICM Workshop on Web Caching*, September 1996. http://w3cache.icm.edu.pl/workshop/talk4/.

[177] Adam Dingle and Thomas Partl. Web cache coherence. In *Proceedings of the 5th International WWW Conference*, Paris, France, May 1996. http://www5conf.inria.fr/fich_html/papers/P2/Overview.html.

[178] James E. Donnelley. WWW media distribution via hopwise reliable multicast. In *Proceedings of the 3rd International WWW Conference*, pages 781–788, April 1995. http://www-atp.llnl.gov/atp/papers/HRM/HRM.html.

[179] Fred Douglis, Thomas Ball, Yih-Farn Chen, and Eleftherios Koutsofios. The AT&T Internet Difference Engine: Tracking and viewing changes on the Web. *World Wide Web*, pages 27–44, January 1998.

[180] Fred Douglis, Anja Feldmann, Balachander Krishnamurthy, and Jeffrey Mogul. Rate of change and other metrics: a live study of the World-Wide Web. In *Proceedings of the 1997 Usenix Symposium on Internet Technologies and Systems (USITS-97)*, pages 147–158, December 1997. http://www.research.att.com/~douglis/papers/roc.ps.gz.

[181] Fred Douglis, Antonio Haro, and Michael Rabinovich. HPP: HTML macro-pre-processing to support dynamic document caching. In *Proceedings of the 1997 Usenix Symposium on Internet Technologies and Systems (USITS-97)*, pages 83–94, December 1997. http://www.research.att.com/~douglis/papers/hpp.ps.

[182] Ronald P. Doyle, Jeffrey S. Chase, Syam Gadde, and Amin Vahdat. The trickle-down effect: Web caching and server request distribution. *Computer Communications*, 25(4):345–356, March 2002.

[183] R. Droms. Dynamic Host Configuration Protocol. RFC 1531, 1993. http://www.ietf.org/rfc/rfc1531.txt.

[184] Ping Du and Jaspal Subhlok. Evaluating the performance of cooperative Web caching with Web Polygraph. In *Proceedings of the 7th International Workshop on Web Content Caching and Distribution*, Boulder, Colorado, August 2002.

[185] Dan Duchamp. Prefetching hyperlinks. In *Proc. Second USENIX Symp. on Internet Technologies and Systems, Boulder, Colorado*, pages 127–138, October 1999.

[186] Bradley M. Duska, David Marwood, and Michael J. Freeley. The measured access characteristics of World-Wide-Web client proxy caches. In *Proceedings of the 1997 Usenix Symposium on Internet Technologies and Systems (USITS-97)*, pages 23–35, Monterey, CA, December 1997. http://www.cs.ubc.ca/spider/marwood/Projects/SPA/wwwap.ps.gz.

[187] Venkata Duvvuri, Prashant Shenoy, and Renu Tewari. Adaptive leases: A strong consistency mechanism for the World Wide Web. In *Proceedings of IEEE INFOCOM'2000*, pages 834–843, March 2000.

[188] S. G. Dykes, K. A. Robbins, and C. L. Jeffery. An empirical evaluation of client-side server selection algorithms. In *Proceedings of INFOCOM*, pages 1361–1370, 2000.

[189] Sandra G. Dykes, Clinton L. Jeffery, and Samir Das. Taxonomy and design analysis for distributed Web caching. In *Proc. of HICSS*, 1999.

[190] Sandra G. Dykes and Kay A. Robbins. A viability analysis of cooperative proxy caching. In *Proceedings of IEEE Infocom*, Anchorage, Alaska, April 2001.

[191] Lars Eggert and John Heidemann. Application-level differentiated services for Web servers. *World Wide Web*, 2(3):133–142, July 1999.

[192] H. Eriksson. MBONE: The Multicast Backbone. *Communications of the ACM*, 37:54–60, 1994.

[193] Jorge Escorcia, Dipak Ghosal, and Dilip Sarkar. A novel cache distribution heuristic algorithm for a mesh of caches and its performance evaluation. *Computer Communications*, 25(3):329–340, February 2002.

[194] Li Fan, Pei Cao, Jussara Almeida, and Andrei Broder. Summary cache: A scalable wide-area Web cache sharing protocol. In *Proceedings of the ACM SIGCOMM'98 conference*, pages 254–265, September 1998. http://www.cs.wisc.edu/~cao/papers/summarycache.html.

[195] Li Fan, Quinn Jacobson, Pei Cao, and Wei Lin. Web prefetching between low-bandwidth clients and proxies: Potential and performance. In *Proceedings of the SIGMETRICS '99 Conference*, pages 178–187, May 1999. http://www.cs.wisc.edu/~cao/papers/prepush.html.

[196] Z. Fei, S. Bhattacharjee, E. W. Zegura, and M. H. Ammar. A novel server selection technique for improving the response time of a replicated service. In *Proceedings of INFOCOM*, pages 783–791, 1998.

[197] Anja Feldmann. Continuous online extraction of HTTP traces from packet traces. Position paper for the W3C Web Characterization Group Workshop, November 1998. http://www.research.att.com/~anja/feldmann/w3c98_httptrace.abs.html.

[198] Anja Feldmann. BLT: Bi-layer tracing of HTTP and TCP/IP. *Computer Networks*, 33(1-6):321–335, June 2000. http://www.elsevier.nl/gej-ng/10/15/22/48/25/47/article.pdf.

[199] Anja Feldmann, Ramon Caceres, Fred Douglis, Gideon Glass, and Michael Rabinovich. Performance of Web proxy caching in heterogeneous bandwidth environments. In *Proceedings of the INFOCOM '99 conference*, pages 107–116, March 1999. http://www.research.att.com/~anja/feldmann/papers/infocom99_proxim.ps.gz.

[200] Robert Fielding, Jim Gettys, Jeff Mogul, Henrik Frystyk, L. Masinter, Paul Leach, and Tim Berners-Lee. Hypertext transfer protocol – HTTP/1.1. RFC 2616, June 1999. http://www.ietf.org/rfc/rfc2616.txt.

[201] Annie Foong, Yu-Hen Hu, and Dennis M. Heisey. Web caching: Locality of references revisited. In *Proceedings of the IEEE International Conference on Networks*, Singapore, September 2000.

[202] Annie P. Foong, Yu-Hen Hu, and Dennis M. Heisey. Essence of an effective Web caching algorithm. In *Proceedings of the International Conference on Internet Computing*, Las Vegas, Nevada, June 2000.

[203] A. Fox and E. A. Brewer. Reducing WWW latency and bandwidth requirements by real-time distillation. *Computer Networks and ISDN Systems*, 28:1445–1456, 1996.

[204] P. Francis, S. Jamin, V. Paxson, L. Zhang, D. Gryniewicz, and Y. Jin. An architecture for a global Internet host distance estimation service. In *Proceedings of INFOCOM*, pages 210–217, 1999.

[205] S. Gadde, J. Chase, and M. Rabinovich. CRISP distributed Web proxy, 1999. http://www.cs.duke.edu/ari/cisi/crisp/.

[206] Syam Gadde, Jeff Chase, and Michael Rabinovich. Directory structures for scalable Internet caches. Technical Report CS-1997-18, Duke university, November 1997. ftp://ftp.cs.duke.edu/dist/techreport/1997/1997-18.ps.gz.

[207] Syam Gadde, Jeff Chase, and Michael Rabinovich. A taste of crispy Squid. In *Proceedings of the Workshop on Internet Server Performance (WISP'98)*, June 1998. http://www.cs.duke.edu/ari/cisi/crisp/crisp-wisp.ps.gz.

[208] Syam Gadde, Jeff Chase, and Michael Rabinovich. Web caching and content distribution: a view from the interior. *Computer Communications*, 24(2):222–231, February 2001.

[209] Syam Gadde, Michael Rabinovich, and Jeff Chase. Reduce, reuse, recycle: An approach to building large Internet caches. In *Proceedings of the HotOS '97 Workshop*, pages 93–98, May 1997. http://www.cs.duke.edu/ari/cisi/crisp-recycle.ps.

[210] Pankaj K. Garg, Kave Eshghi, Thomas Gschwind, Boudewijn R. Haverkort, and Katinka Wolter. Enabling network caching of dynamic Web objects. In *Proc. of Computer Performance Evaluation / TOOLS*, pages 329–338, 2002.

[211] Paul Gauthier. Long term viability of large scale caches. In *Proceedings of the Third International WWW Caching Workshop*, June 1998. http://wwwcache.ja.net/events/workshop/20/ltvc.doc.

[212] Jim Gettys, Tim Berner-Lee, and Henrik Frystyk Nielsen. Replication and caching position statement. http://www.w3.org/Propagation/Activity.html.

[213] Savvas Gitzenis and Nicholas Bambos. Power-controlled data prefetching/caching in wireless packet networks. In *Proceedings of IEEE Infocom*, New York, June 2002.

[214] Steven Glassman. A caching relay for the World Wide Web. *Computer Networks and ISDN Systems*, 27(2):165–173, November 1994.

[215] John Graham-Cumming. Hits and miss-es: A year watching the Web. In *Proceedings of the 6th International WWW Conference*, April 1997.

[216] Cary G. Gray and D. R. Cheriton. Leases: An efficient fault-tolerant mechanism for distributed file cache consistency. In *Proc. of 12th ACM Symposium on Operating Systems Principles*, pages 202–210, Litchfield Park, Arizona, December 1989.

[217] Steven D. Gribble and Eric A. Brewer. System design issues for Internet middleware services: Deductions from a large client trace. In *Proceedings of the 1997 Usenix Symposium on Internet Technologies and Systems (USITS-97)*, pages 207–218, Monterey, CA,

December 1997. http://www.cs.berkeley.edu/~gribble/papers/sys_trace.ps.gz.

[218] C. Grimm, J.-S. Vöckler, and H. Pralle. Load and traffic balancing in large scale cache meshes. *Computer Networks*, 30(16–18):1687–1695, September 1998.

[219] Christian Grimm, Helmut Pralle, and Jens-S. Vöckler. Request routing in cache meshes. *Computer Networks and ISDN Systems*, 30(22-23):2269–2278, November 1998. http://www.elsevier.nl/cas/tree/store/comnet/sub/1998/30/22-23/2048.pdf.

[220] Stephane Gruber, Jennifer Rexford, and Andrea Basso. Protocol considerations for a prefix–caching proxy for multimedia streams. *Computer Networks*, 33(1–6):657–668, June 2000.

[221] Thomas Gschwind and Manfred Hauswirth. NewsCache - a high performance cache implementation for Usenet news. In *Proceedings of USENIX Annual Technical Conference*, Montery, California, June 1999.

[222] Wenzheng Gu and Abdelsalam Helal. Extended Internet Caching Protocol: A foundation for building ubiquitous Web caching. In *Proc. of SAC*, pages 901–907, 2003.

[223] S. Gulwani, A. Tarachandani, D. Gupta, Dheeraj Sanghi, L. P. Barreto, G. Muller, and C. Consel. WebCal a domain specific language for Web caching. *Computer communications*, 24(2):191–201, February 2001.

[224] Meng Guo, Mahmoud Ammar, E. Witte Zegura, and Fang Hao. A probe-based server selection protocol for differentiated service networks. In *Proceedings of the International Conference on Communications (ICC)*, pages 2353–2357, New York, NY, April 2002.

[225] Minaxi Gupta and Mostafa Ammar. A novel multicast scheduling scheme for multimedia server with variable access patterns. In *Proceedings of the International Conference on Communications (ICC)*, Anchorage, Alaska, May 2003.

[226] James Gwertzman. Autonomous replication in wide-area internetworks. Technical Report TR-17-95, Center for Research in Computing Technology, Harvard University, Cambridge, Massachusetts, April 1995. http://www.eecs.harvard.edu/~vino/web/push.cache/.

[227] James Gwertzman and Margo Seltzer. The case for geographical push-caching. In *Proceedings of the HotOS '95 Workshop*, May 1995. http://www.eecs.harvard.edu/~vino/web/hotos.ps.

[228] James Gwertzman and Margo Seltzer. An analysis of geographical push-caching. http://www.eecs.harvard.edu/~vino/web/server.cache/icdcs.ps, 1996.

[229] James Gwertzman and Margo Seltzer. World-Wide Web cache consistency. In *Proceedings of the 1996 Usenix Technical Conference*, pages 141–151, San Diego, CA, January 1996. http://www.eecs.harvard.edu/~vino/web/usenix.196/caching.ps.

[230] Sami Habib, C.P Ravikumar, and A.C Parker. Storage allocation and scheduling problems in Web caching applications. In *Proceedings of the NLANR Web Cache Workshop*, Boulder, Colorado, June 1997.

[231] Hisakazu Hada, Ken ichi Chinen, Suguru Yamaguchi, and Yugi Oie. Behavior of WWW proxy servers in low bandwidth conditions. In *Proceedings of the 4th International Web Caching Workshop*, April 1999. http://www.ircache.net/Cache/Workshop99/ Papers/hada-0.ps.gz.

[232] Martin Hamilton. Multicast approaches to World-Wide Web caching. Technical Report LUT CS-TR 988, Department of Computer Studies, Loughborough University of Technology, Ashby Road, Loughborough Leics, LE11 3TU, UK, August 1995.

[233] Martin Hamilton. Multicast IP and Web caching. In *Proceedings of the Workshop on Web Caching*, Warsaw, Poland, September 1996.

[234] Michael D. Hamilton, P. McKee, and Isi Mitrani. Optimal caching policies for Web objects. In *Proc. of HPCN Europe*, pages 94–103, 2001.

[235] M. Harchol-Balter, M. E. Crovella, and C. D. Murta. On choosing a task assignment policy for a distributed server system. *Journal of Parallel and Distributed Computing*, 59:204–228, 1999.

[236] Hossam Hassanein, Zhengang Liang, and Patrick Martin. Performance comparison of alternate Web caching techniques. In *Proceedings of the IEEE Symposium on Computers and Communications*, Taormina-Giardini Naxos, Italy, July 2002.

[237] Boudewijn R. Haverkort, Rachid El Abdouni Khayari, and Ramin Sadre. A class-based Least-Recently Used caching algorithm for World-Wide Web proxies. In *Proc. of Computer Performance Evaluation / TOOLS*, pages 273–290, 2003.

[238] A. Heddaya, S. Mirdad, and D. Yates. Diffusion based caching along routing paths. In *Proceedings of the 2nd Web Cache Workshop, Boulder, Colarado*, June 1997.

[239] Steven A. Heimlich. Traffic characterization of the NSFNET national backbone. In *Proceedings of the Usenix Winter Conference*, pages 207–27, Washington, D.C., January 1990.

[240] John H. Hine, Craig E. Wills, Anja Martel, and Joel Sommers. Combining client knowledge and resource dependencies for improved World Wide Web performance. In *Proceedings of the INET '98 conference*, July 1998. http://www.isoc.org/inet98/ proceedings/1i/1i_1.htm.

[241] Vegard Holmedahl, Ben Smith, and Tao Yang. Cooperative caching of dynamic content on a distributed Web server. In *Proc. of HPDC*, 1998.

[242] Saied Hosseini-Khayat. Replacement algorithms for object caching. In *Proceedings of the 1998 ACM Symposium on Applied Computing (SAP '98)*, Atlanta, Georgia, February 1998.

[243] Thomas Hou, Jianping Pan, Chonggang Wang, and Bo Li. On prefetching in hierarchical caching systems. In *Proceedings of ICC*, Anchorage, Alaska, May 2003.

[244] Wen-Chi Hou and Suli Wang. Size-adjusted sliding window LFU - a new Web caching scheme. In *Proc. of DEXA*, pages 567–576, 2001.

[245] B. C. Housel, George Samaras, and David B. Lindquist. WebExpress: A client/intercept based system for optimizing Web browsing in a wireless environment. *Mobile Networks and Applications*, 3(4):419–431, January 1999.

[246] Bernardo A. Huberman, Peter L. T. Pirolli, James E. Pitkow, and Rajan M. Lukose. Strong regularities in World Wide Web surfing. *Science*, 280(5360):95–97, April 1998.

[247] Bradley Hufftaker, J. Jung, Evi Nemeth, Duane Wessels, and Kimberly Claffy. Visualization of the growth and topology of the NLANR caching hierarchy. *Computer Networks*, 30(22–23):2131–2139, November 1998.

[248] Christian Huitema and Sam Weerahandi. Internet measurements: The rising trend and the DNS snag. In *ITC Specialist Seminar, IP Traffic Measurement, Modeling and Management, Monterey, CA, USA.*, September 2000.

[249] J. J. Hunt, K. P. Vo, and W. F. Tichy. Delta algorithms: an empirical analysis. *ACM Transactions on Software Engineering and Methodology*, 7:192–214, 1998.

[250] Richard T. Hurley, W. Feng, and B. Y. Li. An analytical comparison of distributed and hierarchical Web-caching architectures. In *Proc. of Computers and Their Applications*, pages 291–295, 2003.

[251] G. Huston. Web caching. *Internet Protocol Journal*, 2(3):2–20, September 1999.

[252] Internet Cache Protocol specification 1.4, 1994. http://excalibur.usc.edu/icpdoc/icp.html.

[253] Internet Cache Protocol (ICP), version 2. RFC 2186, September 1997.

[254] Application of Internet Cache Protocol (ICP), version 2. RFC 2187, September 1997.

[255] D. B. Ingham, S. J. Caughey, and M. C. Little. Fixing the "broken-link" problem: The W3Objects approach. *Computer Networks and ISDN Systems*, 29(8-13):1255–1268,, 1997. http://w3objects.ncl.ac.uk/pubs/fblp/.

[256] D. B. Ingham, S. J. Caughey, and M. C. Little. Supporting highly manageable Web services. *Computer Networks and ISDN Systems*, 29(8-13):1405–1416, 1997. http://w3objects.ncl.ac.uk/pubs/shmws/.

[257] D. B. Ingham, M. C. Little, S. J. Caughey, and S. K. Shrivastava. W3Objects: Bringing object-oriented technology to the Web. *World-Wide Web Journal*, 1, 1995. http://w3objects.ncl.ac.uk/pubs/bootw/.

[258] Hiroyuki Inoue, Kanchana Kanchanasut, and Suguru Yamaguchi. An adaptive WWW cache mechanism in the AI3 network. In *Proceedings of the INET '97 conference*, June 1997. http://www.ai3.net/inet97-w3cache/.

[259] Hiroyuki Inoue, Takeshi Sakamoto, Suguru Yamaguchi, and Yuji Oie. WebHint: An automatic configuration mechanism for optimizing World Wide Web cache system utilization. In *Proceedings of the INET '98 conference*, July 1998. http://www.isoc.org/inet98/proceedings/1i/1i_3.htm.

[260] Sandy Irani. Page replacement with multi-size pages and applications to Web caching. *Algorithmica*, 33(3):384–409, 2002.

[261] A. Iyengar, E. A. MacNair, and T. C. Nguyen. An analysis of Web server performance. In *Proceedings of Globecom*, Phoenix, Arizona, November 1997.

[262] Arun Iyengar. Design and performance of a general-purpose software cache. In *Proceedings of the 18th IEEE International Performance Conference (IPCCC'99)*, February 1999. http://www.research.ibm.com/people/i/iyengar/ipccc99.ps.

[263] Arun K. Iyengar, Mark S. Squillante, and Li Zhang. Analysis and characterization of large-scale Web server access patterns and performance. *World Wide Web*, June 1999. http://www.research.ibm.com/people/i/iyengar/www99.ps.

[264] Quinn Jacobson and Pei Cao. Potential and limits of Web prefetching between low-bandwidth clients and proxies. In *Proceedings of the Third International WWW Caching Workshop*, June 1998. http://wwwcache.ja.net/events/workshop/28/cao-prepush.ps.

[265] V. Jacobson, R. Braden, and D. Borman. TCP extensions for high performance. RFC 1323, 1992. http://www.ietf.org/rfc/rfc1323.txt.

[266] Van Jacobson. How to kill the Internet. Talk at the SIGCOMM '95 Workshop on Middleware, August 1995. ftp://ftp.ee.lbl.gov/talks/vj-webflame.ps.Z.

[267] Sugih Jamin, Cheng Jin, Anthony Kurc, Yuval Shavitt, and Danny Raz. Constrained mirror placement on the Internet. In *Proceedings of the IEEE Infocom conference*, April 2001. http://infocom.ucsd.edu/papers/738-847300932.pdf.

[268] Clinton L. Jeffery, Samir R. Das, and Garry S. Bernal. Proxy-sharing proxy servers. In *Proceedings of the 1st IEEE Conference on Emerging Technologies and Applications in Communications (ETACOM)*, May 1996. http://www.cs.utsa.edu/research/proxy/etacom.ps.

[269] Anxiao Jiang and Jehoshua Bruck. Optimal content placement for en-route Web caching. In *Proc. of NCA*, pages 9–16, 2003.

[270] Zhimei Jiang and Leonard Kleinrock. An adaptive network prefetch scheme. *IEEE Jour. on Selected Areas in Communications*, 16(3):358–368, April 1998.

[271] Zhimei Jiang and Leonard Kleinrock. Web prefetching in a mobile environment. *IEEE Personal Communications*, pages 25–34, October 1998.

[272] S. Jin and A. Bestavros. Sources and characteristics of Web temporal locality. In *Proceedings of 8th International Symposium on Modeling, Analysis and Simulation of Computer and Telecommunication Systems*, pages 28–36, 2000.

[273] Shudong Jin and Azer Bestavros. Popularity-aware greedydual-size algorithms for Web access. In *Proceedings of the 20th International Conference on Distributed Computing Systems (ICDCS)*, April 2000. http://cs-people.bu.edu/jins/Research/popularity-aware.html.

[274] Shudong Jin and Azer Bestavros. Greedydual* Web caching algorithms: exploiting the two sources of temporal locality in Web request streams. *Computer Communications*, 24(2):174–183, February 2001.

[275] Chris W. Johnson. Time and the Web: Representing temporal properties of interaction with distributed systems. In *People and Computers X: Proceedings of HCI'95*, pages 39–50, 1995. http://www.dcs.glasgow.ac.uk/~johnson/papers/HCI95_TAU.ps.Z.

[276] E. Johnson. Increasing the performance of transparent caching with content-aware cache bypass. In *Proceedings of 4th International Web caching Workshop*, 1999.

[277] Kirk L. Johnson, John F. Carr, Mark S. Day, and M. Frans Kaashoek. The measured performance of content distribution networks. In *Proceedings of the 5th International Web Caching and Content Delivery Workshop*, May 2000. http://www.terena.nl/conf/wcw/Proceedings/S4/S4-1.pdf.

[278] John Judge. Estimating peak HTTP request rate for a population of Web users. In *Proceedings of the 10th IEEE Workshop on Local and Metropolitan Area Networks*, pages 108–111, November 1999. http://www.snrc.uow.edu.au/titr/publications/judge_lanman99.pdf.

[279] John Judge, H.W.P. Beadle, and J. Chicharo. Modelling user traffic in the WWW. In *Proceedings of the Australian Telecommunications Networks and Applications Conference*, pages 163–168, December 1995. http://www.snrc.uow.edu.au/titr/publications/jud95b.ps.

[280] John Judge, H.W.P. Beadle, and J. Chicharo. Correlation of HTTP response packet size and estimating confidence intervals for mean packet size and WWW traffic volume. In *Proceedings of the Third Asia-Pacific Conference on Communication (APCC'97)*, pages 382–386, December 1997. http://www.snrc.uow.edu.au/titr/publications/jud97c.ps.

[281] John Judge, H.W.P. Beadle, and J. Chicharo. Modelling World-Wide Web request traffic. In *Proceedings of the IS&T/SPIE Multimedia Computing and Networking Conference*, pages 92–106, February 1997. http://www.snrc.uow.edu.au/titr/publications/jud97a.ps.

[282] John Judge, H.W.P. Beadle, and J. Chicharo. Sampling HTTP response packets for prediction of Web traffic volume statistics. In *Proceedings of the Globecom'98 conference*, November 1998. http://www.snrc.uow.edu.au/titr/publications/jud98a.ps.

[283] John Judge, J. Chicharo, and H.W.P. Beadle. The size of HTTP response packets and calculation of WWW traffic volumes. In *Proceedings of the International Conference on Telecommunications (ICT'97)*, pages 247–262, April 1997. http://www.snrc.uow.edu.au/titr/publications/jud97b.ps.

[284] Jaeyeon Jung and Kilnam Chon. A new approach to scalable network storage system for large objects. In *Proceedings of the 4th International Web Caching Workshop*, April 1999. http://www.ircache.net/Cache/Workshop99/Papers/jung-0.ps.gz.

[285] Jaeyeon Jung and Kilnam Chon. RepliCache: Enhancing Web caching architecture with the replication of large objects. In *Proceedings of the International Conference on Information Networking*, Cheju Island, Korea, January 1999.

[286] Jaeyeon Jung, Dongman Lee, and Kilnam Chon. Proactive Web caching with cumulative prefetching for large multimedia data. *Computer Networks*, 33(1–6):645–655, June 2000.

[287] Jaeyeon Jung, Emil Sit, Hari Balakrishnan, and Robert Morris. DNS performance and the effectiveness of caching. In *Proceedings of ACM SIGCOMM Internet Measurement Workshop*, San Francisco, California, November 2001.

[288] Gail Kalbfleisch, William Deckert, Ranette H. Halverson, and Nelson L. Passos. A brief study on Web caching applied to mobile Web applications. In *Proc. of Computers and Their Applications*, pages 442–445, 2003.

[289] M. Kalyanakrishnan, R.K. Iyer, and J.U. Patel. Reliability of Internet hosts: a case study from the end user's perspective. *Computer Networks and ISDN Systems*, 31(1-2):45–55, January 1999. http://www.elsevier.nl/cas/tree/store/comnet/sub/1999/31/1-2/2035.pdf.

[290] J. Kangasharju, Y. G. Kwon, A. Ortega, X. Yang, and K. Ramchandran. Implementation of optimized cache replenishment algorithms in a soft caching system. In *Proceedings of the IEEE Workshop on Multimedia Signal Processing*, December 1998. http://sipi.usc.edu/~ortega/SoftCaching/MMSP98/.

[291] Jussi Kangasharju, Felix Hartanto, Martin Reisslein, and Keith W. Ross. Distributing layered encoded video through caches. In *Proceedings of IEEE Infocom*, Anchorage, Alaska, April 2001.

[292] Jussi Kangasharju, Young Gap Kwon, and Antonio Ortega. Design and implementation of a soft caching proxy. *Computer Networks and ISDN Systems*, 30(22-23):2113–2121, November 1998. http://www.elsevier.nl/cas/tree/store/comnet/sub/1998/30/22-23/2060.pdf.

[293] Jussi Kangasharju, Keith W. Ross, and James W. Roberts. Locating copies of objects using the domain name system. In *Proceedings of the 4th International Web Caching Workshop*, April 1999. http://www.ircache.net/Cache/Workshop99/Papers/kangasharju-final.ps.gz.

[294] M. Karaul, Y. A. Korilis, and A. Orda. A market-based architecture for management of geographically dispersed, replicated Web servers. In *Proceedings of the 1st International Conf. on Information and Computation Economies*, pages 158–165, 1998.

[295] David Karger, Alex Sherman, Andy Berkheimer, Bill Bogstad, Rizwan Dhanidina, Ken Iwamoto, Brian Kim, Luke Matkins, and Yoav Yerushalmi. Web caching with consistent hashing. *Computer Networks and ISDN Systems*, 31(11-16):1203–1213, May 1999. http://www.elsevier.nl/cas/tree/store/comnet/sub/1999/31/11-16/2181.pdf.

[296] David R. Karger, Eric Lehman, Frank Thomson Leighton, Rina Panigrahy, Matthew S. Levine, and Daniel Lewin. Consistent hashing and random trees: Distributed caching protocols for relieving hot spots on the World Wide Web. In *Proc. of STOC*, pages 654–663, 1997.

[297] E. Katz, M. Butler, and R. McGrath. A scalable Web server: The NCSA prototype. *Computer Networks and ISDN Systems*, 27:155–164, 1994.

[298] Eiji Kawai, Ken ichi Chinen, Suguru Yamaguchi, and Hideki Sunahara. A quantitative analysis of ICP queries at the distributed WWW caching system. In *Proceedings of the INET'99 Conference*, June 1999. http://www.isoc.org/inet99/proceedings/4n/4n_2.htm.

[299] Terence Kelly and Daniel Reeves. Optimal Web cache sizing: Scalable methods for exact solutions. In *Proceedings of the 5th International Web Caching and Content*

Delivery Workshop, May 2000. http://www.terena.nl/conf/wcw/Proceedings/ S2/S2-1.ps.

[300] Terence P. Kelly, Yee Man Chan, Sugih Jamin, and Jeffrey K. MacKie-Mason. Biased replacement policies for Web caches: Differential quality-of-service and aggregate user value. In *Proceedings of the 4th International Web Caching Workshop*, April 1999. http://www.ircache.net/Cache/Workshop99/Papers/kelly-final.ps.gz.

[301] Chris Kenyon. The evolution of Web-caching markets. *IEEE Computer*, 34(11):128–130, 2001.

[302] Anne-Marie Kermarrec, Ihor Kuz, Maarten van Steen, and Andrew S. Tanenbaum. A framework for consistent, replicated Web objects. In *Proceedings of the 18th International Conference on Distributed Computing Systems (ICDCS)*, May 1998. http://www.cs.vu.nl/pub/papers/globe/icdcs.98.pdf.

[303] Anne-Marie Kermarrec, Ihor Kuz, Maarten van Steen, and Andrew S. Tanenbaum. Towards scalable Web documents. Technical Report IR-452, Vrije Universiteit, October 1998. http://www.cs.vu.nl/pub/papers/globe/IR-452.98.ps.Z.

[304] Anne-Marie Kermarrec, Marteen van Steen, and Andrew S. Tanenbaum. A flexible alternative to Web caching. In *Proceedings of the 3rd CaberNet Plenary Workshop*, Rennes, France, April 1997. http://www.cs.vu.nl/~amk/publications/cabernet.ps.

[305] David Siew Chee Kheong and Gang Feng. Efficient setup for multicast connections using tree–caching. In *Proceedings of IEEE Infocom*, Anchorage, Alaska, April 2001.

[306] Heegyu Kim, Kiejin Park, Ji Yung Chung, and Sungsoo Kim. Improving cache hit rate through cooperative caching in cluster-based Web server. In *Proc. of PDPTA*, pages 702–707, 2003.

[307] Ilhwan Kim, Heon Y. Yeom, and Joonwon Lee. Analysis of buffer management policies for WWW proxy. In *Proceedings of the International Conference on Information Networking (ICOIN-12)*, Tokyo, Japan, January 1998. http://arirang.snu.ac.kr/ ~yeom/paper/icoin12b.ps.

[308] R. P. Klemm. Web companion: A friendly client–side Web prefetching agent. *IEEE Trans. on Knowledge and Data Engg.*, 11(4):577–594, 1999.

[309] Ravi Kokku, Praveen Yalagandula, Arun Venkataramani, and Mike Dahlin. A non–interfering deployable Web prefetching system. In *Proc. of the USENIX Symposium on Internet Technologies and Systems*, March 2003.

[310] Keith Kong and D. Ghosal. Pseudo-serving: a user-responsible paradigm for internet access. *Computer Networks*, 29(8–13):1053–1064, September 1997.

[311] Chandra Kopparapu. *Load Balancing Servers, Firewalls, and Caches*. John Wiley and Sons, January 2002.

[312] M. R. Korupolu and M. Dahlin. Coordinated placement and replacement for large–scale distributed caches. In *Proceedings of the IEEE Workshop on Internet Applications*, July 1999.

[313] S. Krashakov and L. Shchur. WWW caching in Russia: Current state and future devel-
      opment. In *Proceedings of the 3rd International Web Caching Workshop*, 1998.

[314] B. Krishnamurthy and J. Rexford. *Web Protocols and Practice: HTTP 1.1, Networking
      Protocols, Caching and Traffic Measurement.* Addison Wesley, 2001.

[315] Balachander Krishnamurthy and Martin Arlitt. PRO-COW: Protocol compliance on
      the Web. Technical Report 990803-05-TM, AT&T Labs, August 1999. http://www.
      research.att.com/~bala/papers/procow-1.ps.gz.

[316] Balachander Krishnamurthy, Jeffrey C. Mogul, and David M. Kristol. Key differences
      between HTTP/1.0 and HTTP/1.1. *Computer Networks and ISDN systems*, 31(11-
      16):1737–1751, May 1999. http://www.elsevier.nl/cas/tree/store/comnet/
      sub/1999/31/11-16/2136.pdf.

[317] Balachander Krishnamurthy and Jia Wang. On network-aware clustering of Web clients.
      In *Proceedings of the SIGCOMM*, August 2000. http://www.acm.org/sigcomm/
      sigcomm2000/conf/paper/sigcomm2000-3-2.pdf.

[318] Balachander Krishnamurthy and Craig E. Willis. Piggyback cache validation for proxy
      caches in the World-Wide Web. In *Proceedings of the 1997 NLANR Web Cache
      Workshop*, June 1997. http://ircache.nlanr.net/Cache/Workshop97/Papers/
      Wills/wills.html.

[319] Balachander Krishnamurthy and Craig Wills. Proxy cache coherency and replacement –
      towards a more complete picture. In *Proceedings of the ICDCS conference*, June 1999.
      http://www.research.att.com/~bala/papers/ccrcp.ps.gz.

[320] Balachander Krishnamurthy and Craig E. Wills. Study of piggyback cache validation
      for proxy caches in the World Wide Web. In *Proceedings of the 1997 Usenix Symposium
      on Internet Technologies and Systems (USITS-97)*, pages 1–12, December 1997. http:
      //www.cs.wpi.edu/~cew/papers/usits97.ps.gz.

[321] Balachander Krishnamurthy and Craig E. Wills. Piggyback server invalidation for
      proxy cache coherency. *Computer Networks and ISDN Systems*, 30(1-7):185–193,
      1998. http://www.elsevier.nl/cas/tree/store/comnet/sub/1998/30/1-7/
      1844.pdf.

[322] Balachander Krishnamurthy and Craig E. Wills. Analyzing factors that influence end-
      to-end Web performance. *Computer Networks*, 33(1-6):17–32, June 2000. http://
      www.elsevier.nl/gej-ng/10/15/22/48/25/28/article.pdf.

[323] P. Krishnan, Danny Raz, and Yuval Shavitt. Transparent en-route caching in WANs?
      In *Proceedings of the 4th International Web Caching Workshop*, April 1999. http:
      //www.ircache.net/Cache/Workshop99/Papers/krishnan-0.ps.gz.

[324] P. Krishnan, Danny Raz, and Yuval Shavitt. The cache location problem. *IEEE/ACM
      Transactions on Networking*, 8(5):568–582, October 2000. http://www.eng.tau.
      ac.il/~shavitt/pub/statToN.pdf.

[325] P. Krishnan and Binay Sugla. Utility of co-operating Web proxy caches. *Computer
      Networks and ISDN Systems*, 30(1-7):195–203, 1998. http://www.elsevier.nl/
      cas/tree/store/comnet/sub/1998/30/1-7/1892.pdf.

[326] Thomas M. Kroeger, Darrell D. E. Long, and Jeffrey C. Mogul. Exploring the bounds of Web latency reduction from caching and prefetching. In *Proceedings of the 1997 Usenix Symposium on Internet Technologies and Systems*, pages 13–22, Monterey, CA, December 1997. http://csl.cse.ucsc.edu/~tmk/ideal.ps.

[327] Thomas M. Kroeger, Jeff Mogul, and Carlos Maltzahn. Digital's Web proxy traces. ftp://ftp.digital.com/pub/DEC/traces/proxy/webtraces.v1.2.html, 1996.

[328] Geoffrey H. Kuenning, G. J. Popek, and Peter Reiher. An analysis of trace data for predictive file caching in mobile computing. In *Proceedings of Usenix Summer Conference*, Boston, MA, June 1994.

[329] Michal Kurcewicz, Wojtek Sylwestrzak, and Adam Wierzbicki. A distributed WWW cache. *Computer Networks and ISDN Systems*, 30(22-23):2261–2267, November 1998. http://www.elsevier.nl/cas/tree/store/comnet/sub/1998/30/22-23/2049.pdf.

[330] Michal Kurcewicz, Wojtek Sylwestrzak, and Adam Wierzbicki. A filtering algorithm for Web caches. *Computer Networks and ISDN Systems*, 30(22-23):2203–2209, November 1998. http://www.elsevier.nl/cas/tree/store/comnet/sub/1998/30/22-23/2047.pdf.

[331] Ihor Kuz, Anne-Marie Kermarrec, Maarten van Steen, and Henk J. Sips. Replicated Web objects: Design and implementation. In *Proceedings of the Fourth Annual ASCI Conference*, June 1998. http://www.cs.vu.nl/pub/papers/globe/asci.98.1.z.

[332] Thomas T. Kwan, Robert E. McGrath, and Daniel A. Reed. NCSA's World Wide Web server: design and performance. *IEEE Computer*, 28(11):68–74, November 1995.

[333] Thomas T. Kwan, Robert E. McGrath, and Daniel A. Reed. User access patterns to NCSA's World Wide Web server. Technical Report UIUCDCS-R-95-1934, Dept. Computer Science, Univ. of Illinois, Urbana-Champaign, February 1995. http://www-pablo.cs.uiuc.edu/Papers/WWW.ps.Z.

[334] Bin Lan, Stéphane Bressan, Beng Chin Ooi, and Kian-Lee Tan. Rule-assisted prefetching in Web-server caching. In *Proc. of CIKM*, pages 504–511, 2000.

[335] Riccardo Lancellotti, Bruno Ciciani, and Michele Colajanni. A scalable architecture for cooperative Web caching. In *Proc. of NETWORKING Workshops*, pages 29–41, 2002.

[336] Nikolaos Laoutaris, Sofia Syntila, and Ioannis Stavrakakis. Meta algorithms for hierarchical Web caches. In *Proceedings of IEEE IPCCC*, Phoenix, Arizona, April 2004.

[337] S. Lawrence and C. L. Giles. Accessibility of information on the Web. *Nature*, 400:107–109, 1999.

[338] Steve Lawrence and C. Lee Giles. Searching the World Wide Web. *Science*, 280(5360):98, 1998.

[339] J. Lee, H. Hwang, Y. Chin, H. Kim, and K. Chon. Report on the costs and benefits of cache hierarchy in Korea. In *Proceedings of the 3rd International Web Caching Workshop*, 1998.

[340] Jeong-Joon Lee, Kyu-Young Whang, Byung Suk Lee, and Ji-Woong Chang. An update-risk based approach to TTL estimation in Web caching. In *Proc. of WISE*, pages 21–29, 2002.

[341] Sung-Ju Lee, Wei-Ying Ma, and Bo Shen. An interactive video delivery and caching system using video summarization. *Computer Communications*, 25(4):424–435, March 2002.

[342] William LeFebvre and Ken Craig. Rapid reverse DNS lookups for Web servers. In *Proceedings of 2nd USENIX Symposium on Internet Technologies and Systems*, Boulder, Colorado, October 1999.

[343] Ulana Legedza and John Guttag. Using network-level support to improve cache routing. *Computer Networks and ISDN Systems*, 30(22-23):2193–2201, November 1998. http://www.elsevier.nl/cas/tree/store/comnet/sub/1998/30/22-23/2054.pdf.

[344] Hui Lei and Dan Duchamp. An analytical approach to file prefetching. In *Proc. USENIX Ann. Technical Conf., USENIX, Anaheim CA*, pages 275–288, January 1997.

[345] Eric Levy-Abegnoli, Arun Iyengar, Junehwa Song, and Daniel Dias. Design and performance of a Web server accelerator. In *Proceedings of IEEE INFOCOM'99*, March 1999. http://www.research.ibm.com/people/i/iyengar/infocom1.ps.

[346] Bo Li, Mordecai Golin, Giuseppe Italiano, Xin Deng, and Kazem Sohraby. On the optimal placement of Web proxies in the Internet. In *Proceedings of the INFOCOM '99 conference*, March 1999. http://www.ieee-infocom.org/1999/papers/09d_01.pdf.

[347] Dan Li and David R. Cheriton. Scalable Web caching of frequently updated objects using reliable multicast. In *Proceedings of the 1999 Usenix Symposium on Internet Technologies and Systems (USITS'99)*, pages 92–103, October 1999. ftp://ftp.dsg.stanford.edu/pub/papers/mmo.ps.gz.

[348] Keqiu Li and Hong Shen. An optimal method for coordinated en-route Web object caching. In *Proc. of ISHPC*, pages 368–375, 2003.

[349] Quanzhong Li and Bongki Moon. Distributed cooperative Apache Web server. In *Proceedings of the 10th International WWW Conference*, Hong Kong, May 2001. http://www10.org/cdrom/papers/pdf/p518.pdf.

[350] Wen-Syan Li, K. Selçuk Candan, Wang-Pin Hsiung, Oliver Po, and Divyakant Agrawal. Engineering high performance database-driven e-commerce Web sites through dynamic content caching. In *Proc. of EC-Web*, pages 250–259, 2001.

[351] Wen-Syan Li, Oliver Po, Wang-Pin Hsiung, K. Selçuk Candan, and Divyakant Agrawal. Freshness-driven adaptive caching for dynamic content Web sites. *Data Knowl. Eng.*, 47(2):269–296, 2003.

[352] Yingjie Li, Cho-Yu Chiang, and M.T. Liu. Effective Web caching for GPRS networks. In *Proceedings of the International Conference on Computer Networks and Mobile Computing*, Beijing, China, October 2001.

[353] Zhengang Liang, Hossam S. Hassanein, and Patrick Martin. Transparent distributed Web caching. In *Proc. of LCN*, pages 225–235, 2001.

[354] Tie Liao. WebCanal: a multicast Web application. *Computer Networks*, 29(8–13):1091–1102, September 1997.

[355] Jochen Liedtke, Vsevolod Panteleenko, Trent Jaeger, and Nayeem Islam. High-performance caching with the Lava hit-server. In *Proceedings of Usenix Annual Technical Conference*, 1998.

[356] Jaeyong Lim and Sanguthevar Rajasekaran. Parallel cache management protocol and algorithm for cooperative Web servers. In *Proc. of ICC*, Anchorage, Alaska, May 2003.

[357] Christoph Lindemann and Oliver P. Waldhorst. Evaluating cooperative Web caching protocols for emerging network technologies. In *Proc. of the Workshop on Caching, Coherence and Consistency (in conjunction with ICS'01)*, Sorrento, Italy, 2001.

[358] M. C. Little, S. K. Shrivastava, S. J. Caughey, and D. B. Ingham. Constructing reliable Web applications using atomic actions. *Computer Networks and ISDN Systems*, 29(8-13), 1997. http://w3objects.ncl.ac.uk/pubs/crwaaa/.

[359] Binzhang Liu, Ghaleb Abdulla, Tommy Johnson, and Edward A. Fox. Web response time and proxy caching. In *Proc. of WebNet*, 1998.

[360] Chengjie Liu and Pei Cao. Strong cache consistency for the World-Wide Web. In *Proceedings of the Works In Progress session of the OSDI '96 conference*, October 1996.

[361] Chengjie Liu and Pei Cao. Maintaining strong cache consistency in the World-Wide Web. In *Proceedings of the ICDCS'97 Conference*, pages 12–21, May 1997. http://www.cs.wisc.edu/~cao/papers/icache.html.

[362] Zhen Liu, Mark S. Squillante, Cathy H. Xia, S. Yu, Li Zhang, Naceur Malouch, and Paul Dantzig. Analysis of caching mechanisms from sporting event Web sites. In *Proc. of ASIAN*, pages 76–86, 2002.

[363] Tong Sau Loon and Vaduvur Bharghavan. Alleviating the latency and bandwidth problems in WWW browsing. In *Proceedings of the 1997 Usenix Symposium on Internet Technologies and Systems (USITS-97)*, pages 219–230, December 1997. http://timely.crhc.uiuc.edu/Papers/usits_v1.ps.

[364] Alejandro López-Ortiz and Daniel M. Germán. A multicollaborative push-caching HTTP procotol for the WWW. Poster for the 5th International WWW Conference, May 1996. http://csg.uwaterloo.ca/~dmg/research/www5/cache.html.

[365] Ying Lu, Avneesh Saxena, and Tarek F. Abdelzaher. Differentiated caching services; a control-theoretical approach. In *Proceedings of the 21st International Conference on Distributed Computing Systems (ICDCS-21)*, Phoenix, AZ, apr 2001. http://www.cs.virginia.edu/~zaher/icdcs01.ps.

[366] Ari Luotonen and Kevin Altis. World-wide Web proxies. *Computer Networks and ISDN Systems*, 27(2):147–154, November 1994.

[367] Anirban Mahanti, Derek Eager, and Carey Williamson. Temporal locality and its impact on Web proxy cache performance. *Performance Evaluation*, 42(2):187–203, September 2000.

[368] Anirban Mahanti, Carey Williamson, and Derek Eager. Traffic analysis of a Web proxy caching hierarchy. *IEEE Network*, 14(3), May 2000.

[369] Mesaac Makpangou and Eric Bérenguier. Relais : un protocole de maintien de cohérence de caches Web coopérants. In *Proceedings of the NoTeRe '97 symposium*, Pau, France, November 1997.

[370] Mesaac Makpangou, Guillaume Pierre, Christian Khoury, and Neilze Dorta. Replicated directory service for weakly consistent replicated caches. In *Proceedings of the 19th IEEE International Conference on Distributed Computing Systems (ICDCS '99)*, pages 92–100, May 1999.

[371] G. Robert Malan, Farnam Jahanian, and Sushila Subramanian. Salamander: A push-based distribution substrate for Internet applications. In *Proceedings of the 1997 Usenix Symposium on Internet Technologies and Systems (USITS-97)*, Monterey, CA, December 1997.

[372] Radhika Malpani, Jacob Lorch, and David Berger. Making World-Wide Web caching servers cooperate. In *Proceedings of the 4th International WWW Conference*, Boston, MA, December 1995. http://www.w3.org/pub/Conferences/WWW4/Papers/59/.

[373] Carlos Maltzahn, Kathy Richardson, and Dirk Grunwald. Performance issues of enterprise level Web proxies. In *ACM SIGMETRICS International Conference on Measurement and Modeling of Computer Systems*, June 1997. http://www.cs.colorado.edu/~carlosm/sigmetrics.ps.gz.

[374] Carlos Maltzahn, Kathy Richardson, and Dirk Grunwald. Reducing the disk I/O of Web proxy server caches. In *Proceedings of the USENIX Annual Technical Conference*, June 1999.

[375] Carlos Maltzahn, Kathy Richardson, Dirk Grunwald, and James Martin. A feasibility study of bandwidth smoothing on the World-Wide Web using machine learning. Technical Report CU-CS-879-99, Dept. of Computer Science, University of Colorado at Boulder, January 1999. http://www.cs.colorado.edu/~carlosm/CU-CS-879-99.ps.gz.

[376] Carlos Maltzahn and Kathy J. Richardson. Comparing the performance of CERN's httpd and Squid. In *Proceedings of the 1997 NLANR Web Cache Workshop*, June 1997. http://www.nlanr.net/Cache/Workshop97/Papers/Maltzahn/maltzahn.ps.

[377] Carlos Maltzahn, Kathy J. Richardson, Dirk Grunwald, and James H. Martin. On bandwidth smoothing. In *Proceedings of the 4th International Web Caching Workshop*, April 1999. http://www.ircache.net/Cache/Workshop99/Papers/maltzahn-final.ps.gz.

[378] Stephen Manley and Margo Seltzer. Web facts and fantasy. In *Proceedings of the 1997 Usenix Symposium on Internet Technologies and Systems (USITS-97)*, pages 125–133, Monterey, CA, December 1997. http://www.eecs.harvard.edu/~vino/web/sits.97.ps.

[379] Evangelos P. Markatos. Main memory caching of Web documents. *Computer Networks*, 28(7–11):893–905, May 1996.

[380] Evangelos P. Markatos and Catherine E. Chronaki. A top 10 approach for prefetching the Web. In *Proceedings of the INET '98 conference*, July 1998. http://www.isoc. org/inet98/proceedings/1i/1i_2.htm.

[381] Evangelos P. Markatos, Manolis G.H. Katevenis, Dionisis Pnevmatikatos, and Michail Flouris. Secondary storage management for Web proxies. In *Proceedings of the 1999 Usenix Symposium on Internet Technologies and Systems (USITS'99)*, October 1999. http://archvlsi.ics.forth.gr/papers/1999.USITS99.web_ proxy_storage.ps.g%z.

[382] Ian Marshall and Chris Roadknight. Linking cache performance to user behavior. *Computer Networks and ISDN Systems*, 30(22-23):2123–2130, November 1998. http:// www.elsevier.nl/cas/tree/store/comnet/sub/1998/30/22-23/2050.pdf.

[383] Kirk Martinez, Steve Perry, and John Cupitt. Object browsing using the Internet imaging protocol. *Computer Networks*, 33(1–6):803–810, June 2000.

[384] Julie A. McCann. The Kendra cache replacement policy and its distribution. *World Wide Web*, 3(4):231–240, December 2000.

[385] Wagner Meira, Jr, Erik Fonseca, Cristina D. Murta, and Virgílio Almeida. Evaluating and configuring WWW cache hierarchies. In *Proceedings of the Third International WWW Caching Workshop*, June 1998. http://wwwcache.ja.net/events/workshop/22/.

[386] Ingrid Melve. Web caching architecture. DESIRE European project. http://www. uninett.no/prosjekt/desire/arneberg/.

[387] Ingrid Melve. Relation analysis, cache meshes. In *Proceedings of the Third International WWW Caching Workshop*, June 1998. http://wwwcache.ja.net/events/ workshop/29/magicnumber.html.

[388] Ingrid Melve. When to kill your siblings: cache mesh relation analysis. *Computer Networks and ISDN Systems*, 30(22-23):2105–2111, November 1998. http://www. elsevier.nl/cas/tree/store/comnet/sub/1998/30/22-23/2058.pdf.

[389] Ingrid Melve, Lars Slettjord, Henny Bekker, and Ton Verschuren. Building a Web caching system - architectural considerations. In *Proceedings of the 1997 NLANR Web Cache Workshop*, June 1997. http://ircache.nlanr.net/Cache/Workshop97/ Papers/Bekker/bekker.ps.

[390] Ingrid Melve, Lars Slettjord, Henny Bekker, and Ton Verschuren. Building a Web caching system - architectural considerations. In *Proceedings of the 8th Joint European Networking Conference*, Edinburgh, Scotland, May 1997. http://www.terena.nl/ conf/jenc8/papers/121.ps.

[391] Daniel Menascé. Scaling Web sites through caching. *IEEE Internet Computing*, 7(4):86–89, 2003.

[392] Jean-Marc Menaud, Valérie Issarny, and Michel Banâtre. A new protocol for efficient cooperative transversal Web caching. In *Proc. of DISC*, pages 288–302, 1998.

[393] Jean-Marc Menaud, Valérie Issarny, and Michel Banâtre. Improving the effective-ness of Web caching. In Springer Verlag, editor, *Recent Advances in Distributed Systems*, volume LNCS 1752. 2000. http://www-rocq.inria.fr/solidor/doc/ps00/Caching.ps.gz.

[394] B. Scott Michel, Konstantinos Nikoloudakis, Peter Reiher, and Lixia Zhang. URL forwarding and compression in adaptive Web caching. In *Proceedings of IEEE INFO-COM'2000 conference*, Tel Aviv, Israel, March 2000. http://www.ieee-infocom.org/2000/papers/282.ps.

[395] Scott Michel, Khoi Nguyen, Adam Rosenstein, Lixia Zhang, Sally Floyd, and Van Jacobson. Adaptive Web caching: towards a new global caching architecture. *Computer Networks and ISDN Systems*, 30(22-23):2169–2177, November 1998. http://www.elsevier.nl/cas/tree/store/comnet/sub/1998/30/22-23/2052.pdf.

[396] Mikhail Mikhailov and Craig E. Wills. Change and relationship-driven content caching, distribution and assembly. Technical Report WPI-CS-TR-01-03, Computer Science Department, Worcester Polytechnic Institute, March 2001. http://www.cs.wpi.edu/~cew/papers/tr01-03.pdf.

[397] P. V. Mockapetris and Kevin J. Dunlap. Development of the domain name system. *ACM Computer Communication Review*, 18(4), August 1988.

[398] J. C. Mogul, F. Douglis, A. Feldmann, and B. Krishnamurthy. Potential benefits of delta encoding and data compression for HTTP. *ACM Computer Communication Review*, 27(4):181–194, October 1997.

[399] Jeffrey Mogul. Squeezing more bits out of HTTP caches. *IEEE Network*, 14(3), May 2000.

[400] Jeffrey Mogul and Paul Leach. Simple hit-metering and usage-limiting for HTTP. RFC 2227, October 1997.

[401] Jeffrey C. Mogul. The case for persistent-connection HTTP. In *Proceedings of the SIGCOMM'95 conference*, Cambridge, MA, August 1995. http://www.acm.org/sigcomm/sigcomm95/papers/mogul.html.

[402] Jeffrey C. Mogul. What's wrong with HTTP (and why it doesn't matter). Slides of a presentation at the 1999 Usenix Technical Conference, June 1999. ftp://ftp.digital.com/pub/DEC/WRL/mogul/usenix1999it_mogul.pdf.

[403] Anelise Munaretto, Mauro Fonseca, and Nazim Agoulmine. Dynamic Web caching. In *Proc. of IMSA*, pages 170–173, 2002.

[404] Cristina Duarte Murta, Virgílio Almeida, and Wagner Meira, Jr. Analyzing performance of partitioned caches for the WWW. In *Proceedings of the 3rd International WWW Caching Workshop*, June 1998. http://wwwcache.ja.net/events/workshop/24/.

[405] Cristina Duarte Murta and Virgilio A. F. Almeida. Using performance maps to understand the behavior of Web caching policies. In *Proceedings of the IEEE Workshop on Internet Applications*, San Jose, CA, July 2001.

[406] Andy Myers, John Chuang, Urs Hengartner, Yinglian Xie, Weiqiang Zhuang, and Hui Zhang. A secure, publisher-centric Web caching infrastructure. In *Proc. of IEEE Infocom*, Anchorage, Alaska, April 2001.

[407] Andy Myers, Peter Dinda, and Hui Zhang. Performance characteristics of mirror servers on the Internet. In *Proceedings of the INFOCOM '99 conference*, pages 304–312, March 1999. http://www.cs.cmu.edu/~acm/papers/anycast-infocom99.pdf.

[408] Masahiko Nabe, M. Murata, and H. Miyahara. Analysis and modelling of World Wide Web traffic for capacity dimensioning of Internet access lines. *Performance Evaluation*, 34(4):249–271, December 1998.

[409] Masaaki Nabeshima. The Japan Cache Project: an experiment on domain cache. *Computer Networks*, 29(8–13):987–995, September 1997.

[410] Yutaka Nakamura, Ken ichi Chinen, Hideki Sunahara, Suguru Yamaguchi, and Yuji Oie. ENMA: The WWW server performance measurement system via packet monitoring. In *Proceedings of the INET'99 Conference*, June 1999. http://www.isoc.org/inet99/proceedings/4n/4n_3.htm.

[411] D. H. Neal. The Harvest object cache in New Zealand. *Computer Networks*, 28(7–11):1415–1430, May 1996.

[412] A. E. Nicholson, I. Zuckerman, and D. W. Albrecht. A decision-theoretic approach for pre-sending information on the WWW. In *Proceedings of the 5th Pacific Rim International Conference on Topics in Artificial Intelligence*, pages 575–586, 1998.

[413] Nicolas Niclausse, Zhen Liu, and Philippe Nain. A new efficient caching policy for the World Wide Web. In *Proceedings of the Workshop on Internet Server Performance (WISP'98)*, June 1998. http://www-sop.inria.fr/mistral/personnel/Nicolas.Niclausse/articles/wisp98/wisp98.ps.gz.

[414] Henrik Frystyk Nielsen, Jim Gettys, Anselm Baird-Smith, Eric Prud'hommeaux, Håkon Lie, and Chris Lilley. Network performance effects of HTTP/1.1, CSS1, and PNG. In *Proceedings of the ACM SIGCOMM '97 Conference*, September 1997. http://www.acm.org/sigcomm/sigcomm97/papers/p102.html.

[415] Norifumi Nishikawa, Takafumi Hosokawa, Yasuhide Mori, Kenichi Yoshida, and Hiroshi Tsuji. Memory-based architecture for distributed WWW caching proxy. *Computer Networks and ISDN Systems*, 30(1-7):205–214, April 1998. http://www.elsevier.nl/cas/tree/store/comnet/sub/1998/30/1-7/1928.pdf.

[416] Mark Nottingham. Optimizing object freshness controls in Web caches. In *Proceedings of the 4th International Web Caching Workshop*, April 1999. http://www.ircache.net/Cache/Workshop99/Papers/nottingham-final.ps.gz.

[417] Alexei Novikov and Martin Hamilton. FTP mirror tracker: First steps towards URN. In *Proceedings of the 5th International Web Caching and Content Delivery Workshop*, May 2000. http://www.terena.nl/conf/wcw/Proceedings/S1/S1-1.ps.

[418] Katia Obraczka, Peter Danzig, Solos Arthachinda, and Muhammad Yousuf. Scalable, highly available Web caching. Technical Report 97-662, USC Computer Science Department, 1997. ftp://usc.edu/pub/csinfo/tech-reports/papers/97-662.ps.Z.

[419] Masato Oguchi and Kinji Ono. A proposal for a World-Wide Web caching proxy mechanism. In *Proceedings of the Third International Symposium on Interworking (IN-TERWOKING '96)*, pages 531–540, October 1996. http://www.sail.t.u-tokyo. ac.jp/~oguchi/PAPERS/INTERWORKING/camera_ready.ps.

[420] Masato Oguchi and Kinji Ono. A study of caching proxy mechanisms realized on wide area distributed networks. In *Proceedings of the Fifth IEEE International Symposium on High Performance Distributed Computing (HPDC-5)*, pages 443–449, August 1996. http://www.sail.t.u-tokyo.ac.jp/~oguchi/PAPERS/ IEEE_HPDC96/paper.ps.

[421] J. Padhye, V. Firoiu, D. Towsley, and J. Kurose. Modeling TCP throughput. In *Proceedings of the ACM SIGCOMM Conference*, pages 303–314, 1998.

[422] Venkata N. Padmanabhan. Improving World Wide Web latency. Technical Report UCB/CSD-95-875, University of California at Berkeley, Computer Science Division, May 1995. http://www.cs.berkeley.edu/~padmanab/papers/masters-tr. ps.gz.

[423] Venkata N. Padmanabhan and Jeffrey C. Mogul. Improving HTTP latency. In *Proceedings of the 3rd International WWW Conference*, Chicago, October 1994. http://www. ncsa.uiuc.edu/SDG/IT94/Proceedings/DDay/mogul/HTTPLatency.html.

[424] Venkata N. Padmanabhan and Jeffrey C. Mogul. Using predictive prefetching to improve World-Wide Web latency. In *Proceedings of the ACM SIGCOMM '96 Conference*, pages 26–36, Stanford University, CA, July 1996. http://www.cs.berkeley.edu/ ~padmanab/papers/ccr-july96.ps.gz.

[425] Venkata N. Padmanabhan and Lili Qiu. The content and access dynamics of a busy Web site: Findings and implications. In *Proceedings of the SIGCOMM conference*, August 2000. http://www.research.microsoft.com/~padmanab/papers/ sigcomm2000.ps.

[426] V. S. Pai, M. Aron, G. Banga, M. Svendsen, P. Druschel, and W. Zwaenepol. Locality-aware request distribution in cluster-based network servers. In *Proceedings of the 8th International Conference on Architectural Support for Programming Languages and Operating Systems*, pages 205–216, 1998.

[427] Vivek S. Pai, Peter Druschel, and Willy Zwaenepoel. Flash: An efficient and portable Web server. In *Proceedings of the USENIX 1999 Annual Technical Conference*, June 1999. http://www.cs.rice.edu/~vivek/flash99/.

[428] Henry Novianus Palit. Using TCOZ for modeling Web caching. In *Proc. of APSEC*, 2001.

[429] Themistoklis Palpanas and Alberto Mendelzon. Web prefetching using partial match prediction. In *Proceedings of the 4th International Web Caching Workshop*, April 1999. http://www.ircache.net/Cache/Workshop99/Papers/palpanas-0.ps.gz.

[430] Chel Park, Haeyoung Yoo, Joong Soon Jang, Gihyun Jung, and Kyunghee Choi. A heuristic caching strategy for Web servers based on the binary knapsack model. In *Proc. of Intl. Conf. on Internet Computing*, pages 688–691, May 2003.

[431] Tomas Partl and Adam Dingle. A comparison of WWW caching algorithm efficiency. http://webcache.ms.mff.cuni.cz:8080/paper/paper.html, 1996.

[432] Sanjoy Paul and Zongming Fei. Distributed caching with centralized control. *Computer communications*, 24(2):256–268, February 2001.

[433] V. Paxson and Sally Floyd. Why we don't know how to simulate the Internet. In *Proceedings of the 1997 Winter Simulation Conference*, pages 1037–1044, December 1997. ftp://ftp.ee.lbl.gov/papers/wsc97.ps.

[434] Stéphane Perret, John Dilley, and Martin Arlitt. Performance evaluation of the distributed object consistency protocol. Technical Report HPL-1999-108, Hewlett-Packard Laboratories, September 1999. http://www.hpl.hp.com/techreports/1999/HPL-1999-108.html.

[435] Guillaume Pierre. Conception d'un système de cache Web adapté aux spécificités des utilisateurs. In *Proceedings of the 1998 NoTeRe colloquium*, October 1998.

[436] Guillaume Pierre. *Architecture et dimensionnement d'infrastructures de caches Web pour Intranets décentralisés*. PhD thesis, Université d'Evry-Val d'Essonne, Evry (France), June 1999.

[437] Guillaume Pierre, Ihor Kuz, and Maarten van Steen. Adaptive replicated Web documents. Technical Report IR-477, Vrije Universiteit, Amsterdam, September 2000. http://www.cs.vu.nl/~gpierre/publi/ARWD_ir477.php3.

[438] Guillaume Pierre, Ihor Kuz, Maarten van Steen, and Andrew S. Tanenbaum. Differentiated strategies for replicating Web documents. *Computer Communications*, 24(2):232–240, February 2001. http://www.cs.vu.nl/~gpierre/publi/DSRWD_comcom.php3.

[439] Guillaume Pierre and Mesaac Makpangou. A flexible hybrid concurrency control model for collaborative applications in large scale settings. In *Proceedings of the 7th ACM SIGOPS European Workshop*, Renvyle, Ireland, September 1996.

[440] Guillaume Pierre and Mesaac Makpangou. Saperlipopette!: a distributed Web caching systems evaluation tool. In *Proceedings of the 1998 Middleware conference*, pages 389–405, September 1998.

[441] Guillaume Pierre and Maarten van Steen. Globule: a platform for self-replicating Web documents. In *Proceedings of the 6th International Conference on Protocols for Multimedia Systems*, pages 1–11, October 2001. http://www.cs.vu.nl/~gpierre/publi/GPSRWD_proms2001.php3.

[442] Guillaume Pierre, Maarten van Steen, and Andrew S. Tanenbaum. Self-replicating Web documents. Technical Report IR-486, Vrije Universiteit, Amsterdam, February 2001. http://www.cs.vu.nl/~gpierre/publi/SRWD_ir486.php3.

[443] Peter L.T. Pirolli and James E. Pitkow. Distributions of surfers' paths through the World Wide Web: Empirical characterizations. *World Wide Web*, 2(1–2):29–45, January 1999.

[444] James Pitkow. In search of reliable usage data on the WWW. *Computer Networks*, 29(8–13):1343–1355, September 1997.

[445] James E. Pitkow. Summary of WWW characterizations. *Computer Networks and ISDN Systems*, 30(1-7):551–558, April 1998. http://www.elsevier.nl/cas/tree/store/comnet/sub/1998/30/1-7/1877.pdf.

[446] James E. Pitkow. Summary of WWW characterizations. *World Wide Web*, 2(1–2):3–13, January 1999.

[447] James E. Pitkow and Margaret M. Recker. A simple yet robust caching algorithm based on dynamic access patterns. In *Proceedings of the 3rd International WWW Conference*, Chicago, October 1994. http://www.ncsa.uiuc.edu/SDG/IT94/Proceedings/DDay/pitkow/caching.html.

[448] S. Podlipnig and L. Böszörmenyi. A survey of Web cache replacement strategies. *ACM Computing Surveys*, 35(4):374–398, December 2003.

[449] Marco Emilio Poleggi, Bruno Ciciani, and Michele Colajanni. Global caching mechanisms in clusters of Web servers. In *Proc. of MASCOTS*, pages 421–426, 2002.

[450] D. Povey and J. Harrison. A distributed Internet cache. In *Proceedings of the 20th Australian Comp. Sci. Conf., Sydney, Australia*, February 1997.

[451] Konstantinos Psounis. Class-based delta-encoding: A scalable scheme for caching dynamic Web content. In *Proc. of ICDCS Workshops*, pages 799–805, 2002.

[452] Konstantinos Psounis and Balaji Prabhakar. A randomized Web-cache replacement scheme. In *Proceedings of IEEE Infocom*, Anchorage, Alaska, April 2001.

[453] Lili Qiu, Venkata Padmanabhan, and Geoffrey Voelker. On the placement of Web server replicas. In *Proceedings of the IEEE Infocom conference*, April 2001. http://infocom.ucsd.edu/papers/839-4067851989.ps.

[454] M. Rabinovich, I. Rabinovich, R. Rajaraman, and A. Aggarwal. A dynamic object replication and migration protocol for an Internet hosting service. In *Proceedings of the 19th IEEE International Conference on Distributed Computing Systems*, pages 101–113, 1999.

[455] M. Rabinovich and O. Spatscheck. *Web Caching and Replication*. Addison Wesley, 2001.

[456] Michael Rabinovich. Issues in Web content replication. *Data Engineering Bulletin (invited paper)*, 21(4), December 1998. http://www.research.att.com/~misha/otherPubs/web_repl.ps.gz.

[457] Michael Rabinovich and Amit Aggarwal. RaDaR: A scalable architecture for a global Web hosting service. In *Proceedings of the 8th International WWW Conference*, pages 467–483, Toronto, Canada, May 1999. http://www8.org/w8-papers/4c-server/radar/radar.pdf.

[458] Michael Rabinovich, Jeff Chase, and Syam Gadde. Not all hits are created equal: cooperative proxy caching over a wide-area network. *Computer Networks and ISDN Systems*, 30(22-23):2253–2259, November 1998. http://www.elsevier.nl/cas/tree/store/comnet/sub/1998/30/22-23/2055.pdf.

[459] Sampath Rangarajan, Shalini Yajnik, and Pankaj Jalote. WCP – a tool for consistent on-line update of documents in a WWW server. *Computer Networks and ISDN Systems*, 30(1-7):327–336, April 1998. http://www.elsevier.nl/cas/tree/store/comnet/sub/1998/30/1-7/1858.pdf.

[460] Mike Reddy and Graham P. Fletcher. Intelligent control of dynamic caching strategies for Web servers and clients. In *Proc. of WebNet*, 1997.

[461] Mike Reddy and Graham P. Fletcher. Exp1: a comparison between a simple adaptive caching agent using document life histories and existing cache techniques. *Computer Networks and ISDN Systems*, 30(22-23):2149–2153, November 1998. http://www.elsevier.nl/cas/tree/store/comnet/sub/1998/30/22-23/2044.pdf.

[462] Mike Reddy and Graham P. Fletcher. Intelligent Web caching using document life histories: A comparison with existing cache management techniques. In *Proceedings of the Third International WWW Caching Workshop*, June 1998. http://wwwcache.ja.net/events/workshop/12/3W3cache/MSWord/3W3cache.ps.

[463] Reza Rejaie and Jussi Kangasharju. Mocha: A quality adaptive multimedia proxy cache for internet streaming. In *Proceedings of NOSSDAV*, Port Jefferson, New York, June 2001.

[464] J. Rexford, S. Sen, and A. Basso. A smoothing proxy service for variable-bit-rate streaming video. In *Proceedings of the Global Internet Symposium*, 1999.

[465] J. Rexford and D. Towsley. Smoothing variable-bit-rate video in an Internetwork. *IEEE/ACM Transactions on Networking*, 7:202–215, 1999.

[466] Sean C. Rhea, Kevin Liang, and Eric A. Brewer. Value-based Web caching. In *Proc. of WWW Conf.*, pages 619–628, 2003.

[467] Luigi Rizzo and Lorenzo Vicisano. Replacement policies for a proxy cache. Technical Report RN/98/13, UCL-CS, 1998. http://www.iet.unipi.it/~luigi/lrv98.ps.gz.

[468] Philippe Rochat and Stuart Thompson. Proxy caching based on object location considering semantic usage. In *Proceedings of the 4th International Web Caching Workshop*, April 1999. http://www.ircache.net/Cache/Workshop99/Papers/rochat-final.ps.gz.

[469] P. Rodriguez, K.W. Ross, and E. Biersack. Distributing frequently-changing documents in the Web: Multicasting or hierarchical caching. *Computer Networks and ISDN Systems*, 30, November 1998. http://www.eurecom.fr/~ross/multicast.ps.

[470] Pablo Rodriguez, Ernst Biersack, and Keith W. Ross. Automated delivery of Web documents through a caching infrastructure. In *Proc. of EUROMICRO*, pages 233–240, 2003.

[471] Pablo Rodriguez, Ernst W. Biersack, and Keith W. Ross. Improving the WWW: Caching or multicast. In *Proceedings of the Third International WWW Caching Workshop*, June 1998. http://wwwcache.ja.net/events/workshop/03/MC_vs_Cache.ps.

[472] Pablo Rodriguez, Andreas Kirpal, and Ernst W. Biersack. Parallel-access for mirror sites in the Internet. In *Proceedings of IEEE INFOCOM'2000*, pages 864–873, March 2000. http://www.eurecom.fr/~rodrigue/papers/parallel_Info99.ps.

[473] Pablo Rodriguez and Sandeep Sibal. SPREAD: Scalable platform for reliable and efficient automated distribution. *Computer Networks*, 33(1-6):33–49, June 2000. http://www.elsevier.nl/gej-ng/10/15/22/48/25/29/article.pdf.

[474] Pablo Rodriguez, Sandeep Sibal, and Oliver Spatscheck. TPOT: translucent proxying of TCP. *Computer Communications*, 24(2):249–255, February 2001.

[475] Pablo Rodriguez, Christian Spanner, and Ernst W. Biersack. Web caching architectures: Hierarchical and distributed caching. In *Proceedings of the 4th International Web Caching Workshop*, April 1999. http://www.ircache.net/Cache/Workshop99/Papers/rodriguez-final.ps.gz.

[476] Pablo Rodriguez, Christian Spanner, and Ernst W. Biersack. Analysis of Web caching architectures: hierarchical and distributed caching. *IEEE/ACM Trans. on Networking*, 9(4):404–418, August 2001.

[477] K. W. Ross. Hash-routing for collections of shared Web caches. *IEEE Network Magazine*, 11(6):37–44, November 1997. http://www.seas.upenn.edu/~ross/hash.ps.

[478] A. Rousskov and D. Wessels. High-performance benchmarking with Web Polygraph. *Software Practice and Experience*, 34:187–211, 2004.

[479] Alex Rousskov and Valery Soloviev. A performance – of the Squid proxy on HTTP/1.0. *World Wide Web*, 2(1–2):47–67, January 1999.

[480] Alex Rousskov and Duane Wessels. Cache digests. *Computer Networks and ISDN Systems*, 30(22-23):2155–2168, November 1998. http://www.elsevier.nl/cas/tree/store/comnet/sub/1998/30/22-23/2057.pdf.

[481] Alex Rousskov, Duane Wessels, and Glenn Chisholm. The first IRCache Web cache bake-off – the official report, April 1999. http://bakeoff.ircache.net/bakeoff-01/.

[482] Mark Russell and T. P. Hopkins. CFTP: a caching FTP server. *Computer Networks*, 30(22–23):2211–2222, November 1998.

[483] Maytham Safar. Classification of Web caching systems. In *Proc. of ICWI*, pages 768–773, 2002.

[484] Victor Y Safranov. Optimizing Web servers using page rank prefetching for clustered accesses. Master's thesis, Graduate school, New Brunswick, Rutgers, The State University Of New Jersey, May 2001.

[485] Victor Safronov and Manish Parashar. Optimizing Web servers using page rank prefetching for clustered accesses. *World Wide Web*, 5(1), March 2002.

[486] Françoise Sailhan and Valérie Issarny. Energy-aware Web caching for mobile terminals. In *Proc. of ICDCS Workshops*, pages 820–825, 2002.

[487] Jr. Santos and David Wetherall. Increasing effective link bandwidth by suppressing replicated data. In *Proceedings of Usenix Annual Technical Conference*, New Orleans, Louisiana, June 1998.

[488] Nakul Saraiya and R. Vasudevan. Measuring network cache performance. In *Proceedings of the 4th International Web Caching Workshop*, April 1999. http://www.ircache.net/Cache/Workshop99/Papers/saraiya-0.ps.gz.

[489] Prasenjit Sarkar and John Hartman. Efficient cooperative caching using hints. In *Proceeding of the 2nd ACM Symposium on Operating Systems Design and Implementation (OSDI)*, Seattle, WA, November 1996. http://www.cs.arizona.edu/swarm/papers/ccache/.

[490] M. Sayal, Y. Breitbart, P. Scheuermann, and R. Vingralek. Selection algorithms for replicated Web servers. In *Proceedings of the Workshop on Internet Server Performance*, 1998.

[491] Stuart Schechter, Murali Krishnan, and Michael D. Smith. Using path profiles to predict HTTP requests. *Computer Networks and ISDN Systems*, 30(1-7):457–467, April 1998. http://www.elsevier.nl/cas/tree/store/comnet/sub/1998/30/1-7/1917.pdf.

[492] P. Scheuermann, Junho Shim, and Radek Vingralek. A case for delay-conscious caching of Web documents. *Computer Networks*, 29(8–13):997–1005, September 1997.

[493] Andrew Sears, Julie A. Jacko, and Michael S. Borella. Internet delay effects: How users perceive quality, organization, and ease of use of information. In *Proceedings of the CHI '97 conference*, 1997. http://condor.depaul.edu/~asears/publications/FullPapers/UserPerceptions1.html.

[494] Jeff Sedayao. "Mosaic will kill my network!" - studying network traffic patterns of Mosaic use. In *Proceedings of the 3rd International WWW Conference*, Chicago, October 1994. http://www.ncsa.uiuc.edu/SDG/IT94/Proceedings/DDay/sedayao/mos_traf_paper.html.

[495] Jeff Sedayao. World Wide Web network traffic patterns. In *Proceedings of the COMPCON '95 conference*, 1995.

[496] S. Selvakumar and P. Prabhakar. Implementation and comparison of distributed caching schemes. *Computer Communications*, 24(7-8):677–684, April 2001. http://www.elsevier.nl/gej-ng/10/15/19/47/31/32/abstract.html.

[497] P. Sember, T. R. Mueller, N. Baker, M. C. Flower, B. Raskutti, and W. Wen. Web cache focussing devices. *Computer Networks*, 30(1–7):682–684, April 1998.

[498] Sourav Sen and Y. Narahari. Improving Web server performance by network aware data buffering and caching. In *Proc. of HiPC*, pages 242–251, 2002.

[499] Dimitrios N. Serpanos, George Karakostas, and W. H. Wolf. Effective caching of Web objects using Zipf's law. In *Proc. of IEEE International Conference on Multimedia and Expo (II)*, pages 727–730, 2000.

[500] Anees Shaikh, Renu Tewari, and Mukesh Agrawal. On the effectiveness of DNS-based server selection. In *Proceedings of the IEEE Infocom conference*, April 2001. http://infocom.ucsd.edu/papers/806-3339248951.pdf.

[501] Junho Shim, Peter Scheuermann, and Radek Vingralek. Proxy cache design: Algorithms, implementation and performance. *IEEE Transactions on Knowledge and Data Engineering*, 1999. http://www.ece.nwu.edu/~shimjh/publication/tkde98.ps.

[502] B. A. Shirazi, A. R. Hurson, and K. M. Kavi. *Scheduling and load balancing in parallel and distributed systems*. IEEE Computer Society Press, New York, 1995.

[503] Elizabeth Shriver, Eran Gabber, Lan Huang, and Christopher A. Stein. Storage management for Web proxies. In *Proc. of the Usenix Annual Technical Conference*, Boston, MA, June 2001.

[504] J. Simonson, D. Berleant, X. Zhang, M. Xie, and H. Vo. Version augmented URIs for reference permanence via an Apache module design. *Computer Networks and ISDN Systems*, 30(1-7):337–345, April 1998. http://www.elsevier.nl/cas/tree/store/comnet/sub/1998/30/1-7/1879.pdf.

[505] Ben Smith, Anurag Acharya, Tao Yang, and Huican Zhu. Exploiting result equivalence in caching dynamic Web content. In *Proceedings of the 1999 Usenix Symposium on Internet Technologies and Systems (USITS'99)*, Boulder, Colorado, October 1999. http://www.cs.ucsb.edu/research/swala/usits99/paper.ps.

[506] Neil G. Smith. The UK national Web cache - the state of the art. *Computer Networks*, 28(7–11):1407–1414, May 1996.

[507] Mirjana Spasojevic, C. Mic Bowman, and Alfred Spector. Using wide-area file systems within the World-Wide Web. In *Proceedings of the 3rd International WWW Conference*, Chicago, October 1994. http://www.ncsa.uiuc.edu/SDG/IT94/Proceedings/DDay/spasojevic/paper.html.

[508] S. E. Spero. HTTP performance problems. In *Proceedings of the 2nd International WWW Conference, Chicago, USA*, October 1994.

[509] Simon E. Spero. Analysis of HTTP performance problems. http://metalab.unc.edu/mdma-release/http-prob.html.

[510] Mike Spreitzer and Bill Janssen. HTTP "next generation". *Computer Networks*, 33(1-6):593–607, June 2000. http://www.elsevier.nl/gej-ng/10/15/22/48/25/66/article.pdf.

[511] David Starobinski and David Tse. Probabilistic methods for Web caching. *Performance Evaluation*, 46(2–3):125–137, October 2001.

[512] Hung-Min Sun, X. Zang, and K. S. Trivedi. The effect of Web caching on network planning. *Computer Communications*, 22(14):1343–1350, September 1999.

[513] N. Swaminathan and S. V. Raghavan. Intelligent prefetch in WWW using client behavior characterization. In *Proceedings of IEEE MASCOTS*, San Francisco, California, August 2000.

[514] CISCO Systems. Web Cache Control Protocol. White Paper, 1997.

[515] Wenting Tang, Fan Du, Matt W. Mutka, Lionel M. Ni, and Abdol-Hossein Esfahanian. Supporting global replicated services by a routing-metric-aware DNS. In *Proceedings of the 2nd International Workshop on Advanced Issues of E-Commerce and Web-Based Information Systems (WECWIS 2000)*, pages 67–74, June 2000. ftp://ftp.cse.msu.edu/pub/acs/mutka/papers/wecwis2k.ps.

[516] Xueyan Tang and Samuel T. Chanson. Coordinated en-route Web caching. *IEEE Trans. Computers*, 51(6):595–607, 2002.

[517] Xueyan Tang and Samuel T. Chanson. On caching effectiveness of Web clusters under persistent connections. *J. Parallel Distrib. Comput.*, 63(10):981–995, 2003.

[518] T. T. Tay, Yanjun Feng, and M. N. Wijeysundera. A distributed Internet caching system. In *Proceedings of IEEE Conf. on Local Computer Networks*, Tampa, Florida, November 2000.

[519] R. Tewari, H.M. Vin, A. Dan, and D. Sitaram. Resource-based caching for Web servers. In *Proceedings of ACM/SPIE Multimedia Computing and Networking (MMCN'98)*, January 1998. http://www.cs.utexas.edu/users/dmcl/projects/trellis/papers/ps/MMCN98-RBC.ps.

[520] Renu Tewari, Michael Dahlin, Harrick Vin, and John Kay. Beyond hierarchies: Design considerations for distributed caching on the Internet. Technical Report TR98-0, University of Texas, February 1998. http://www.cs.utexas.EDU/users/dahlin/papers/tr98-04.ps.

[521] David Thaler and Chinya Ravishankar. Using name-based mappings to increase hit rates. *IEEE/ACM Transactions on Networking*, 6(1):1–14, February 1998.

[522] Faber Theodore, Joseph D. Touch, and W. Yue. The TIME-WAIT state in TCP and its effect on busy servers. In *Proceedings of IEEE Infocom*, New York, March 1999.

[523] K. Thompson, G. Miller, and R. Wilder. Wide–area internet traffic patterns and characteristics. In *Proceedings of the 3rd International Web Caching Conference*, 1998.

[524] Gary Tomlinson, Drew Major, and Ron Lee. High-capacity Internet middleware: Internet cache system architectural overview. In *Proceedings of the Workshop on Internet Server Performance (WISP99)*, May 1999.

[525] Joe Touch. The LSAM proxy cache - a multicast distributed virtual cache. In *Proceedings of the Third International WWW Caching Workshop*, June 1998. http://wwwcache.ja.net/events/workshop/14/lsam-arch.pdf.

[526] Bhuvan Urgaonkar, Anoop Ninan, Prashant Shenoy Mohammad Raunak, and Krithi Ramamritham. Maintaining mutual consistency for cached Web objects. In *Proceedings of the 21st International Conference on Distributed Computing Systems (ICDCS-21)*, Phoenix, AZ, apr 2001. http://lass.cs.umass.edu/papers/ps/ICDCS01.ps.

[527] Amin Vahdat, Tom Anderson, Mike Dahlin, Eshwar Belani, David Culler, Paul Eastham, and Chad Yoshikawa. WebOS: Operating system services for wide area applications. In *Proceedings of the Seventh Symposium on High Performance Distributed Computing*, July 1998. http://www.cs.utexas.edu/users/dahlin/papers/hpdc98.ps.

[528] Amin Vahdat, Michael Dahlin, and Thomas Aderson. Turning the Web into a computer. http://www.cs.utexas.edu/users/dahlin/papers/webComputer.ps, May 1996.

[529] Athena Vakali. An evolutionary scheme for Web replication and caching. In *Proceedings of the 4th International Web Caching Workshop*, April 1999. http://www.ircache.net/Cache/Workshop99/Papers/vakali-0.ps.gz.

[530] Athena Vakali. Proxy cache replacement algorithms: A history-based approach. *World Wide Web*, 4(4), December 2001.

[531] Athena Vakali. Evolutionary techniques for Web caching. *Distributed and Parallel Databases*, 11(1):93–116, 2002.

[532] Vinod Valloppillil and Keith W. Ross. Cache Array Routing Protocol v1.0. Internet draft, February 1998. http://www.ietf.org.

[533] Rob van der Mei, Willa Ehlich, Paul Reeser, and John Francisco. A decision support system for tuning Web servers in distributed object oriented network architectures. In *Proceedings of the Workshop on Internet Server Performance (WISP99)*, May 1999. http://www.cc.gatech.edu/fac/Ellen.Zegura/wisp99/papers/vandermei.doc.

[534] Maarten van Steen, Philip Homburg, and Andrew S. Tanenbaum. Globe: A wide-area distributed system. *IEEE Concurrency*, 7(1):70–78, January-March 1999. http://www.cs.vu.nl/pub/papers/globe/ieeeconc.99.org.ps.Z.

[535] Maarten van Steen, Andrew S. Tanenbaum, Ihor Kuz, and Henk J. Sips. A scalable middleware solution for advanced wide-area Web services. *Distributed Systems Engineering*, 6(1):34–42, March 1999. http://www.cs.vu.nl/pub/papers/globe/dsej.99.ps.Z.

[536] Arun Venkataramani, Ravi Kokku, and Mike Dahlin. TCP Nice: A mechanism for background transfers. In *Proc. of the USENIX Operating Systems Design and Implementation (OSDI) conference*, December 2002.

[537] Arun Venkataramani, Praveen Yalagandula, Ravindranath Kokku, Sadia Sharif, and Mike Dahlin. The potential costs and benefits of long-term prefetching for content distribution. *Computer Communications*, 25(4):367–375, March 2002.

[538] Dinesh C. Verma. *Content Distribution Networks: An Engineering Approach*. John Wiley and Sons, January 2002.

[539] Olivier Verscheure, Chitra Venkatramani, Pascal Frossard, and Lisa Amini. Joint server scheduling and proxy caching for video delivery. *Computer Communications*, 25(4):413–423, March 2002.

[540] Radek Vingralek, Yuri Breitbart, Mehmet Sayal, and Peter Scheuermann. Web++: A system for fast and reliable Web service. In *Proceedings of 1999 USENIX Annual Technical Conference*, pages 171–184, June 1999. http://lilac.ece.nwu.edu:1024/publications/USENIX/WebPlus.ps.

[541] Jia Wang. A survey of Web caching schemes for the Internet. *ACM Computer Communication Review*, 25(9):36–46, October 1999. http://www.cs.cornell.edu/Info/People/jiawang/web-survey.ps.

[542] Xiaoyu Wang, Wee Siong Ng, Beng Chin Ooi, Kian-Lee Tan, and Aoying Zhou. BuddyWeb: A P2P-based collaborative Web caching system. In *Proc. of NETWORKING Workshops*, pages 247–251, 2002.

[543] Z. Wang. CacheMesh: A distributed cache system for the world wide web. In *Proceedings of the 2nd NLANR Web Caching Workshop, Boulder, Colorado*, June 1997.

[544] Zhen Wang and Jon Crowcroft. Prefetching in World Wide Web. In *Proceedings of Global Internet*, pages 28–32, London, England, November 1996.

[545] R. Weber. On the optimal assignment of customers to parallel servers. *Journal of Applied Probability*, 15:406–413, 1978.

[546] D. Wessels. *Web Caching*. O'Reilly and Associates, 2001.

[547] D. Wessels. *Squid: The Definitive Guide*. O'Reilly and Associates, 2004. (to be published in 2004).

[548] Duane Wessels. Intelligent caching for World-Wide Web objects. In *Proceedings of the INET '95 conference*, Honolulu, Hawaï, June 1995. http://www.nlanr.net/~wessels/Papers/wessels-inet95/wessels-inet95.ps.gz.

[549] Duane Wessels. Evolution of the NLANR cache hierarchy: Global configuration challenges. http://www.nlanr.net/Papers/Cache96/, November 1996.

[550] Duane Wessels and K Claffy. ICP and the Squid Web cache. *IEEE Journal on Selected Areas in Communication*, 16(3):345–357, April 1998. http://www.ircache.net/~wessels/Papers/icp-squid.ps.gz.

[551] Bert Williams. Transparent Web caching solutions. In *Proceedings of the 3rd International WWW Caching Workshop*, Manchester, England, June 1998.

[552] Stephen Williams, Marc Abrams, Charles R. Standridge, Ghaleb Abdulla, and Edward A. Fox. Removal policies in network caches for World-Wide Web documents. In *Proceedings of the ACM SIGCOMM '96 Conference*, pages 293–305, Stanford University, CA, August 1996. http://ei.cs.vt.edu/~succeed/96sigcomm/.

[553] Carey Williamson and Mudashiru Busari. On the sensitivity of Web proxy cache performance to workload characteristics. In *Proceedings of IEEE Infocom*, Anchorage, Alaska, April 2001.

[554] Carey L. Williamson. On filter effects in Web caching hierarchies. *ACM Trans. Internet Techn.*, 2(1):47–77, 2002.

[555] C. E. Wills and Mikhail Mikhailov. Studying the impact of more complete server information on Web caching. *Computer Communications*, 24(2):184–190, February 2001.

[556] Craig E. Wills and Mikhail Mikhailov. Characterizing Web resources and server responses to better understand the potential of caching. In *Proceedings of the Web Characterization Workshop*, Cambridge, MA, November 1998. World Wide Web Consortium. http://www.cs.wpi.edu/~cew/papers/wcw98.html.

[557] Craig E. Wills and Mikhail Mikhailov. Examining the cacheability of user-requested Web resources. In *Proceedings of the 4th International Web Caching Workshop*, April

1999. http://www.ircache.net/Cache/Workshop99/Papers/wills-final. ps.gz.

[558] Craig E. Wills and Mikhail Mikhailov. Towards a better understanding of Web resources and server responses for improved caching. *Computer Networks and ISDN Systems*, 31(11-16):1231–1243, May 1999.

[559] Craig E. Wills, Mikhail Mikhailov, and Hao Shang. N for the price of 1: Bundling Web objects for more efficient content delivery. In *Proceedings of the 10th International WWW Conference*, Hong Kong, May 2001. http://www.cs.wpi.edu/~cew/ papers/www01.pdf.

[560] Craig E. Wills and Hao Shang. The contribution of DNS lookup costs to Web object retrieval. Technical Report WPI-CS-TR-00-12, Worcester Polytechnic Institute, July 2000. http://www.cs.wpi.edu/~cew/papers/tr00-12.ps.gz.

[561] Alec Wolman, Geoff Voelker, Nitin Sharma, Neal Cardwell, Molly Brown, Tashana Landray, Denise Pinnel, Anna Karlin, and Henry Levy. Organization-based analysis of Web-object sharing and caching. In *Proceedings of the 1999 Usenix Symposium on Internet Technologies and Systems (USITS'99)*, pages 25–36, October 1999. http: //bauhaus.cs.washington.edu/homes/wolman/papers/usits99.pdf.

[562] Alec Wolman, Geoff Voelker, Nitin Sharma, Neal Cardwell, Anna Karlin, and Henry Levy. On the scale and performance of cooperative Web proxy caching. In *Proceedings of the 17th ACM Symposium on Operating Systems Principles (SOSP'99)*, pages 16–31, December 1999. http://www.cs.washington.edu/research/networking/ websys/pubs/sosp99/sosp99.ps.gz.

[563] A. Woodruff, P. M. Aoki, E. Brewer, P. Gauthier, and L. A. Rowe. An investigation of documents from the WWW. In *Proceedings of the 5th World Wide Web Conference*, pages 963–979, 1996.

[564] Roland P. Wooster and M. D. Abrams. Proxy caching that estimates page load delays. *Computer Networks*, 29(8–13):977–986, September 1997.

[565] Roland Peter Wooster. Optimizing response time, rather than hit rates, of WWW proxy caches. Master's thesis, Virginia Tech, December 1996. http://scholar.lib.vt. edu/theses/available/etd-34131420119653540/.

[566] Kurt Jeffery Worrell. Invalidation in large scale network objects caches. Master's thesis, Faculty of the graduate school of the University of Colorado, 1994. ftp://ftp.cs. colorado.edu/pub/cs/techreports/schwartz/WorrellThesis.ps.Z.

[567] Kun-Lung Wu and Philip S. Yu. Latency-sensitive hashing for collaborative Web caching. *Computer Networks*, 33(1-6):633–644, June 2000. http://www.elsevier.nl/ gej-ng/10/15/22/48/25/69/article.pdf.

[568] Kun-Lung Wu, Philip S. Yu, and Joel L. Wolf. Segment-based proxy caching of multimedia streams. In *Proceedings of the 10th International WWW Conference*, Hong Kong, May 2001. http://www10.org/cdrom/papers/pdf/p183.pdf.

[569] Yi-Hung Wu and Arbee L. P. Chen. Prediction of Web page accesses by proxy server log. *World Wide Web*, 5(1), March 2002.

[570] Yinglian Xie and David O'Hallaron. Locality in search engine queries and its implications for caching. In *Proceedings of IEEE Infocom*, New York, NY, June 2002.

[571] J. Yang, W. Wang, R. Muntz, and J. Wang. Access driven Web caching. Technical Report 990007, UCLA, 1999.

[572] Jiong Yang, Wei Wang, and Richard R. Muntz. Collaborative Web caching based on proxy affinities. In *Proc. of SIGMETRICS*, pages 78–89, 2000.

[573] Qiang Yang and Henry Haining Zhang. Web-log mining for predictive Web caching. *IEEE Trans. Knowl. Data Eng.*, 15(4):1050–1053, 2003.

[574] Qiang Yang, Henry Haining Zhang, and Ian Tian Yi Li. Mining Web logs for prediction models in WWW caching and prefetching. In *Proc. of KDD*, pages 473–478, 2001.

[575] Qiang Yang, Henry Haining Zhang, Ian Tian Yi Li, and Ye Lu. Mining Web logs to improve Web caching and prefetching. In *Proc. of Web Intelligence*, pages 483–492, 2001.

[576] Qiang Yang and Henry Hanning Zhang. Integrating Web prefetching and caching using prediction models. *World Wide Web*, 4(4), December 2001.

[577] J. Yin, L. Alvisi, M. Dahlin, and C. Lin. Using leases to support server-driven consistency in large-scale systems. In *Proceedings of the 18th International Conference on Distributed Computing System (ICDCS '98)*, May 1998. http://www.cs.utexas. EDU/users/dahlin/papers/icdcs98.ps.

[578] J. Yin, L. Alvisi, M. Dahlin, and C. Lin. Volume leases for consistency in large-scale systems. *IEEE Transactions on Knowledge and Data Engineering*, 11:563–576, 1999.

[579] Jian Yin, Lorenzo Alvisi, Mike Dahlin, and Arun Iyengar. Engineering server-driven consistency for large scale dynamic Web services. In *Proceedings of the 10th International WWW Conference*, Hong Kong, May 2001. http://www10.org/cdrom/papers/pdf/p264.pdf.

[580] Jian Yin, Lorenzo Alvisi, Mike Dahlin, and Calvin Lin. Hierarchical cache consistency in a WAN. In *Proceedings of the 1999 Usenix Symposium on Internet Technologies and Systems (USITS'99)*, October 1999. http://www.cs.utexas.edu/users/dahlin/papers/usits99-YinAlvisiDahlinLin%.ps.

[581] Ken Yocum and Jeff Chase. Payload caching: high–speed data forwarding for network intermediaries. In *Proceedings of USENIX Annual Technical Conference*, Boston, MA, June 2001.

[582] C. Yoshikawa, B. Chun, P. Eastham, A. Vahdat, T. Anderson, and D. Culler. Using smart clients to build scalable services. In *Proceedings of the 1997 USENIX Technical Conference*, pages 105–117, 1997.

[583] Hyong youb Kim, Vijay S. Pai, and Scott Rixner. Increasing Web server throughput with network interface data caching. In *Proc. of ASPLOS*, pages 239–250, 2002.

[584] Haobo Yu, Lee Breslau, and Scott Shenker. A scalable Web cache consistency architecture. In *Proceedings of the ACM SIGCOMM'99 Conference*, pages 163–174, September 1999.

[585] Philip S. Yu and Edward A. MacNair. Performance study of a collaborative method for hierarchical caching in proxy servers. *Computer Networks and ISDN Systems*, 30(1–7):215–224, April 1998. http://www.elsevier.nl/cas/tree/store/comnet/sub/1998/30/1-7/1829.pdf.

[586] Jun-Li Yuan and Chi-Hung Chi. Web caching performance: How much is lost unwarily? In *Proc. of Human*, pages 23–33, 2003.

[587] Junbiao Zhang, Rauf Izmailov, Daniel Reininger, and Maximilian Ott. Web caching framework: Analytical models and beyond. In *Proceedings of the IEEE Workshop on Internet Applications*, San Jose, CA, July 1999.

[588] Junbiao Zhang, Rauf Izmailov, Daniel Reininger, and Maximilian Ott. WebCASE: A simulation environment for Web caching study. In *Proceedings of the 4th International Web Caching Workshop*, April 1999. http://www.ircache.net/Cache/Workshop99/Papers/zhang-final.ps.gz.

[589] Lixia Zhang, Sally Floyd, and Van Jacobson. Adaptive Web caching. In *Proceedings of the 1997 NLANR Web Cache Workshop*, June 1997. http://ircache.nlanr.net/Cache/Workshop97/Papers/Floyd/floyd.ps.

[590] Huican Zhu and Tao Yang. Class-based cache management for dynamic Web content. In *Proceedings of IEEE Infocom*, Anchorage, Alaska, April 2001.

[591] G. K. Zipf. *Human behavior and the principle of least-effort*. Addison Wesley, Cambridge, MA, 1949.

[592] Qing Zou, Patrick Martin, and Hossam Hassanein. Transparent distributed Web caching with minimum expected response time. In *Proceedings of the IEEE International Performance, Computing, and Communications Conference*, Phoenix, AZ, April 2003.

[593] I. Zuckerman, D. Albrecht, and A. Nicholson. Predicting users' requests on the WWW. In *Proceedings of the 7th International Conference on User Modeling*, pages 275–284, 1999.

Index